SPRINGER PUBLISHING

AF712173

GET THE MOST FROM YOUR BOOK

SPRINGER PUBLISHING CONNECT™

VOUCHER CODE:

W5YU6DVD

Online Access

Your print purchase of *Culturally Responsive Counselor Education: Multicultural Education, Curricula Design, and Praxis* includes **online access via Springer Publishing Connect**™ to increase accessibility, portability, and searchability.

Insert the code at http://connect.springerpub.com/content/book/978-0-8261-6541-1 or scan the QR code and insert the voucher code today!

Having trouble? Contact our customer service department at cs@springerpub.com

Instructor Resource Access for Adopters

Let us do some of the heavy lifting to create an engaging classroom experience with a variety of instructor resources included in most textbooks SUCH AS:

INSTRUCTOR MANUAL

POWERPOINTS

TEST BANK

Visit **https://connect.springerpub.com/** and look for the **"Show Supplementary"** button on your **book homepage** to see what is available to instructors! First time using Springer Publishing Connect? Email **textbook@springerpub.com** to create an account and start unlocking valuable resources.

CULTURALLY RESPONSIVE COUNSELOR EDUCATION

Sherritta Hughes, PhD, LPC, ACS, CWC, has been making a profound impact in the field of counseling since 2010 with a passion for fostering mental wellness and championing cultural responsiveness. A licensed professional counselor, she embarked on her journey at Morgan State University, where she earned her Bachelor of Science degree. She further honed her expertise with a Master of Science in Clinical Psychology, Counselor License Track, from Alabama A&M University. Committed to advancing her knowledge and influence, Dr. Hughes achieved her doctorate in Counselor Education and Supervision from The Chicago School of Professional Psychology, Washington DC Campus.

Dr. Hughes's dedication to multicultural counseling and leadership has been recognized through prestigious accolades, notably receiving The Rita L. Robinson Multicultural Counseling Award for her exemplary contributions. Her leadership roles are a testament to her commitment to the profession and the communities she serves. She has presided over esteemed organizations such as the North Atlantic Region of Counselor Educators and Supervisors, the New Jersey Counseling Association, the Maryland Association for Multicultural Counseling, and the New Jersey Multicultural Counseling Association.

Deeply invested in community well-being, Dr. Hughes has been actively involved in Somerset, New Jersey, serving on the Freeholder's Boards to address local needs and initiatives. In 2016, she launched Counselor Education, Supervision, and Development, LLC, a pioneering venture where she designs National Board of Certified Counselors (NBCC)–approved continuing education and training content for counselors nationwide. This platform underscores her commitment to elevating the standards of counselor education and fostering professional growth.

Amid the challenges of the COVID-19 pandemic in 2020, Dr. Hughes recognized the amplified need for accessible mental health services. She founded Hughes Integrative Wellness, Org., a nonprofit organization dedicated to providing culturally responsive treatment modalities. This initiative not only serves clients seeking empathetic, personalized care but also offers recent graduates invaluable opportunities to work and learn how to run a private practice rooted in cultural responsiveness.

In academia, Dr. Hughes has excelled as both faculty and program director of a Clinical Mental Health Counseling (CMHC) master's program. Currently, she enriches minds as an adjunct faculty member at the University of Southern California, sharing her wealth of knowledge and practical insights with the next generation of school counselors. Her research agenda is dynamic and impactful, focusing on wellness interventions and counseling practices for athletes and communities that are underrepresented in academic literature.

Today, Dr. Hughes's private practice operates in Somerset and Trenton, New Jersey, where her work is centered on holistic wellness, self-care, sociocultural identity development, and addressing social dilemmas that impact mental health and well-being. Her approach is integrative and compassionate, reflecting her belief in the power of culturally responsive interventions to transform lives.

Dr. Hughes's journey is one of dedication, leadership, and an unwavering commitment to advocacy and education. Her contributions continue to shape the field of counseling, empowering both professionals and clients to navigate the complexities of mental health with confidence and cultural sensitivity.

CULTURALLY RESPONSIVE COUNSELOR EDUCATION

Multicultural Education, Curricula Design, and Praxis

Sherritta Hughes, PhD, LPC, ACS, CWC

SPRINGER PUBLISHING

Springer Publishing Company, LLC
902 Carnegie Center/Suite 140, Princeton, NJ 08540
www.springerpub.com
connect.springerpub.com

Acquisitions Editor: Mindy Okura-Marszycki
Production Editor: Claire Kramer
Compositor: Thomson Digital

ISBN: 978-0-8261-7682-0
eBook ISBN: 978-0-8261-6541-1
DOI: 10.1891/9780826165411

SUPPLEMENTS:

SPRINGER PUBLISHING CONNECT™ | **A robust set of instructor resources designed to supplement this text is located at http://connect.springerpub.com/content/book/978-0-8261-6541-1. Qualifying instructors may request access by emailing textbook@springerpub.com.**

Instructor Materials:
LMS Common Cartridge With All Instructor Resources ISBN: 978-0-8261-5149-0
Instructor's Manual ISBN: 978-0-8261-6772-9
Instructor Test Bank ISBN: 978-0-8261-6056-0
Instructor Chapter PowerPoints ISBN: 978-0-8261-6189-5
Instructor Sample Syllabus ISBN: 978-0-8261-7687-5
CACREP Competency Mapping ISBN: 978-0-8261-0068-9

25 26 27 28 / 5 4 3 2 1

Library of Congress Cataloging-in-Publication Data

Names: Hughes, Sherritta author
Title: Culturally responsive counselor education : multicultural education, curricula design, and praxis / Sherritta Hughes, PhD, LPC, ACS, CWC.
Description: First Springer Publishing edition. | Princeton, NJ : Springer Publishing Company, 2026. | Includes bibliographical references and index.
Identifiers: LCCN 2025020650 (print) | LCCN 2025020651 (ebook) | ISBN 9780826176820 | ISBN 9780826165411 ebook
Subjects: LCSH: Educational counseling--Study and teaching | Culturally relevant pedagogy | Curriculum planning | Multicultural education
Classification: LCC LB1027.5 .H79 2026 (print) | LCC LB1027.5 (ebook)
LC record available at https://lccn.loc.gov/2025020650
LC ebook record available at https://lccn.loc.gov/2025020651

Publisher's Note: **New and used products purchased from third-party sellers are not guaranteed for quality, authenticity, or access to any included digital components.**

Printed in the United States of America by Gasch Printing.

CONTENTS

PREFACE

In a world that grows more interconnected each day, the importance of culturally responsive teaching (CRT) in counselor education cannot be overstated. As our societies become more diverse, the need for educators who can navigate and embrace this diversity in their classrooms is crucial. It is within this context that *Culturally Responsive Counselor Education: Multicultural Education, Curricula Design, and Praxis* was conceived.

This book is a result of extensive research, reflection, and a commitment to fostering equity and inclusivity in the field of counselor education. It aims to provide both aspiring and seasoned counselor educators with the knowledge and tools necessary to create affirming, equitable, and effective learning environments for their students.

OVERALL GOAL OF THE BOOK

The overarching goal of this book is to equip counselor educators with the principles, strategies, and tools to effectively implement CRT in their programs. By doing so, we aim to prepare future counselors to work compassionately and competently with diverse client populations.

DISTINGUISHING FEATURES

This book stands out for its comprehensive approach to culturally responsive counselor education. It integrates theoretical frameworks with practical applications, providing readers with a robust understanding of what CRT is and how to implement it. Key distinguishing features include:

- in-depth exploration of multicultural education and CRT principles
- practical strategies for creating inclusive learning environments
- detailed discussions on the role of artificial intelligence (AI) in counselor education
- example assignments and rubrics for measuring cultural responsiveness
- instructor resources

In its support of counselor educators across their journey toward cultural responsiveness, this book includes a variety of instructor resources:

- reflection questions for critical thinking
- sample course descriptions based on CRT

- further reading recommendations
- sample assignments and rubrics that align with CRT principles

INTENDED AUDIENCE

This book is intended for a wide range of readers within the field of counselor education, including:

- counselor education and supervision (CES) doctoral students
- junior faculty members
- seasoned faculty members

PART I: ON BECOMING CULTURALLY RESPONSIVE IN COUNSELOR EDUCATION

Chapter 1: Culturally Responsive Teaching, Counselor Education, and Curricula Reform

This chapter introduces the rationale for the significance of CRT and examines its role as an element of meaning within educational reform, which constitutes an ongoing process in the preparation of counselor education curricula.

Chapter 2: Preparing for Teaching as Counselor Educators: Creating Affirming and Equitable Learning Environments for Learners and Educators

This chapter examines essential preparatory aspects for instructors in CES programs, emphasizing cultural awareness, pedagogical philosophy, adaptability, personal well-being, and continuous education. It underscores the importance of self-examination, development, and adaptation in becoming a culturally responsive counseling educator.

PART II: ON BEING INFORMED, AWARE, AND READY TO APPLY CULTURALLY RESPONSIVE TEACHING IN COUNSELOR EDUCATION

Chapter 3: Shifting a Curricula Paradigm: Addressing a Growing Diversity in Counselor Education Through the Foundations of Culturally Responsive Teaching Approaches

This chapter examines the shift toward CRT approaches in counselor education to address growing diversity in student populations. It explores key principles and models of CRT, and provides strategies for overcoming contextual challenges.

Chapter 4: Culturally Responsive Counselor Education: Tools for Teaching

This chapter explores essential tools and strategies for fostering CRT in counselor education programs. It provides a comprehensive guide for developing skills for the use of these tools, which include cultural humility, empathy, advocacy, and reflective practice.

PART III: EVALUATING CULTURALLY RESPONSIVE TEACHING THROUGH THE COUNSELOR EDUCATION PROGRAMMING: SYSTEMS, METRICS, AND ARTIFICIAL INTELLIGENCE

Chapter 5: Culturally Responsive Teaching Across the Required Coursework

This chapter presents the application of CRT across counselor education curricula. It includes example assignments demonstrating cultural responsiveness and uniquely designed rubrics that correspond to these assignments.

Chapter 6: Culturally Responsive Teaching in the Era of Artificial Intelligence

This chapter examines emerging and contemporary applications of AI programs as tools within counselor education. It provides detailed descriptions of these AI programs and tools, and discusses how they can be ethically integrated to enhance cultural responsiveness.

This book is a call to action for counselor educators to engage in continuous reflection, professional development, and praxis. It underscores the necessity of self-examination, growth, and adaptation in the journey toward becoming a culturally responsive educator. My hope is that this work will inspire and guide CES faculty in their efforts to cultivate inclusive, compassionate, and effective educational settings.

Sherritta Hughes

INTRODUCTION

This first edition companion textbook, *Culturally Responsive Counselor Education: Multicultural Education, Curricula Design, and Praxis,* focuses on the preparation of counselor educators who aspire to faculty and leadership positions in counselor preparation programs, with an emphasis on CRT. The primary context where the information may be applied is counselor education programs where students pursue master's degrees that fulfill educational requirements for licensure as mental health counselors. The text addresses interconnected subtopics, including practical elements and applications of the relationships between implementing multicultural education throughout counselor preparation curricula and pedagogical praxis principles within a framework of CRT.

This textbook is a contribution to the existing body of literature that supports pedagogical approaches and enhances understanding of learning processes in counselor preparation programs–Atieno Okech & Rubel (2019); Curran (1972); Barrio Minton, Gibson, & Wachter Morris, (2016); Brotherton (1996); Haddock & Whitman (2018); Vela (2020); West, Bubenzer, Cox, & McGlothlin (2013). Collectively, these publications have, in part, established the foundation for the present companion textbook by providing fundamental insights into the significance of addressing teaching and learning in counselor education through theoretical frameworks, practical applications, and clinical implications grounded in empirical literature across counselor education and supervision scholarship.

In alignment with scholars who have aimed at instructing faculty in counselor education (Barrio-Minton, Atieno Oketch, West, Vela, and so forth), the emphasis here is on the provision of elements that reflect the importance of preparing future counselor educator faculty to teach through pedagogical principles that adeptly demonstrate applications of culturally responsive praxis across the entire curriculum. As preparation for the classroom environment is wrapped up in an ethos of teaching skills that vary across disciplines in terms of theoretical models and strategies to implement for learning and course designs, this book is designed to capture or demonstrate preparational foundations to begin practicing instructional skills. Several key and interconnected general objectives of this book constitute a compilation of reflections and critical analyses derived from the author's teaching experiences, insights gained from studying praxis, and considerations of culturally diverse student cohorts engaged in teaching and learning counseling curricula. These key and general objectives are:

1. Intentionally incorporate learning materials that reflect social and cultural diversity, representing learners, counselors, educators, and supervisors both within and outside the learning environment.
2. Establish multicultural learning environments that are designed and evaluated as safe spaces for learners who identify at intersections of identity where marginalization, discrimination, and oppressive experiences occur; particularly for those who occupy positions reflecting minoritized and racialized ethnic identities.
3. Engage courageously in meaningful faculty-learner discourse on the current social, racial, and political climate that also exists in counselor preparation classrooms.
4. Lastly, embed cultural responsiveness into comprehensive teaching practices, conceptually described to include pedagogy used to frame and strategize teaching, learning materials and course book selections, program or department policy, learning objectives, course syllabi, assignment feedback and rubrics, assessments, and evaluations.

GROUNDING

In higher education institutions across the United States, there is a continuous increase in social and cultural diversity among students and faculty (Sabela et al., 2023). Sabela et al. (2023) emphasize the significance of addressing the growing diversity in higher education, asserting that when properly managed, it will enhance student access, success rates, and performance in educational settings. As the diversity among students and faculty expands in higher education, the imperative to meet the learning needs of diverse classrooms has precipitated a call for reform across college and university campuses, including graduate level programs in counselor education.

Culturally responsive reform is frequently met with apprehension, disapproval, and rhetoric that advocates for the preservation of traditional teaching methodologies and learning content as the established norm, often expressed as "this is the way we have done it and that is how we will continue." Much of the traditional teaching methodologies and learning content is predicated upon a Eurocentric, male, cisgender-dominated perspective, whereby higher education classrooms tend to be marginalizing and oppressive for learners who identify with minoritized social and cultural groups. According to Martinez-Acosta and Favero (2018), a genuine evaluation and examination of inclusive strategies must be conducted on our campuses to ensure we adequately address the requirements of our entire student body. Consequently, educators in higher education learning environments are encouraged to recognize this not only as a fundamental problem but also as a systemic issue that necessitates reform-oriented action across disciplines (Cochrane et al., 2017).

The apprehension surrounding the teaching of diversity in higher education stems from various factors, including misconceptions, resistance to change, concerns about potential impacts on traditional curricula, and sheer racist views on including diverse scholarship, narratives, and perspectives on historical and present accounts of issues and dynamics being taught. However, understanding and embracing diversity are crucial in every aspect across all levels of higher education for several reasons:

- At the institutional level, diversity education fosters an inclusive campus environment, preparing students for a globalized workforce. It enhances the institution's reputation, attracts a diverse student body and faculty, and promotes innovation through varied perspectives.
- At the departmental level, incorporating diversity into curricula enriches academic discourse, encourages critical thinking, and broadens the scope of research. It helps departments stay relevant and responsive to societal changes and industry demands.
- At the classroom level, diversity education improves student engagement, promotes empathy and cultural competence, and prepares students for diverse professional environments. It also challenges educators to adopt inclusive teaching practices and address unconscious biases.
- At the individual level, exposure to diversity enhances personal growth, develops intercultural communication skills, and cultivates a more nuanced understanding of complex social issues.
- Implementing diversity education across these system levels is essential for creating a more equitable, inclusive, and effective higher education landscape that better serves all students and prepares them for success in an increasingly diverse world.

Educational reform further pertains to equity in the classroom in order to better meet learning needs of culturally diverse students and the intentional use of culturally responsive instruction and pedagogical approaches. This is not a novel concept, but one that has been in existence throughout the history of the United States, especially during the height of the Civil Rights Era. At that time it was cast as a political agenda, when it has always been a human equity agenda (which is commonly considered political in and of itself). Educational reform advocates for the use of multicultural education, emphasizing the importance of learning materials that reflect all learners, particularly those who are representative of ethnically and racially diverse students.

Educational reform in the context of CRT practices is exemplified in the works of Paulo Freire, bell hooks, Zaretta Hammond, James A. Banks, and Gloria Ladson-Billings, among others. It is imperative that we as CES faculty become more familiar with these pedagogy scholars:

- Freire is a Brazilian educational scholar most recognized for his book, *Pedagogy of the Oppressed* (1970). Across his advocacy for educational reform, Freire emphasized the importance of culture, use of (and teaching learners to practice) critical consciousness, and a liberatory praxis designed for instructional freedom that addresses society.
- bell hooks is a feminist and educational advocate and scholar, whose views within educational reform are about teaching educators to create empowering learning environments that respect and value learners from all backgrounds. hooks wrote a series of books that communicate how to incorporate feminist pedagogy as a strategy that serves

to disrupt the oppressed-oppressor relationship, oppose White supremacy, and design learning environments that are designed for equitable and just higher education.

- Hammond is the author of *Culturally Responsive Teaching and the Brain* (2015), which focuses on how educators can use brain science to create more inclusive and effective learning environments. Through her scholarship, Hammond teaches practical guides that offer directions for what to do and critical points that serve as how it works among learners.
- Banks, who was a pioneer of multicultural education and teaching scholar-practitioner, formulated a series of frameworks to integrate CRT in education policy, requirements for teaching, and praxis for what educators are to do with skill. As founder of the Center for Multicultural Education at the University of Washington, Banks developed the four levels of multicultural curriculum reform, which is infused with theory on educational and social justice that supports learners and professional development for educators.
- Gloria Ladson-Billings, a significant scholar-practitioner in CRT, is an expert in culturally relevant pedagogy for social and cultural diverse learning environments. Known as a pedagogical theorist, Ladson-Billings introduced the concept of culturally responsive pedagogy (CRP) in a groundbreaking article, "Toward a Theory of Culturally Relevant Pedagogy" (Ladson-Billings, 1995). CRP is considered to be a fundamental approach necessary for multidisciplinary educators and contains three main components: critical consciousness, cultural competence, and academic success.

These and other culturally responsive education scholars are examined throughout the text, with explorations about how their works can be used to inform implications for pedagogical principles in CRT within counselor education. Collectively, their perspectives form a foundation for preparing counselor educators to use methodologies that reflect CRP in teaching counselor education curricula at both the doctoral and master's level of education.

In alignment with the comprehensive tenets of educational reform of curricula and instructional methods in higher education, the discipline of CES has a lineage of scholars and practitioners who assert that instruction in pedagogical methods is crucial in preparing faculty to implement more intentional, culturally responsive counselor education. The following are a few scholars in CES who have made significant contributions to CRT:

- Dr. Renae D. Mayes: widely recognized for her contributions to culturally responsive counseling. Her extensive publications in this field have earned her multiple accolades.
- Dr. Cheryl Holcomb-McCoy: significant contributions to the field of school counseling with her emphasis on cultural responsiveness. Her studies and written works have had a substantial impact on many professionals in this area.
- Dr. Laveria Hutchison: published on CRT in higher education and its application in counselor education.
- Dr. Meghan Comstock: produced research that explored the relationship between professional learning, teacher beliefs, and CRT practices.

Themes across CES scholarship that demonstrate this alignment pertain to instructional approaches, curriculum development, and teaching and learning theory, with the latter being central to the content of this textbook.

PEDAGOGY IN COUNSELOR EDUCATION

Teaching theory is regarded as the conceptual application of pedagogy that encompasses the principles and methods that form the foundation for effective teaching and learning. It provides a framework for educators to design, implement, and evaluate instructional practices. In counselor education (CE), there is not one specific pedagogy taught or generally applied. Pedagogy is described and applied broadly in CE yet can be categorized similarly to a taxonomy of pedagogies, and similarly to those considered among the critical pedagogies. *The Critical Pedagogy Reader* (2003), edited by Darder, Baltodano, and Torres, argues that pedagogies should go beyond merely shaping teaching methods, educational principles, and instructional approaches, which often align with learning theories and are backed by empirical research. Instead, they should strive to incorporate a wide range of diverse perspectives and viewpoints. This approach aims to enhance the ability of progressive educators to critically examine how capitalism and gender and racialized relations affect students from historically marginalized communities.

CE, as a social science, integrates teaching constructs and material from psychology, philosophy, education, sociology, and anthropology. These interconnected disciplines address human development and concerns, forming a holistic framework that can be experienced across the curricula of CE. Hence, it is important to use multiple learning and teaching materials to capture the comprehensive scope of CE curricula. This utility will involve preparing lessons and courses in CE via interconnections among these other disciplines to formulate intentional pedagogy that supports counseling practice. To do this, some educators have formed integrative educational frameworks based on cultural relationships that promote connections between educators, learners, and the taught subject. Harriet L. Schwartz implements an example of this in her 2019 book, *Connected Teaching: Relationship, Power, and Mattering in Higher Education.*

In the context of higher education, Schwartz (2019) explores relational cultural theory (RCT) in terms of how fostering meaningful relationships between teachers and students can enhance the learning experience. Schwartz emphasizes the importance of emotional and intellectual connections, arguing that these relationships are crucial for student development and academic success. She also addresses the dynamics of power and authenticity in the classroom, highlighting the concept of "mattering" and its impact on the student-teacher relationship. This latter focus is in alignment with critical pedagogy, which is shaped into the foundation of what is being encouraged to use in preparing Counselor Education and Supervision (CES) for teaching in this era of the 21st century.

As pedagogy in CES becomes increasingly significant in the preparation of learning materials and course design that supports practitioners and their future clients, it is imperative that the profession evolves and further develops with intentionality to address the teaching and learning needs of culturally diverse adult learners. The objective is for counselor educators and supervisors to establish effective relationships with students, imparting the importance of critical thinking and emphasizing that progressing through the curricula is not solely about achieving high grades but, rather, developing the capacity to engage with clients and colleagues through a culturally responsive perspective.

BOOK OVERVIEW

Themes

The primary themes of this book are centrally aligned in a bidirectional manner with CRT at the core. The central alignment of themes serves to illustrate the content as being interrelated and connected and having bidirectional impact. The first theme focuses on CRT. It will be delineated according to a definition, acknowledging principles outlined in research for teaching in higher education. Practical examples of CRT will be presented as they pertain to preparing culturally responsive counselor educators (CRCE) who will teach CE curricula. The objective for this theme is to construct an action-oriented guide and tool for doctoral students and faculty to use across pedagogical practices for a shift toward a multicultural education lens of teaching.

The second theme pertains to the specific focus on the significance of deeper understanding of CRT as an approach to equip current and prospective CES educators who elect to pursue faculty positions. A set of multimodal resources will serve as instructional teaching interventions that value and affirm the social and cultural backgrounds of all learners, addressing an educational reform imperative for counselor education to incorporate inclusive pedagogy based on a multicultural perspective. This approach will subsequently enhance the use of diverse representation within and across learning content used in counselor education coursework. This theme aims to elucidate the critical issue of educating counselor educators on teaching methods that acknowledge the historical perpetuation of social and cultural biases in counselor education curricula, which have been oppressive, exclusionary, and predominantly taught through a Western Eurocentric cisgender White male framework.

The third and final theme proposed for the book aims to describe how CRT serves as an asset for doctoral students and their future students to see themselves and their cultures reflected in the CE curriculum. On the basis of the author's experience as an educator in and outside of the formal classroom, a mental healthcare provider, a colleague with a strong CES identity, and an African American woman, there has been an observed gradual increase in social and cultural diversity among master's and doctoral degree stakeholders (e.g., students, faculty, leadership, and staff). Although this development is encouraging, much of the CE learning content remains static. Furthermore, the approaches to student engagement and limited representation of racially and minoritized scholarly learning content persist. Consequently, this theme intends to objectively illustrate what will be termed "snapshots" of CES experiences in the classroom. In the context of this book, snapshots will serve as case examples of CRT being needed or applied across career work.

Key Features of Each Chapter

- Snapshot–A counselor educator's experience in the classroom
- Quote from a CES
- Content Summaries
- Culturally Responsive Counselor Educator (CRCE) Skills Textbox
- Further Reading

USER'S GUIDE

Book Content Outline

Part I	On Becoming Culturally Responsive in Counselor Education	
Chapter 1	Culturally Responsive Teaching, Counselor Education, and Curricula Reform	This chapter introduces the rationale for the significance of CRT and examines its role as an element of meaning within educational reform, which constitutes an ongoing process in the preparation of counselor education curricula.
Chapter 2	Preparing for Teaching as Counselor Educators: Creating Affirming and Equitable Learning Environments for Learners and Educators	This examines essential preparatory aspects for instructors in CES programs, emphasizing cultural awareness, pedagogical philosophy, adaptability, personal well-being, and continuous education. Key elements include understanding personal and student cultural identity formation to create inclusive learning environments. Intersectionality helps analyze how various identities shape experiences. A CRT approach necessitates introspection about one's beliefs and biases to establish equitable classrooms that respect diverse viewpoints. A growth mindset enables educators to view obstacles as development opportunities and refine their pedagogical techniques. Prioritizing self-care and preventing burnout are vital for maintaining effectiveness and modeling healthy habits for students, involving awareness of burnout indicators, self-care practices, and seeking support. Continuous learning through professional growth, flexibility, and self-reflection enhances educators' cultural competence. This preparation enables CES faculty to foster inclusive, compassionate, and effective educational settings, equipping counseling students to work with diverse clients. It underscores the importance of self-examination, development, and adaptation in becoming a culturally responsive counseling educator.

(continued)

Part II	On Being Informed, Aware, and Ready to Apply Culturally Responsive Teaching in Counselor Education	
Chapter 3	Shifting a Curricula Paradigm: Addressing a Growing Diversity in Counselor Education Through the Foundations of Culturally Responsive Teaching Approaches	This chapter examines the shift toward CRT approaches in counselor education to address growing diversity in student populations. It explores key principles and models of CRT, including Gloria Ladson-Billings' CRP, Geneva Gay's CRT model, and Django Paris and H. Samy Alim's culturally sustaining pedagogy (CSP). Discussion is offered on the importance of multicultural competence, evidence-based teaching practices, and reflective supervision in counselor education. A highlight is an outline on the contextual challenges in implementing CRT and a provision of strategies for overcoming them. The chapter also introduces assessment tools for measuring cultural responsiveness in curricula and teaching practices. By integrating these frameworks, approaches, and assessments, counselor educators can create more inclusive, equitable learning environments that prepare future counselors to work effectively with diverse populations. An emphasis is based on the need for ongoing reflection, professional development, and praxis to continually improve cultural responsiveness in counselor education programs.
Chapter 4	Culturally Responsive Counselor Education: Tools for Teaching	This chapter is centric to our increasingly diverse and interconnected world. Content explores what makes culturally responsive counselor education paramount for preparing future counselors to effectively serve diverse populations. The chapter explores essential tools and strategies for fostering CRT in counselor education programs. The teaching tools addressed are (a) awareness of sociocultural complexities in teaching, (b) hidden curriculum, (c) social and cultural capital, (d) cultural humility, (e) empathy and advocacy, (f) reflective practice, (g) multicultural competence, (h) pedagogical practice, (i) language barriers, (j) technology use in counselor education, and (k) advocacy-focused teaching. Content of the chapter further provides a comprehensive guide for counselor educators who are preparing to teach a breakdown of the tool, shaped to illustrate a practical approach for developing skills for use of the tools

(continued)

Part III	Evaluating Culturally Responsive Teaching Throughout the Counselor Education Programming: Systems, Metrics, and Artificial Intelligence	
Chapter 5	Culturally Responsive Teaching Across the Required Coursework	This chapter presents the application of CRT across counselor education curricula. The curricula comprise core courses mandated by the National Board of Certified Counselors (NBCC) and most state boards of examiners for professional counseling. NBCC and state boards of examiners are institutions that regulate aspects of the licensing process for individuals who (a) complete counselor education curricula at the master's level, and (b) review applications for required course completion to obtain the master's degree in counseling. In addition to the core courses in counselor education, the more common elective courses based on areas of specialization are included. In alignment with the CRT applications across counselor education curricula, example assignments demonstrating cultural responsiveness and uniquely designed rubrics that correspond to the assignments are provided. Furthermore, this chapter incorporates a summary of the most current Council for Accreditation of Counseling and Related Educational Programs (CACREP) Standards (2024) that align with the culturally responsive course learning objectives, which are suggested as a guide for CES faculty to formulate their own.
Chapter 6	Culturally Responsive Teaching in the Era of Artificial Intelligence	This chapter examines emerging and contemporary applications of AI programs as tools within counselor education. It provides detailed descriptions of these AI programs and tools, elucidating how faculty may use them appropriately and instruct students in their ethical use, in accordance with strategies proposed by the American Counseling Association (ACA). The chapter's content focuses on the use of AI as an ethical responsibility, an analysis of potential challenges associated with AI implementation, proposed solutions to these challenges, the application of AI in assessment and evaluation processes, and strategies for maintaining relevance in the current AI-driven era.

REFERENCES

Barrio Minton, C. A., Gibson, D. M., & Wachter Morris, C. A. (Eds.). (2016). *Evaluating student learning outcomes in counselor education*. American Counseling Association.

Brotherton, S. J. (1996). *Counselor education for the twenty-first century*. Bergin & Garvey.

Cochrane, T., Narayan, V., & Oldfield, J. (2017). Designing authentic student learning experiences through technology-enhanced learning design frameworks. *Journal of Interactive Learning Research, 28*(2), 137–157.

Curran, C. A. (1972). *Counseling-learning: A whole-person model for education*. New York: Grune & Stratton.

Darder, A., Baltodano, M., & Torres, R. D. (2003). Critical pedagogy: An introduction. In A. Darder, M. Baltodano, & R. D. Torres (Eds.), *The critical pedagogy reader* (pp. 1–20). Routledge.

Freire, P. (1970). *Pedagogy of the oppressed. Penguin Modern Classics*. Penguin Classics.

Haddock, L. R., & Whitman, J. S. (Eds.). (2018). *Preparing the educator in counselor education: A comprehensive guide to building knowledge and developing skills*. Routledge.

Hammond, Z. L. (2015). *Culturally responsive teaching and the brain*. Corwin Press.

Ladson-Billings, G. (1995). Toward a theory of culturally relevant pedagogy. *American Educational Research Journal, 32*(3), 465–491. https://doi.org/10.2307/1163320

Martinez-Acosta, V. G., & Favero, C. B. (2018). A discussion of diversity and inclusivity at the institutional level: The need for a strategic plan. *Journal of Undergraduate Neuroscience Education, 16*(3), A252–A260. PMID: 30254540; PMCID: PMC6153014.

Okech, J. E. A., & Rubel, D. J. (Eds.). (2019). *Counselor education in the 21st century: Issues and experiences*. American Counseling Association.

Sabela, P. T., Masuku, M. M., & Mthembu, Z. (2023). Diversity and its implications for teaching and learning in higher educational institutions. In M. O. Maguvhe & M. M. Masuku (Eds.), *Using African epistemologies in shaping inclusive education knowledge*. Palgrave Macmillan. https://doi.org/10.1007/978-3-031-31115-4_22

Schwartz, H. L. (2019). *Connected teaching: Relationship, power, and mattering in higher education* (1st ed.). Stylus Publishing, LLC.

Vela, J. C. (2020). *Teaching and learning in counselor education*. American Counseling Association.

West, J. D., Bubenzer, D. L., Cox, J. A., & McGlothlin, J. M. (Eds.). (2013). *Teaching in counselor education: Engaging students in learning*. Association for Counselor Education and Supervision.

INSTRUCTOR RESOURCES

SPRINGER PUBLISHING CONNECT™ | A robust set of instructor resources designed to supplement this text is located at **http://connect.springerpub.com/content/book/978-0-8261-6541-1**. Qualifying instructors may request access by emailing **textbook@springerpub.com**.

- **LMS Common Cartridge With All Instructor Resources**
- **Instructor's Manual:**
  - Learning Activities for each chapter
  - Teaching Tips
- **Instructor Sample Syllabus** containing a course overview and sample course syllabus for a 15-week course with course descriptions, course objectives, readings, assignments, course schedules, and more.
- **Instructor Chapter PowerPoints** summarizing chapter content.
- **Instructor Test Bank** with more than **50** multiple-choice questions (including full rationales).
- **CACREP Competency Mapping**

PART I

ON BECOMING CULTURALLY RESPONSIVE IN COUNSELOR EDUCATION

CHAPTER 1

CULTURALLY RESPONSIVE TEACHING, COUNSELOR EDUCATION, AND CURRICULA REFORM

Multicultural education is a reform movement designed to create equal educational opportunities for all students, regardless of their cultural background. It seeks to transform the curriculum, teaching methods, and school environment to reflect the diverse cultural backgrounds of students.

—James A. Banks

LEARNING OBJECTIVES After studying this chapter, you will be able to:

- Articulate the meaning and characteristics of culturally responsive teaching (CRT) in relation to its interconnectivity to multicultural education (ME) and critical pedagogy (CP) to conceptually ground reasoning for it being important for the preparation of teaching in counselor preparation programs.
- Compile a concise overview of key insights of ME that grounds CRT as a pedagogical approach that stems from culturally responsive pedagogy.
- Introduce scholars of culturally responsive educators who examine, integrate, and publish pedagogical research that forms the basis for curriculum reform in counselor education and who highlight supporting concepts for developing a framework of CRT practices.

SNAPSHOT: A counselor educator's career experience

In my Advanced Psychopathology course, I frequently emphasize cultural responsiveness when teaching diagnostic skills. My instructional approach highlights direct verbiage published in the *Diagnostic and Statistical Manual of Mental Disorders* (5th edition text revision; *DSM-5-TR; American Psychiatric Association [APA], 2022)* that explains how diagnosis is a crucial aspect of mental healthcare that affects individuals with minority racial identities in negative ways. Recently, I have made it a priority to address the updates in the *DSM-5-TR* (APA, 2022) that explore (a) institutional racism and bias, (b) histories of overdiagnosing and wrongly diagnosing African American men with symptoms of psychosis, (c) a new public awareness of inclusive language being necessary for an address of gender diversity, and (d) historically othering persons as *non-White*, now recognizing the use of such a terminology is marginalizing and oppressive. I explain that under the guidance of Dr. Althea Stewart, the 145th APA president (2018–2019), the psychiatric field implemented changes focused on increasing cultural inclusivity and addressing healthcare professionals' potential racist and exclusionary biases, which can limit access to quality care for people of all sociocultural backgrounds. My course takes a multidisciplinary approach, incorporating materials from psychiatric medicine, biology, social psychology, and counseling. Invariably, a student questions the importance of cultural responsiveness in these areas, often in a rhetorical and insensitive manner. In one instance, a student repeatedly raised this question throughout the semester, suggestive of a disguised comment rather than genuine inquiry. What strategies would you use for students enrolled in counselor education programs who struggle to accept the existence of various forms of racism within their chosen profession? How would you address their skepticism toward culturally responsive teaching methods that emphasize these issues, especially when they find such concepts difficult to believe?

INTRODUCTION

This chapter delineates an introduction to culturally responsive teaching (CRT) and its foundational principles and characteristics. More in-depth descriptions are examined throughout the context of this book. Additionally, this chapter provides accounts of the counselor education and supervision (CES) discipline in terms of it harnessing CRT across preparing educators, one of three central role constructs of CES. Chapter 2 addresses the other two central constructs—counselor and supervisor—as they are also integral to CES preparation.

To ground this chapter, I begin by introducing the concept and meaning of multicultural education (ME). Its purpose is to guide understanding of a complex practicality of, and meaning-making for, use of CRT in counseling education curricula. Garnering use and understanding ME is in relation to intersecting propositions that are based on (a) CES development as faculty with strong professional counselor identity, (b) intentional curriculum design that supports reflection of the increasingly diverse counselors-in-training cohorts and future consumers whom they will have cross-cultural encounters with for therapeutic services, and lastly, (c) program evaluation that is less punitive and more aligned with support of culturally responsive pedagogical practices and applied approaches.

MULTICULTURAL EDUCATION

ME is practical and applicable to information on the growing cultural diversity in U.S. classrooms (K–12 and in higher education). It is gaining in traction for teaching preparation for counselor training programs because of societal events that are often impacting students in counselor education (CE) graduate programs and that exemplify presenting problems of clients with whom they will work across their careers and in the more experiential courses like practicum and internship. Conceptually, ME is characterized in numerous contexts that elucidate pedagogical practices and theoretical paradigms. It constitutes an interactive and continuous process that systematically aims to include and affirm diversity by promoting educational equity for all students. It encompasses the instructional design that considers all students regarding their worldviews, histories in the shared society, and ways that the learning materials have historically left out many conditions that illustrate oppression, marginalization, and various other -isms. Essentially, ME fosters an intentional inclusive educational environment.

In the 10th edition of their influential textbook, *Multicultural Education: Issues and Perspectives*, Banks and Banks (2019) conceptualize ME as a prescriptive reform aimed at addressing educational inequalities rooted in racism. The foundation of the ME approach is predicated on several concepts, commencing with the fundamental principle that all students possess a legal and equal right to education. This core precept has subsequently expanded to encompass the necessity for broader equality across educational institutions, extending beyond racial issues or the exclusion of African Americans to incorporate individuals with diverse cultural and social identities who experience disadvantages and lack power.

The concept of "lacking power" is within the context of privilege and refers to the systemic and structural inequalities that exist in society, where certain groups hold unearned advantages and benefits (privilege) while others face systemic disadvantages and marginalization (lack of power). Privilege is often invisible to those who possess it, as it is embedded within societal norms and structures. This dynamic creates power imbalances that affect access to resources, opportunities, and social privileges. For example, individuals who belong to commonly considered "dominant" groups (e.g., White, male, able-bodied) often have greater access to education, employment, and healthcare, whereas those from marginalized groups (e.g., so-called people of color, women, individuals with disabilities) face barriers and discrimination. These power imbalances perpetuate cycles of disadvantage and inequality, making it difficult for marginalized groups to achieve the same level of success and well-being as their privileged counterparts. These experiences of power are often in action within our classrooms, operating as undercurrents that are not always obvious. However, ME helps educators realize this as a dynamic, shifting the power differences in ways to empower students.

In contemporary discourse, ME has evolved to become multicontextual, addressing inequalities based on a wide range of factors including gender, race, nationality, socioeconomic status, ability, language, religion, sexual orientation, and ethnicity. From the advancements of ME, Banks and Banks (2019) purport that it is necessary because historic capitalistic systems of White supremacy have awarded particular learners better educational experiences and tools necessary in classrooms. The latter idea is based on the fact that education, as an institution, has systematically marginalized and oppressed racially minoritized cultural groups of learners, thereby reducing the chances of equal and equitable educational opportunities. Having this knowledge lends to educators being more accountable for their selection of learning materials, determining how classroom experiences play out, and gaining a level of competence to address systemic complexities that are in effect and require dismantling. For example, the gap in access to learning material is reflective across histories and contemporary worldviews of students who have been systemically othered because of White supremacy, institutional racism, and other marginalizing and oppressive conditions that implicitly exist and have been perpetrated via policy and in the justice system (Bhavnani, Mirza, & Meetoo, 2005). Counselor educators often hesitate to address these issues because of diverse viewpoints among adult learners, concerns about administrative repercussions, and job security worries for non-tenured faculty. Consequently, providing useful strategies during the preparatory stages will assist educators at all levels in discussing the practical implications of their curriculum and its impact on students.

ME is a reform movement across all levels of formal education, including CE programs. In K–12, it is prescriptive in addressing how educators are encouraged and currently being trained to provide instruction to meet the learning and educational needs of culturally diverse classrooms and apply those lessons in broader society. In the United States, educational reform is driven by the necessity to address pedagogical challenges arising from interactions between teachers and students. These challenges encompass limited or superficial relationships, as well as oppressive cross-cultural encounters involving learners, educators, and institutions, especially in higher education context.

In the past, ME aimed to tackle the problem of educational resources and subject matter that failed to adequately reflect the wide-ranging ethnic, cultural, social, socioeconomic, sociopolitical, and linguistic backgrounds of the student population. However, this objective is undergoing a significant transformation in the current social environment and is becoming increasingly politicized. Efforts to undermine the goals of ME are now occurring through legislative actions at both state and federal governmental levels. Therefore, actively attending to these experiences between learner and educator, as well as addressing culturally homogeneous (e.g., based on a singular or so-called "standard" cultural group) learning material, would demonstrate an intentional inclusion of diverse worldviews and lived experiences at macro and micro levels of society. Furthermore, a historic and contemporary pedagogical challenge that pertains to ME is entrenched in approaches to teaching that tend to remain static; these are centered on a male, White, dominant Western perspective. This type of continuity fails to capture or address the sociocultural diversity in the classroom or learning environment, and even the diversity among faculty who require training that supports competency development in preparation for challenging discussions and discourse on the sociopolitical and sociocultural climate.

For example, consider a series of ongoing conflicts in which graduate students in CES classrooms may possess national identities reflective of, and potentially connected to, these conflicts (e.g., familial ties, attending school on a visa).

- Russia-Ukraine Conflict: This conflict commenced in 2022 when Russia initiated a military invasion of Ukraine, resulting in significant armed engagements and humanitarian crises.
- Yemeni Civil War: This ongoing conflict initiated in 2014, involved multiple factions, and culminated in a severe humanitarian crisis.
- Syrian Civil War: This complex armed conflict began in 2011 and involved the Syrian government, various opposition groups, and international actors.
- Tigray Conflict in Ethiopia: This conflict originated in 2020 between the Ethiopian government and the Tigray People's Liberation Front.

- Sudanese Conflict: Persistent armed clashes in Sudan, particularly in Darfur, have been ongoing for years, with recent escalations.
- Myanmar Conflict: Various ethnic groups and the Myanmar military have been engaged in armed conflict for decades, with recent escalations since 2021.
- Libyan Civil War: This ongoing armed conflict involving multiple factions and foreign powers has been ongoing since 2011.
- Israeli-Palestinian Conflict: This protracted conflict has featured recent escalations in Gaza (Ravid, 2025).
- Conflict in the Sahel Region: Various insurgencies and militant groups are active in countries such as Mali and Niger.

Upon reviewing the aforementioned list, which international conflicts have garnered the most attention in your experience? Which of these conflicts may have relevance to the field of counseling, and for what reasons? What factors determine which conflicts receive the most prominence in media coverage? What criteria are used to establish this hierarchy of importance?

The evolving sociocultural and sociopolitical landscapes, collectively, create both obstacles and opportunities for addressing diversity in higher education via innovative and productive ways. ME equips current and prospective educators with a comprehensive understanding of complex cultural concepts, enhances their effectiveness in diverse classroom settings, and encourages them to view race, class, gender, social status, and other cultural factors as interconnected elements.

ME strategically endeavors to transform components of the learning environment, creating relevance for education that is responsive to culture via pedagogy, policy, and programming. ME aims to support students in their development of knowledge, attitudes, and skills necessary to function within their own microcultures, the U.S. macro culture, other micro cultures, and the global community. When implemented, ME may be conceptualized as a relational, social, and inclusive system that comprehensively undergoes ongoing transformation. In this way, ME would reduce exclusivity and "the way we've always done it" attitudes among the following working parts of our educational dynamics:

- institutional policy and politics
- faculty and staff—attitudes, perceptions, beliefs, and actions
- teaching styles and strategies
- curriculum and course of study
- instructional materials
- standardized assessment and testing procedures
- institutional culture and hidden curriculum
- languages and linguistic diversity
- community relationships and partnerships

Each of the aforementioned components are of educational institutions representing areas where ME creates opportunities to address (a) student experiences in the classroom,

(b) the impact that the macro level of society has on learning content, and (c) the role educators play in educational reform. Fundamentally, when not methodically addressed through ME, these components are aspects within institutional or systemic programming that impede pedagogical improvement in teaching and learning outcomes. To achieve strategic outcomes, ME is implemented by stakeholders at every level of a college or university, functioning to disrupt and dismantle bias, oppressive learning conditions, exclusionary practices, hidden curriculum, and traditional perspectives that value resistance to change, ethnocentrism, and perpetuation of institutional biases.

Relative to CE, there is ME implementation that is reflected in the Multicultural and Social Justice Counseling Competencies (MSJCC). This set of competencies has been adopted by the American Counseling Association (ACA); faculty who teach in counselor preparation programs (e.g., Clinical Mental Health master's degree programs) teach these competencies primarily in a required course to examine multiculturalism within the context of counseling. Most recently, social justice has been collaboratively integrated with multicultural dynamics that are embedded within cross-cultural encounters at micro and macro levels of our historic and contemporary pluralistic and sociopolitical society. The embeddedness is often not taught via means of instructional praxis, but as aspirational endeavors.

Moreover, most multicultural counseling courses are structured from an issues perspective and a separatist approach. However, content of the multicultural course is increasingly being incorporated into the full scope of the curricula of counselor preparation programming. Nevertheless, among CES faculty, there is no established pedagogical approach identified to teach ME content or the provision of metrics for CES faculty who identify as ME educators to assess the effectiveness of their implementation across instructional practices. Throughout this book, I propose the adoption of CRT and pedagogy by CES to prepare faculty for teaching CE curricula at the master's and doctoral levels for students entering the counseling profession.

WHAT IS CULTURALLY RESPONSIVE TEACHING?

CRT is conceptualized by numerous scholars who prepare educators for K–12 classrooms and faculty who instruct in higher education settings (Ladson-Billings, 2021). Two scholars most known for CRT are Geneva Gay and Gloria Ladson-Billings. In her groundbreaking book, Gay (2018) defined CRT as an educational strategy that emphasizes the significance of incorporating students' cultural backgrounds into all learning aspects, thereby providing teaching implications that are grounded in theory.

Throughout their research on CRT methods (e.g., Ladson-Billings, 1995a, 1995b, 2004, 2006), Ladson-Billings characterizes it as an approach that strives to establish a learning setting where students' cultural heritage, linguistic diversity, and personal experiences are respected and woven into the educational content. Conceptually, CRT is grounded in ME and culturally responsive pedagogy in order to facilitate student engagement with challenging academic material and enhances their advanced cognitive abilities by linking new information to their preexisting knowledge and lived experiences. This is an aspect of skill development that contributes to CE preparation, enabling faculty to better engage students in transformational conversations about systemic issues prevalent in mental healthcare. It will also support greater competency in addressing current and historical sociocultural and political dynamics that influence the professional counselor's work.

CRT is also an approach posing as an umbrella concept that reflects critical pedagogy (CP; Ladson-Billings, 1995a). A first account of CP is attributed to Henry Giroux in his publication, *Theory and Resistance in Education: A Pedagogy for the Opposition* (1983). Giroux, along with other critical pedagogists—Peter McLaren, Paulo Freire, bell hooks, Maxine Greene, Donaldo Macedo, Michelle Fine—were central to educational reform of education in the United States as they endeavored to prepare teachers in a manner that was intended to be transformative for social action in the interest of oppressed communities. In reflection of this aspect of CRT, Zaretta Hammond defines CRT according to greater awareness of the diversity centric to language. This importance, in part, is reflective of the growing immigrant communities that enter the U.S. institution of education (e.g., K–12 classrooms and in higher education). Hammond, a prominent teacher educator, is known for her groundbreaking book, *Culturally Responsive Teaching and the Brain: Promoting Authentic Engagement and Rigor Among Culturally and Linguistically Diverse Students* (2015).

Hammond's definition of CRT is critical to the educator's abilities, specifically to recognize students' cultural displays of learning and meaning-making and to respond positively and constructively with teaching strategies that use cultural knowledge as a scaffold to connect students' existing knowledge to new concepts and content, thereby promoting effective information processing. Furthermore, Hammond asserts that while CRT is an approach educators should implement, they must simultaneously understand the importance of establishing relationships with students to foster healthy socioemotional connections, thus creating a safe space for learning (Hammond, 2015).

Hammond offers CRT as "one of our most powerful tools for helping students" successfully navigate the academic achievement gap that exists in and across the institution of education in the United States (p. 15). There are students who are extensively recognized in pedagogical literature as falling in the achievement gap. These students are characterized as those who are racially minoritized, possessing intersecting identities characterized by their religion, abilities, ethnicities, gender and affectionate orientations, socioeconomic status, nationality, and language. In an address of this characterization, Hammond posits that the achievement gap is not attributable to students' pluralistic identities, but rather to school policies and teacher practices that provide inadequate opportunities in the learning environment. Such positioning sits in an ethos of pedagogy that demonstrates CP, which is a composite of pedagogies that include ME and CRT.

In alignment with multicultural education (ME), critical pedagogy (CP)—a foundational component of critical race theory (CRT)—seeks to empower students from historically oppressed populations and functions as a transformative framework for challenging institutional biases through activist-oriented teaching (Darder et al., 2003; Ladson-Billings, 2014). Through teaching practices and preparation activities, CP is what Freire (2020) advocated for in *Pedagogy of the Oppressed.* Freire urged teachers to educate students according to a developing volition of freedom (that was historically suppressed) to question concepts of power, culture, and oppression that exist in the curriculum and learning materials, as though education in formal classrooms exists in isolation and without attention to the sociopolitical world beyond the classroom. Freire's groundbreaking *Pedagogy of the Oppressed,* which was first published in 1970, has had three subsequent reprints and is translated in numerous languages.

In preparation for multidisciplinary teaching, CP posits a central theme wherein students and educators establish relationships and create communities that facilitate the use of diverse instructional approaches, grounding pedagogical praxis to address the learning needs of all students (hooks, 1994; Ladson-Billings, 2004, 2023). In the *Teaching to Transgress* series of books—specifically *Teaching Community: A Pedagogy of Hope* (hooks, 2003)—bell hooks expands on this central theme by proposing that there is transformative power in the educator's role and emphasizing the importance of fostering a sense of community within educational settings. hooks underscores the necessity for educators to cultivate an environment that values diversity, dialogue, and collaboration.

hooks articulates personal experiences as an educator and examines how pedagogical practices can manifest in diverse contexts, extending beyond traditional classroom environments. She proposes a pedagogical approach grounded in love, care, commitment, knowledge, responsibility, respect, and trust (2007). Through this holistic methodology, hooks posits that educators can establish optimal conditions for learning and facilitate students' profound engagement with the subject matter.

In *Teaching Community: A Pedagogy of Hope*, hooks (2003) examines topics such as racism, the role of spirituality in education, and the necessity for progressive social change. Such themes and elective courses are now incorporated into CE programs. Consider Monmouth University in New Jersey as an illustration. Their Clinical Mental Health Counseling (CMHC) Master's of Science program includes an optional course titled "Spirituality in Counseling." This course explores global religions and various spiritual practices in which clients might engage, examining how these elements can influence client well-being and shape treatment strategies. Typically, this subject matter is only briefly addressed in multicultural counseling courses within CE curricula. To grasp the significance of such an elective, one can turn to hooks' perspective. She advocates for educators to view the entire world as a learning environment, recognizing that education can occur in diverse settings and circumstances, with spirituality and religion playing crucial roles.

hooks and other critical pedagogists posit that for institutional transformation to be effective through pedagogical praxis, the individuals engaged in both learning and teaching are integral to the process. CP is an extension within the context of CRT, by acknowledging that sociopolitical and sociocultural forces at the macro level of society (mirrored in classroom or micro levels) have maintained implicit and explicit exclusionary teaching strategies (Ladson-Billings, 1995b, 2021). An example of the implicit and explicit teaching strategies can be explained via hidden curriculum. A series of critical pedagogists explore characteristics of the hidden curriculum in order to decrease its negative impact on students' experiences of isms lending to their intersecting identities and complexities of how these students experience society in relation to their intersecting identities.

According to Giroux (Kärner & Schneider, 2024), the hidden curriculum emphasizes how schools transmit social norms and values that reinforce existing oppressive social hierarchies. Penna, a colleague of Giroux, highlights that the hidden curriculum plays a role in maintaining social inequities (Giroux & Penna, 1979). Phillp W. Jackson, who introduced the term in his 1968 publication *Life in Classrooms*, discusses how students learn unspoken norms and values through their school experiences. Thinking critically, reflect back to the reasons why ME became an educational reform in the United States and the rationale for training educators in CRT. This may be explored via histories of the institution of education and where it is in contemporary times.

Moreover, as a strategy to begin critically considering the meaning of developing teaching in CE programs, see the comparisons in Table 1.1, which includes descriptions of ME, CRT, and critical pedagogy to conceptualize how they are interconnected with each other.

Historic Relevance of Culturally Responsive Teaching

A historic relevance of CRT begins in a number of contexts. However, the two highlighted here are the social protests for racial equity and equality of the 1960s and 1970s and ME, which informs and is resultant of the former.

The social protests for racial equity and equality of the 1960s and 1970s exemplified the complex sociopolitical history of the United States. Beginning with the era of Reconstruction, then Jim Crow laws, to the Civil Rights era, and now where we are in the 21st century of our sociopolitical landscape in the United States, each of these time frames captured historic events that involved the institution of education, leading to the culmination of what makes CRT, pedagogy, and teaching vital to advancement for all students and necessary when preparing to teach CE curricula. Each of these eras are described in the text that follows in relation to education.

Reconstruction

Education became particularly important during the Reconstruction era (1865–1877). After the Civil War, newly freed African Americans saw education as a crucial step toward achieving equality, independence, and prosperity. African Americans sought opportunities to learn, despite facing significant challenges such as poverty and opposition from White supremacy movements (National Park Service, n.d.). During this era, the Fourteenth Amendment was added to the Constitution in 1868, which "specified that both blacks and whites had the same rights" (Currie, 2010, p. 29). Still, laws called Black Codes were being formulated in southern states. For example, Black Code law in Louisiana, sec. 5, stated no public meetings or congregations of negroes shall be allowed after sunset (Currie, 2010).

African Americans established schools with the help of Northern aid societies and the federal government's Freedmen's Bureau (Butchart, 2010). These schools were not just for children but also for adults and older adults who wanted to learn to read and write. Education was seen as a way to improve economic circumstances, protect against fraud and exploitation, and prepare for civic participation.

In direct correlation with education, the era of Reconstruction was based on broader efforts to rebuild the South and provide equal educational opportunities for descendants of slavery in the United States. Specific efforts were state constitution revisions, instituting federal funding for education, and racial integration. Many Southern states rewrote their constitutions during Reconstruction to include provisions for public

TABLE 1.1 Comparison of ME, CRT, and CP

Pedagogical Concept	Definition	Goals	Practices
Multicultural education (ME)	ME aims to respect and affirm diversity by promoting educational equity for all students. It involves teaching students about different cultural perspectives and histories to create a more inclusive environment.	Its primary objective is to ensure that all students, regardless of their cultural backgrounds, have equal opportunities to learn and succeed.	Features curriculum reforms to include diverse perspectives, teaching practices that reflect cultural diversity, and policies that support diversity and inclusion.
Culturally responsive teaching (CRT)	CRT involves using students' cultural knowledge, prior experiences, and performance styles to make learning more relevant and effective. It's about recognizing and valuing students' cultural backgrounds in the teaching process.	To enhance students' learning experiences by connecting new information to their existing cultural context, thus improving engagement and academic achievement.	Adapting teaching methods to meet the cultural, emotional, and academic needs of students, and integrating students' cultural references in all aspects of learning.
Critical pedagogy (CP)	CP is an educational approach that encourages students to question and challenge domination, and the beliefs and practices that dominate. It's based on the ideas of Paulo Freire, who advocated for education as a practice of freedom.	To empower students to become critical thinkers and agents of change by addressing and dismantling power imbalances and social injustices.	Engaging students in dialogue, encouraging critical thinking about societal issues, and fostering a sense of agency to address and transform oppressive structures.
Interconnections			
	Shared Goals	Complementary Practices	
Interconnectivity of each concept that supports development of teaching praxis	Equity in Education: Ensuring all students, regardless of their cultural background, have access to fair and equal educational opportunities. Cultural Awareness: Promoting understanding, respect, and appreciation for diverse cultural perspectives. Empowerment: Encouraging students to become active participants in their learning and in their communities.	Inclusive Curriculum: Integrating diverse cultural perspectives and content into the curriculum to reflect the backgrounds of all students. Student-Centered Learning: Tailoring instruction to meet the diverse needs, interests, and cultural contexts of students. Reflective Teaching: Encouraging educators to reflect on their own biases and to continuously adapt their teaching strategies to be more inclusive and equitable.	

(continued)

TABLE 1.1 Comparison of ME, CRT, and CP *(continued)*

Pedagogical Concept	Definition	Goals	Practices
	Critical Thinking: Fostering students' abilities to question, analyze, and challenge societal norms and injustices.	Critical Dialogue: Creating opportunities for students to engage in discussions about social justice, power dynamics, and cultural issues. Community Engagement: Building strong connections with students' families and communities to support a holistic approach to education.	

Note: ME, CRT, and CP are interconnected pedagogical concepts within the realm of education, each with its focus yet sharing common goals of inclusivity, equity, and social justice. Table 1.1 shows how they relate to each other.
CP, critical pedagogy; CRT, culturally responsive teaching; ME, multicultural education.

education. For example, Mississippi's 1868 constitution required the state to establish a uniform system of free public schools. Similarly, Florida's constitution mandated the state to provide education for all children without distinction or preference. Relative to federal funding, the Reconstruction Acts of 1867 and 1868 provided federal funding for the establishment of public schools in the South. This funding was essential for building schools and hiring teachers to educate both Black and White students. And in terms of racial integration, which would be a long-standing legal fight in the United States, states such as Louisiana and South Carolina explicitly prohibited racial segregation in their constitutions during Reconstruction. However, this commitment to integration was later undermined during the Jim Crow era, which is described next in relation to education (Currie, 2010).

Jim Crow

Subsequent to the era of Reconstruction in American history and in relation to the grounding purpose of culturally responsive education is the era of Jim Crow. During the Jim Crow era (late 19th century to mid-20th century), education became a critical battleground for African Americans (Currie, 2010; Steptoe, 2015). Some states mandated that African American students receive vocational training instead of academic education, reinforcing racial stereotypes and limiting their future opportunities. During this era, the Supreme Court decision to establish the "separate but equal" doctrine went into effect, allowing states to maintain segregated public facilities, including schools. This ruling provided legal justification for segregated education systems.

African Americans recognized education as a crucial tool for social and economic advancement, even in the face of oppressive segregation laws and systemic inequities (Anderson, 2019). With limited resources and under challenging circumstances, Black communities established their own educational institutions, which became hubs of resilience and resistance, offering quality learning experiences and cultivating a sense of empowerment. During this period, numerous historically Black colleges and universities (HBCUs) were established to provide higher education opportunities for Black students, including Howard University (1867), Morehouse College (1867), and Spelman College (1881).

The Black church played a vital role in this era, with organizations like the African Methodist Episcopal (AME) Church and other Black religious institutions often running their own schools to educate African American children. These educational facilities were essential in areas where public schooling was either underfunded, nonexistent, or against the law. Such laws were in existence because states were able to make up their own laws during this time frame.

It would be years later, and because of the Civil Rights era, when the federal government would make official attempts to reduce this unconstitutional power with the implementation of the United States Department of Education (USDE). The USDE was established on October 17, 1979, when President Jimmy Carter signed the Department of Education Organization Act into law. The department began operating on May 4, 1980, following the split of the Department of Health, Education, and Welfare into the Department of Education and the Department of Health and Human Services.

Civil Rights Era

Culminating information from the eras of Reconstruction and Jim Crow bleeds into a series of historical events pertaining to the U.S. institution of education and other U.S. institutions (Goldman, 2023). Many accounts that are situated in the institution of education are ongoing and present today as African Americans set the precedent during this era for other racialized minorities to gain access to equity in education (Danns & Purdy, 2015). This is the case even in2025 with news concerning attempts to alter the sociopolitical landscape to diminish diversity, equity, and inclusion practices in higher education and to cut cultural studies and student programs. An example of this is the politics concerning the state of education and learning materials that are instructional to diverse cultural histories (ABC News, 2024; EdTrust, 2023).

During the Civil Rights era (1950s–1960s), education became a central focus of the movement. The fight for desegregation and equal educational opportunities was a major goal (Currie, 2010). The landmark Supreme Court case *Brown v. Board of Education* (1954) declared that segregated schools were inherently unequal and ordered the desegregation of public schools.

Despite the ruling, many schools remained segregated for years, and the struggle for integration was met with significant resistance. African American students and their families, along with civil rights organizations like the National Association for the Advancement of Colored People (NAACP), played a crucial role in pushing for change. The efforts of these individuals and groups helped to dismantle the legal framework of segregation and paved the way for greater educational equality.

Greater Educational Equality—Immigrants and Increasing Diversity Among Learners

With an overlap of the Civil Rights era into ME reform, the social protests continued into the 1970s. This form of educational advocacy for greater educational equality began to result in policies to capture other minoritized, oppressed, and marginalized sociocultural groups.

Higher education advocacy for immigrants began to gain significant momentum in the mid-20th century, particularly around the 1960s. This period saw a growing recognition of the importance of diversity and inclusion in higher education institutions (Academic Leadership Institute, 2021). The Civil Rights Movement played a crucial role in highlighting the need for equal educational opportunities for all, including immigrants and other marginalized groups.

One notable milestone was the passage of the Immigration and Nationality Act of 1965, which abolished the national origins quota system and opened the doors to a more diverse group of immigrants. This led to an increase in the number of international students and faculty in U.S. higher education institutions.

A number of programs and initiatives that came out of this comprehensive ME reform are:

- The Presidents' Alliance on Higher Education and Immigration: This alliance of American college and university leaders works to increase public understanding of how immigration policies impact students, campuses, and communities. They provide resources and advocate for policies that support immigrant, international, and refugee students.
- Higher Education Immigration Portal: This initiative integrates data, policies, resources, and effective practices about DACA (Deferred Action for Childhood Arrivals) and undocumented, other immigrant, international, and refugee students to fuel change at the federal, state, and campus levels.
- Ethnic and Racial Disparities in Education: This resource from the American Psychological Association (APA) focuses on understanding and reducing disparities in education for ethnic and racial minority groups. It provides strategies to redress disparities associated with poverty in early childhood and empower immigrant families to be informed consumers of the U.S. educational system.
- Toolkit for Higher Education for Immigrant Students: The National Immigration Law Center (NILC) offers a toolkit with resources for students, advocates, and legislators interested in improving access to in-state tuition, financial aid, and scholarships for immigrant students.

Many of the persons advocating for ME reform were student-led groups and faculty in higher education. Although hundreds exist, several of these advocacy groups are spotlighted to highlight the importance of understanding how purposive curricula reform is, has been, and will be during contemporary times of our nation. A list of these advocacy groups follows:

- Student Nonviolent Coordinating Committee (SNCC): Founded in 1960 by Ella Baker, SNCC played a major role in the Civil Rights Movement through organizing sit-ins and freedom rides and advocating for voting rights and educational equality.

- NAACP Youth & College Division: Led by Mary White Ovington, this division focuses on engaging and mobilizing youth and college students in the fight for civil rights and social justice.
- Feminist Majority Foundation (FMF): Founded in 1987 by Toni Carabillo, Peg Yorkin, Katherine Spillar, and Eleanor Smeal, FMF works to empower women and girls through advocacy, education, and research, including efforts to promote gender equality in higher education.
- Lambda Legal: Started by Bill Thom, Arthur Leonard, and Evan Wolfson, this organization has been advocating for the rights of LGBTQ+ individuals since 1973, including fighting for equal educational opportunities and protections for LGBTQ+ students.
- American Indian Higher Education Consortium (AIHEC): Established in 1972 by a group of tribal college presidents—Gerald One Feather, David Reisling, Pat Locke, and Helen Schierbeck—AIHEC represents tribal colleges and universities, advocating for the educational needs and rights of Native American students.
- Dream Alliance: This organization focuses on supporting undocumented students, advocating for their rights and access to higher education.

CURRICULA REFORM ACROSS THE INSTITUTION OF EDUCATION: ACCOUNTING FOR MULTICULTURAL EDUCATION, CULTURALLY RESPONSIVE TEACHING, AND CRITICAL PEDAGOGY

An evolving ME made a shift toward curricula reform, which refers to the process of revising and updating educational curricula to make it more relevant, inclusive, and effective. Though discussed among scholars of CP and ME—Freire and Banks—it builds upon ME by reevaluating the content, teaching methods, and assessment strategies used in schools and other educational institutions. The goals of curricula reform can vary across disciplines, but they generally include:

- Incorporating Diverse Perspectives: Ensuring that the curriculum reflects the experiences and contributions of people from various backgrounds, including different races, ethnicities, genders, and socioeconomic statuses.
- Promoting Critical Thinking: Encouraging students to think critically and independently, rather than simply memorizing facts.
- Integrating Technology: Updating the curriculum to include new technologies and digital literacy skills that are essential for the modern workforce.
- Addressing Current Issues: Including contemporary topics such as climate change, social justice, and global citizenship to make learning more relevant to students' lives.
- Improving Equity and Access: Ensuring that all students have access to high-quality education, regardless of their background or circumstances.

Curricula reform is a continuous process that seeks to adapt education to the changing needs of society and the individual student. Furthermore, when curricula reform is intentional around culture and the increasing diversity among students in higher education, it is reflective of the sociopolitical landscape that impacts colleges and universities at many levels, including the way faculty approaches the learning environment.

Curricula reform is especially important in the context of growing diversity across colleges and universities. This involves making the educational content more inclusive and reflective of the diverse backgrounds and experiences of students. Here are some key aspects of curricula reform in this context:

- Inclusive Content: Integrating the histories, contributions, and perspectives of marginalized and underrepresented groups into the curriculum. This ensures that all students see themselves represented in what they are learning.
- Cultural Competence: Developing courses and programs that teach cultural competence, thereby helping students understand, appreciate, and navigate diverse cultural backgrounds and perspectives.
- Interdisciplinary Approaches: Incorporating interdisciplinary approaches that highlight the interconnectedness of different fields and how they intersect with issues of diversity and inclusion.
- Language and Accessibility: Ensuring that curriculum materials are accessible to students with different linguistic and learning needs, including providing resources in multiple languages and formats.
- Representation in Faculty and Staff: Hiring diverse faculty and staff who bring varied perspectives and experiences to the classroom, thereby enriching the educational environment.
- Support Services: Establishing support services such as mentoring, counseling, and academic assistance tailored to the needs of diverse student populations.
- Community Engagement: Encouraging partnerships with diverse communities to bring real-world perspectives and experiences into the educational setting.

These reforms help create an educational environment where all students feel valued, respected, and empowered to succeed. CRT is deeply intertwined with curricula reform, especially in the context of growing diversity in higher education. In the next section on CRT in higher education, some ways in which these reforms support CRT are provided.

CULTURALLY RESPONSIVE TEACHING IN HIGHER EDUCATION

From a practical sense, CRT is an educational approach that acknowledges and incorporates the diverse cultural backgrounds of students in the learning process as well as faculty who are teaching and leading the students within classrooms. As a method, it aims to create an inclusive and equitable classroom environment where all students feel valued and respected as adults with various lived experiences that can inform the learning material and instructional practices. Key elements include:

- Cultural Awareness: Educators recognize their own cultural biases and understand the cultural backgrounds of their students.

- Curriculum Inclusion: Teaching materials and content reflect the diverse cultures and experiences of students, promoting representation and relevance.
- High Expectations: Teachers hold high expectations for all students, believing in their potential to succeed regardless of their cultural background.
- Critically Responsive Pedagogy: Instructional strategies and classroom interactions are adapted to be culturally relevant and responsive to students' needs.
- Adult Learning Awareness: Learning experiences are designed to be meaningful and engaging from an andragogical perspective, often drawing on students' cultural knowledge and experiences that allow space for them to use social and cultural capital.

By narrowing in on CRT as a manner for implementation into CE curricula. instructors will be able to center on what adult learners need and how faculty apply pedagogical approaches and praxis geared for preparing culturally responsive counselors. In CE, CRT can be a vital approach for creating an inclusive and equitable academic environment. The following starting points indicate where CRT is suggested to be applied in CE faculty development:

- Curriculum Development: Universities and colleges incorporate diverse perspectives into their courses. This means including readings, case studies, and examples from a variety of cultural backgrounds. For example, history courses might cover not only Western civilizations but also Asian, African, and Indigenous histories.
- Faculty Training: Professors and instructors receive training on cultural competence and inclusive teaching strategies. This helps them recognize and address their own biases, understand their students' cultural contexts, and use teaching methods that are effective across different cultures.
- Student Engagement: Courses are designed to be relevant and engaging for students from diverse backgrounds. This can involve group projects, discussions, and assignments that allow students to bring their cultural perspectives into the classroom.
- Support Services: Higher education institutions provide resources such as cultural centers, mentoring programs, and counseling services tailored to the needs of minority and international students. These services help create a supportive community and address any unique challenges these students might face.
- Research and Outreach: Universities often conduct research on issues related to diversity and inclusion, and they engage with local communities to better understand and address the needs of diverse populations.
- Policy Advocacy: Higher education institutions advocate for policies that support diversity and inclusion, such as affirmative action, scholarships for underrepresented students, and inclusive campus policies.

By implementing these practices, CES faculty leadership sets an aim to create a learning environment where all students feel valued and can succeed. Moreover, in the social sciences, where counselor preparation programs commonly exist in higher education, there is nuance and great room for CRT in action. Here are ways CRT can be implemented from a multidisciplinary approach (i.e., psychology, sociology, anthropology, public health):

- Inclusive Curriculum: Courses are designed to include diverse perspectives and contributions from various cultural backgrounds.
- Contextual Learning: Teaching methods are adapted to connect course content with students' cultural contexts. This might involve using case studies, examples, and research that are relevant to the students' own experiences and backgrounds.
- Critical Pedagogy: Educators encourage students to critically analyze societal structures and issues, including those related to race, gender, and class. This helps students develop a deeper understanding of social inequalities and their own roles in addressing them.
- Collaborative Learning: Group projects and discussions are used to foster collaboration among students from different cultural backgrounds. This promotes mutual respect and understanding, as well as the exchange of diverse ideas and perspectives.
- Supportive Environment: Creating a classroom environment where all students feel safe and valued is essential. This includes establishing norms for respectful communication and providing support services tailored to the needs of diverse students.
- Faculty Development: Professors and instructors receive training on CRT practices, helping them to better understand and address the diverse needs of their students.

CULTURALLY RESPONSIVE TEACHING SCHOLARS

There are a growing number of scholars who train and study CRT. Notable individuals who have laid the groundwork for understanding and implementing CRT by helping educators create more inclusive and effective learning environments include Gloria Ladson-Billings, Geneva Gay, James A. Banks, and Sonia Nieto, to name a few. In Table 1.2, there is a description of what these CRT scholars offer to educators.

Critical reflections on how to integrate a synthesis of information is based on what CRT in CE looks like. To this end, consider the following questions:

1. How can CRT harness the ability to shape safe learning environments with an appreciation of greater social and cultural diversity?
2. What historical accounts support the rationale for moving educators away from oppressive teaching approaches that historically and presently sustain dominant versus nondominant identities and systems?
3. Where would you begin to liberate learners so that they can develop informed insights from critical, creative, and conscious perspectives?
4. What resources might you consult to locate suitable CE teaching materials that reflect marginalized and minoritized identities and lived experiences?

TABLE 1.2 Influential Scholars Who Have Defined and Contributed to the Practice of CRT

Scholar	Key Contribution	Notable Works
Gloria Ladson-Billings	Pioneering work on culturally relevant pedagogy	*The Dreamkeepers: Successful Teachers of African American Children*
Geneva Gay	Research on CRT	*Culturally Responsive Teaching: Theory, Research, and Practice*
James A. Banks	Models for integrating cultural content in curriculum	*Cultural Diversity and Education: Foundations, Curriculum, and Teaching*
Sonia Nieto	Advocating for CRT practices	*Affirming Diversity: The Sociopolitical Context of Multicultural Education*
Joy Lawson Davis	CRT for gifted learners	*Bright, Talented & Black: A Guide for Families of African American Gifted Learners*
H. Richard Milner, IV	Role of race in education	*Start Where You Are, But Don't Stay There: Understanding Diversity, Opportunity Gaps, and Teaching in Today's Classrooms*
Zaretta Hammond	CRT and the brain, and linguistic diversity	*Culturally Responsive Teaching and the Brain*
Linda Darling-Hammond	CRT practices to support diverse learners	*The Flat World and Education: How America's Commitment to Equity Will Determine Our Future*
Sharlene Voogd Cochrane, Meenakshi Chhabra, Majorie A. Jones, and Deborah Spragg	CRT among faculty in higher education; The Cultural and Literacy Curriculum Institute	*Culturally Responsive Teaching and Reflection in Higher Education: Promising Practices From the Cultural Literacy Curriculum Institute*

CRT, culturally responsive teaching.

CONCLUSION

In conclusion, the integration of ME and CRT is paramount in preparing educators to meet the diverse needs of their students. By understanding and applying the tenets of CRT, CES can create inclusive and equitable learning environments that respect and value the unique cultural identities of all students. The historical context, from the eras of Reconstruction, Jim Crow, and the Civil Rights Movement, underscores the enduring need for CRT to address systemic inequities and promote social justice. With the increasing diversity caused by immigration, there is a heightened imperative for equity in education. As higher education institutions embark on curricula reform, the principles of ME and CRT must be central to these efforts, ensuring that all students have the opportunity to succeed and thrive in an inclusive educational landscape.

In the profession of CES, the principles of ME and CRT are particularly significant. Current sociocultural-political issues are reflected in classrooms, where students with diverse views, identities, and sometimes conflicting viewpoints engage with the CE curricula in ways that are best to facilitate without force or encouragement to follow "old guard" ways of understanding and learning. This is considered to be oppressive and lacking in liberation, essentially limiting space to think critically and independently. To address this complexity, training future counselors to be culturally responsive is essential. The CRT approach to covering learning across CE curricula ensures that they are equipped to understand and address the multifaceted identities of their clients and about themselves.

By incorporating these principles into CE curricula, programs can foster the development of counselors who are not only skilled in therapeutic techniques but also deeply committed to social justice and equity. This comprehensive approach helps future counselors become advocates for their clients, promoting mental health and well-being in diverse communities. As the demographic landscape continues to evolve, the need for culturally competent counselors becomes increasingly critical, underscoring the importance of integrating these educational strategies into counselor training programs.

CHAPTER RESOURCES

Culturally Responsive Counselor Educator Skills

CRCE Skills to Further Develop From This Chapter	
10 Core Tenets of CRT	Faculty Development Areas to Implement CRT
Student-Centered Learning: Focus on students' cultural backgrounds and experiences	Cultural Awareness Training: Workshops and Seminars—Focus on understanding and valuing the diverse cultural backgrounds of college students. Topics could include implicit bias, microaggressions, and intercultural communication. Professional Development Programs—Encourage faculty to participate in continuous learning opportunities that focus on cultural competence.
Cultural Competence: Teachers' understanding and appreciation of diverse cultural backgrounds	Professional Development: CRT Strategies—Offer training sessions specifically designed for higher education contexts, addressing issues like diverse learning styles and culturally relevant pedagogical practices.
High Expectations: Setting high academic expectations for all students	Curriculum Design: Inclusive Curriculum Development—Provide resources and training on how to incorporate diverse perspectives and materials into college-level courses. Curriculum Review—Establish committees to review and revise existing curricula to ensure cultural relevance and inclusivity.

(continued)

CRCE Skills to Further Develop From This Chapter ***(continued)***	
Cultural Relevance: Integrating students' cultural references into the curriculum	Classroom Management: Effective Strategies—Adapt classroom management techniques for large lectures and smaller seminars to ensure an inclusive and respectful learning environment.
Critical Consciousness: Encouraging students to question and challenge societal norms	Assessment Practices: Fair and Culturally Sensitive Assessments—Develop guidelines and training for creating assessments that are fair to all students and consider cultural differences. Alternative Assessment Methods—Encourage the use of diverse assessment methods such as portfolios, presentations, and reflective essays.
Inclusive Curriculum: Using diverse and multicultural learning materials	Classroom Engagement: Student Engagement—Train faculty on strategies to engage students from diverse backgrounds actively.
Positive Relationships: Building strong, respectful relationships with students and their communities	Community Engagement: Community Partnerships— Promote building partnerships with community organizations that support diverse student populations. Alumni Networks—Engage alumni from diverse backgrounds to mentor current students and provide insights into navigating higher education.
Equity and Access: Ensuring all students have equal opportunities to succeed	Equity Training: Promoting Educational Equity—Offer workshops on understanding and addressing systemic inequalities in higher education. Inclusive Policies—Develop and promote policies that ensure all students have equal access to educational resources and opportunities.
Collaborative Learning: Promoting cooperative learning environments	Collaborative Learning Techniques: Group Work and Peer Learning—Train faculty on facilitating effective group work and peer learning activities that respect and leverage cultural diversity. Cross-Cultural Collaboration—Encourage faculty to design projects that require cross-cultural collaboration among students.
Reflective Practice: Continuously reflecting on and improving teaching practices	Critical Pedagogy: Empowering Students—Train faculty in the principles of CP to encourage students to question and challenge societal norms. Dialogical Teaching—Promote teaching methods that involve dialogue and critical thinking, enabling students to become active participants in their education.

CP, critical pedagogy; CRCE, culturally responsive counselor educator; CRT, culturally responsive teaching.

CONTENT SUMMARY

- The need for multicultural education (ME) strategies in K–12 and higher education settings in the United States stems partly from the nation's history of educational reform and increasing cultural diversity among students. Significant historical events and constitutional amendments have paved the way for advocacy movements promoting social justice, as well as social, political, and racial equity and equality across educational environments. These movements also emphasize the importance of connecting the diverse histories and worldviews of both students and educators.
- Leveraging the unique cultural traits, backgrounds, and viewpoints of students from diverse ethnic groups can enhance their learning experience. Culturally responsive teaching (CRT) methods can be understood as instructional approaches that address the distinct cultural attributes that differentiate students from one another and from their instructor.
- Teaching methods that are sensitive to cultural diversity highlight the significance of weaving students' cultural heritage and life experiences into educational strategies. This approach aims to create a learning environment that is both inclusive and fair. By implementing these culturally aware techniques, educators can boost student participation and academic success while also nurturing an atmosphere of acceptance and appreciation for varied cultural viewpoints.
- The goal of ME reform is to reshape educational institutions, ensuring equal opportunities for success among students from diverse cultural, racial, and socioeconomic backgrounds. This involves adjusting curricula, teaching methods, and policies to acknowledge and appreciate the varied experiences and identities of students, ultimately fostering educational fairness and social equity.
- A crucial component of ME is the incorporation of diverse cultural content into the curriculum. By presenting varied perspectives and histories in educational materials, counselor preparation programs can offer a more comprehensive and inclusive worldview, reflecting the cultural dynamics both inside and outside the classroom that influence learning and feelings of inclusion. This approach enables students from different backgrounds to leverage their social and cultural capital, recognizing themselves in their studies, which can boost their self-confidence and academic involvement.
- The effective preparation and continuous learning of counselor educators (CEs) are essential for implementing teaching methods that are culturally sensitive, using inclusive and critical pedagogical approaches, and delivering ME. It is vital for CEs to acquire the necessary expertise and abilities to comprehend and respond to their students' varied requirements. Regular training sessions and assistance can aid CEs in cultivating culturally responsive techniques, confronting their personal prejudices, and fostering more inclusive learning spaces.

Advanced Reflection Questions

1. How can CRT practices be integrated into CES curricula to enhance the learning experiences of master's level counselors-in-training (CIT) from diverse backgrounds? Discuss specific strategies and potential challenges.
2. In what ways can CE faculty and doctoral level students critically examine and address their own biases to create a more inclusive and equitable classroom environment? Provide examples from your teaching experiences or observations.
3. Analyze the impact of ME on student engagement and achievement. How can counselor preparation programs and universities measure the effectiveness of their ME praxis?
4. Discuss the role of CP in fostering social justice and equity in CES. How can CES balance the need for academic rigor with the goal of empowering CIT to challenge systemic inequalities?
5. Reflect on a CRT framework you have studied or implemented. What were its key components, and how did it influence your approach to teaching and student interactions? (You will need to explore CRT pedagogies to find ones that help respond to this question.)

Further Reading

Betters-Bubon, J., Brunner, T., & Kansteiner, A. (2016). Success for all? The role of the school counselor in creating and sustaining culturally responsive positive behavior interventions and supports programs. *The Professional Counselor, 6*(3), 263–277. https://doi.org/10.15241/jbb.6.3.263

Betters-Bubon, J., & Kansteiner, A. (2018). Culturally responsive school counseling: A case study of a culturally responsive PBIS program. *Journal of School Counseling, 16*(3), 1–20.

Irvine, T., Labarta, A., & Emelianchik-Key, K. (2021). Using a relational-cultural and Adlerian framework to enhance multicultural pedagogy. *The Professional Counselor, 11*(2), 233–247. https://doi.org/10.15241/ti.11.2.233

Lee, C. C. (2019). Multicultural competence: A framework for counselor education. *Journal of Counseling & Development, 97*(4), 456–468. https://doi.org/10.1002/jcad.12294

Ratts, M. J., & Green, J. L. (2015). Multicultural competence and social justice: A national survey of school counselors. *Journal of Multicultural Counseling and Development, 43*(1), 3–15.

Ratts, M. J., & Pedersen, P. B. (2014). A counselor's guide to social justice: Promoting equity and advocacy. *Journal of Multicultural Counseling and Development, 42*(1), 3–16.

Samuels, A. J. (2017). Exploring culturally responsive pedagogy: Teachers' perspectives on fostering equitable and inclusive classrooms. *Journal of Education Research, 14*(2), 123–135. https://files.eric.ed.gov/fulltext/EJ1166706.pdf

Sue, D. W., Arredondo, P., & McDavis, R. J. (1992). Multicultural counseling competencies and standards: A call to the profession. *Journal of Multicultural Counseling and Development, 20*(2), 64–88. https://onlinelibrary.wiley.com/doi/10.1002/j.1556-6676.1992.tb01642.x

Worthington, R. L., Soth-McNett, A. M., & Moreno, J. (2007). Culturally responsive counseling interventions: A review of the literature. *Journal of Counseling & Development, 85*(3), 299–310.

REFERENCES

Academic Leadership Institute. (2021, June 25). *The history of diversity in higher education.* ALI Series Part I. https://sites.lsa.umich.edu/leadership-institute/2021/06/25/the-history-of-diversity-in-higher-education-ali-series-part-i/

ABC News. (2024, April 5). *Map: The impact of anti-DEI legislation.* ABC News. https://abcnews.go.com/US/map-impact-anti-dei-legislation/story?id=108795967

American Psychiatric Association. (2022). *Diagnostic and statistical manual of mental disorders* (5th ed., text rev.). https://doi.org/10.1176/appi.books.9780890425787

Anderson, J. D. (2019). *The education of Blacks in the South, 1860–1935: A source book.* University of North Carolina Press.

Banks, J. A., & Banks, C. A. M. (Eds.). (2019). *Multicultural education: Issues and perspectives* (10th ed.). Wiley.

Bhavnani, R., Mirza, H. S., & Meetoo, V. (2005). *Tackling the roots of racism: Lessons for success.* Policy Press.

Butchart, R. E. (2010). *Schooling the freed people: Teaching, learning, and the struggle for Black freedom, 1861–1876.* University of North Carolina Press.

Currie, S. (2010). *The struggle for equality: Landmark court cases.* Lucent Books.

Danns, D., & Purdy, M. A. (2015). Historical perspectives on African American education, civil rights, and Black power. *Journal of African American History, 100*(4), 621–642. https://doi.org/10.5323/jafriamerhist.100.4.0573

Darder, A., Torres, R. D., & Baltodano, M. (Eds.). (2003). *The critical pedagogy reader.* Routledge.

EdTrust. (2023, November 15). *A map of anti-DEI efforts on college campuses across the U.S.* EdTrust. https://edtrust.org/rti/a-map-of-anti-dei-efforts-on-college-campuses-across-the-u-s/

Freire, P. (2020). *Pedagogy of the oppressed: 50th anniversary edition*. Bloomsbury Academic.

Gay, G. (2018). *Culturally responsive teaching: Theory, research, and practice* (3rd ed.). Teachers College Press.

Giroux, H. A. (1983). *Theory and resistance in education: A pedagogy for the opposition.* Bergin & Garvey.

Giroux, H. A., & Penna, A. N. (1979). Social education in the classroom: The dynamics of the hidden curriculum. *Theory and Research in Social Education, 7*(1), 21–42. https://doi.org/10.1080/00933104.1979.10506048

Giroux, H. A. (2024). *Teachers as intellectuals: Toward a critical pedagogy of learning.* Bloomsbury Publishing.

Goldman, S. A. (2023). *One more war to fight: Union veterans' battle for equality through Reconstruction, Jim Crow, and the lost cause.* Rowman & Littlefield.

Hammond, Z. (2015). *Culturally responsive teaching and the brain: Promoting authentic engagement and rigor among culturally and linguistically diverse students.* Corwin Press.

hooks, b. (1994). *Teaching to transgress: Education as the practice of freedom*. Routledge.

hooks, b. (2003). *Teaching community: A pedagogy of hope*. Routledge.

hooks, b. (2007). *Teaching critical thinking: Practical wisdom*. Routledge.

Jackson, P. W. (1968). *Life in classrooms*. Holt, Rinehart and Winston.

Kärner, T., & Schneider, G. (2024). A scoping review on the hidden curriculum in education. *Research in Education Curriculum and Pedagogy: Global Perspectives, 1*(1). https://doi.org/10.56395/recap.v1i1.1

Ladson-Billings, G. (1995a). But that's just good teaching! The case for culturally relevant pedagogy. *Theory Into Practice, 34*(3), 159–165. https://doi.org/10.1080/00405849509543675

Ladson-Billings, G. (1995b). Toward a theory of culturally relevant pedagogy. *American Educational Research Journal, 32*(3), 465–491. https://doi.org/10.3102/00028312032003465

Ladson-Billings, G. (2004). *Crossing over to Canaan: The journey of new teachers in diverse classrooms*. John Wiley & Sons.

Ladson-Billings, G. (2006). From the achievement gap to the education debt: Understanding achievement in US schools. *Educational Researcher, 35*(7), 3–12. https://doi.org/10.3102/0013189X035007003

Ladson-Billings, G. (2014). Culturally relevant pedagogy 2.0: Aka the remix. *Harvard Educational Review, 84*(1), 74–84. https://doi.org/10.17763/haer.84.1.p2rj131485484751

Ladson-Billings, G. (2021). *Culturally relevant pedagogy: Asking a different question*. Teachers College Press.

Ladson-Billings, G. (2023). "Yes, but how do we do it?": Practicing culturally relevant pedagogy. In A. D. Dixson & C. K. McKoy (Eds.), *White teachers/diverse classrooms: Culturally responsive pedagogy* (pp. 33–46). Routledge.

National Park Service. (n.d.). *African Americans and education during reconstruction. Author*. Retrieved November 20, 2024, from https://www.nps.gov/articles/african-americans-and-education-during-reconstruction-the-tolson-s-chapel-schools.htm

Northeastern University. (n.d.). *Culturally responsive teaching strategies*. Retrieved June 8, 2025, from https://graduate.northeastern.edu/resources/culturally-responsive-teaching-strategies

Ravid, B. (2025, August 8). *Israeli security cabinet approves plan to occupy Gaza City: Report*. MSN. https://www.msn.com/en-us/news/world/israeli-security-cabinet-approves-plan-to-occupy-gaza-city-report/ar-AA1K7UZu

Sanjakdar, F., & Apple, M. W. (Eds.). (2024). *Engaging critical pedagogy in education: Global phenomenon, local praxis*. Routledge.

Shapin, S. (2012). The Ivory Tower: The history of a figure of speech and its cultural uses. *The British Journal for the History of Science, 45*(1), 1–27. https://doi.org/10.1017/S0007087412000118

Steinberg, S. R., & Down, B. (Eds.). (2020). *The SAGE handbook of critical pedagogies*. SAGE Publications.

Steptoe, T. L. (Ed.). (2015). *Jim Crow: Voices from a century of struggle, 1876–1919*. Library of America.

CHAPTER 2

PREPARING FOR TEACHING AS COUNSELOR EDUCATORS: CREATING AFFIRMING AND EQUITABLE LEARNING ENVIRONMENTS FOR LEARNERS AND EDUCATORS

Crisis does three things. It reveals character. It exposes weakness. But it also creates opportunity . . .

—Dr. Thomas Parham

LEARNING OBJECTIVES After studying this chapter, you will be able to

- Construct intrapersonal ideas around what it means to develop a sense of cultural identity in relation to cross-cultural encounters with students, learning materials used to teach, and an awareness of how these elements intersect and impact on one another.
- Understand foundational knowledge of the counselor education and supervision (CES) discipline as it pertains to its unique tripartite ethos—counselor, educator, and supervisor—via personal and professional identity development through the framework of intersectionality.
- Demonstrate the ability to identify, describe, and formulate a teaching philosophy incorporating content fundamental to knowledge of self and culturally responsive teaching (CRT) to be practiced in counseling education programs.
- Develop the empirical application of self-care, burnout prevention, and meaning-making strategies for lifelong learning.

SNAPSHOT: A counselor educator's career experience

At the outset of my teaching career, I was like many new faculty members—still working on my dissertation. I secured a full-time tenure-track position at a 4-year university while completing my doctoral studies. On my first evening of teaching, I experienced a mix of emotions, feeling invigorated and enthusiastic. One of my courses that evening was on multicultural issues in counseling. During my doctoral program, I learned that this course was typically assigned to junior faculty and faculty members of color. However, after about three sessions, my initial enthusiasm waned as I began to feel unprepared. I felt daunted by the all-White adult student cohort, the tensions surrounding the course material, and my status as the first Black faculty member in the Clinical Mental Health Counseling master's program. This shift was also influenced by the textbook content and the students' limited understanding of racism and other systemic and historical forms of discrimination experienced by various sociocultural groups and individuals. As the semester progressed, I realized I needed to investigate my department's culture. Although departmental and institutional culture is crucial, I had neglected to inquire about it during my interview. My excitement about obtaining the faculty position had caused me to overlook the ongoing issues of racism, oppression, and lack of social justice in society. Our nation was grappling with police killings of numerous Black individuals (Freddy Gray, Tamir Rice, Michael Brown, Eric Garner, Alton Sterling, Philando Castile) and mass shootings (Emanuel African Methodist Episcopal Church, the San Bernadino attack, Pulse Nightclub shooting, Washington Navy Yard shooting). These injustices and senseless killings occurred while I was pursuing my doctorate in counselor education and supervision (CES; 2013–2016). I now realize that during my interview process, I failed to ask how the university or program had addressed any of these incidents.

INTRODUCTION

The introductory quote addresses the concept of teacher preparation. Dr. Thomas A. Parham is a highly respected figure in the field of counseling and psychology. He is currently the president of California State University, Dominguez Hills (CSUDH). Dr. Parham has had a long and distinguished career, with over 40 years of experience as a scholar and practitioner. He has made significant contributions to the field, particularly in the areas of identity development, African psychology, and multicultural counseling. Dr. Parham has authored numerous journal articles, book chapters, and books, including *Psychological Storms: The African American Struggle for Identity* and *Counseling Persons of African Descent: Raising the Bar of Practitioner Competence*. The quote that introduces this chapter is from a speech where Dr. Parham emphasized the significance of being educators who are resilient and adaptable in higher education. Educators frequently encounter unforeseen obstacles and emergencies, ranging from classroom management issues to curriculum modifications or broader societal concerns. These circumstances often reveal educators' true cultural identities, nature, and capabilities, showcasing their devotion, ability to solve problems, and dedication to their students. Such circumstances will also impact where educators demonstrate areas of angst, as well as feeling and being unprepared to address societal concerns that impact the profession of counseling. Specifically, this impact affects students who are matriculating counselor training curricula in a way that possibly hinders the student and their future clients whom they will serve as mental health counselors.

Moreover, crises occurring across our nation that are brought up in classroom discussion tend to uncover areas where educators may require additional growth or assistance, such as enhancing their cultural awareness and humility, refining communication abilities, or embracing new instructional techniques. Identifying these limitations provides opportunities for focused professional development and the chance to address and overcome them. It also is a call for greater personal awareness of how to methodically create safe learning spaces to address sociocultural inequities that uncover held biases and other isms of students and colleagues in the profession of counseling.

In essence, the quote suggests that crises can be transformative experiences that create opportunities for learning and development, uncover blind spots of bias, and even call for gatekeeping practices. By equipping counselor educators to navigate and capitalize on these challenges, institutions of higher learning can cultivate an environment of ongoing improvement and innovation, ensuring that faculty members are well-prepared to deliver high-quality education to their students. To capture the essence of what Parham shares, this chapter aims to engage in cultural identity development (personal and professional) that is fundamental to preparing counselor education and supervision (CES) for the complex educational ethos of counselor preparation programs of this era of the 21st century (25 years in). A key aspect of this subject is developing a comprehensive approach that fosters educational growth, specifically tailored for instructing in counselor training programs.

Comprehensively, the chapter addresses (a) shaping a healthy, informed, and conscious personal cultural identity; (b) developing a culturally responsive teaching (CRT) philosophy; (c) strategic planning for self-care and burnout prevention; and (d) developing an aptitude for lifelong learning that extends beyond graduate studies. The focus will be on developing and maintaining a healthy mindset that can be interpreted into a conscious sense of self so as to mentally prepare for becoming a counselor educator-practitioner-scholar who can transition seamlessly across roles such as mentor, leader, content creator, disruptor, advocate, researcher, and developer. Insight on how to psychologically prepare for teaching will also be provided in terms of what is being communicated about self in a teaching philosophy and what is important to attend to when sociocultural issues manifest in faculty and student dialogue and discourse. The chapter will conclude with a summary of ideas that elucidate what future faculty counselor educators can do to holistically feel and skillfully be ready for a multifaceted teaching.

DEVELOPING A HEALTHY SENSE OF SELF IN PREPARATION FOR TEACHING AND LEARNING FROM A CULTURALLY RESPONSIVE PERSPECTIVE

In this context, fostering a robust sense of self intertwines personal and professional cultural identities. Tools to consider in developing a healthy self-concept include cultivating a mindset and awareness of how sociocultural and political issues, as well as global events occurring beyond the classroom, will manifest within it and warrant attention. The environments where a healthy self-concept can flourish and these proposed tools are examined in the text that follows, focusing on their manifestation in counselor education programs and methods for implementing culturally sensitive teaching approaches.

Cultural Identity Development

According to Jean Phinney and other cultural identity scholars—Deborah Rivas-Drake; William Cross, Jr.; and Rene V. Galliher, to name a few—the formation and evolution of one's cultural identity is a complex process that involves developing a sense of self in relation to one's cultural, racial, and ethnic heritage. Cross et al. (1991) and Helms (1990), in their groundbreaking literature, teach that this journey entails comprehending and assimilating the customs, ideologies, and traditions of one's cultural background, as well as recognizing oneself as part of that cultural community. While the initial stages of identity development occur during the early phases of life, such as infancy, childhood, and adolescence, the process continues to evolve as individuals age and have a series of encounters with others and the world (Phinney, 1989). Our cultural identities are not static; they can transform through interactions with others and life experiences. Additionally, the significance of various aspects of our identity may fluctuate depending on the context, with certain elements becoming more prominent or valuable as social or cultural capital in different situations. Essentially, understanding of cultural identity development will:

- Help on a personal level to be more aware of:
  - self in cross-cultural encounters with students and colleagues
  - biases held about sociocultural-political worldviews of others who are different from you
  - areas of growth where perspective-taking would be helpful in navigating discourse where differing views and values are being communicated
- Help on a professional level to practice intentional teaching that:
  - lends to building relationships with students from various backgrounds and styles of learning
  - incorporates learning materials that allow for students to use their social and cultural capital to wrestle with new and difficult curricula content
  - dismantles systemic or institutional isms that surface in instructional materials being used in counselor preparation programs (e.g., ethnocentristic ideas about who experts are in the profession) and that exist in mental healthcare

Hence, cultural identity development, when understood and applied in teaching and counseling practices, may be used at a conscious level to support personal and professional development when preparing to teach counselor preparation curricula, building relationships with students and selecting learning materials used to teach. However, to comprehend a more comprehensive conceptual framework of cultural identity development, it is essential to examine its origins in greater depth.

Several scholars, including Drs. Janet Helms and William Cross, have conducted groundbreaking theoretical and empirical research on the development of cultural identity. Their work explores how individuals evolve into their current and future selves. Helms (1990) is particularly renowned for developing Black and White racial identity development models. For instance, in the White racial identity developmental model, Helms delineates stages through which persons of this ethnic cultural group come to recognize their racial identity and the associated advantages. The model consists of two primary phases: abandonment of racism and evolution of a non-racist identity. Each phase encompasses multiple stages that illustrate the progression from racial unawareness and ignorance of privilege to active engagement in combating racism.

Helms' work is an extension of the scholarship of Dr. William Cross. Cross (1971) developed the Nigrescence model, which focuses on the identity development process for African Americans. The model describes five stages: preencounter, encounter, immersion-emersion, internalization, and internalization-commitment. The process begins with a lack of awareness about racial identity, followed by an encounter that challenges this view, leading to a deep immersion in Black culture, and eventually to a balanced and committed integration of one's racial identity.

Both Helms and Cross emphasize the importance of understanding and addressing racial identity as a dynamic and ongoing process that influences individuals' interactions with society and their own self-concept. Nationalities are also significantly important to cultural identity, whereby it has a broader complexity of development, including language, sense of belonging, cultural heritage, socialization, and even legal frameworks. With greater cultural diversity represented across the United States, student bodies, and cultural studies in higher education, more cultural identity development models are being formulated. Across the more contemporary cultural identity frameworks, ethnicity and nationality are being considered and interconnected across development. These models come at the behest of active education reform and the importance of educators knowing how to meaningfully support earlier stages of development that are inclusive of cultural, not just socioemotional, cognitive, and physical, development (Vedder & van Geel, 2017).

A few of the more contemporary cultural identity development models and scholars of cultural identity development are in the table that follows. The table includes scholars who are less commonly referenced in counselor training programs and interconnected topics that are relative to cultural identity development (i.e., scholars who have created assessment tools concerning cultural identity development).

Table 2.1 offers a diverse range of insights into aspects related to the significance of cultural identity formation that extends beyond race. Understanding various elements of cultural identity development is crucial for developing self-awareness and the awareness of others. Furthermore, it helps to conceptualize that we all have a pluralistic identity that shapes how we consider self and others, and a means to take up or hold spaces that reflects who is in the room (e.g., context). Objectively, the importance here is to understand that various factors of cultural identity development are related to intersectionality. The text that follows features a synopsis of intersectionality that is being considered to ground the critical nature of (a) enhancing the conceptualization of personal cultural identity, (b) developing a confident response to inquiries regarding one's cultural identity development, and (c) examining the intersections within an individual's cultural identity where experiences of conflicting and adjacent cultural identity factors contribute to privilege, power, oppressor-oppressed dynamics, marginalization, and minoritization.

TABLE 2.1 Key Scholars in Cultural Identity, Their Research on Development, and Further Exploration of Their Empirical and Conceptual Models

Cultural Identity Development Scholar	Topical Research on Cultural Identity Development	Further Reading on the Topic
Adriana J. Umaña-Taylor	Studies examine the formation of ethnic-racial identity in Latinx adolescents, emphasizing the crucial roles played by family members, social circles, and cultural environments.	Umaña-Taylor, A. J. (2013). Ethnic-racial identity development and adjustment in adolescence: A review of research and implications for education. In C. E. Santos & A. J. Umaña-Taylor, *Studying ethnic identity: Methodological and conceptual approaches across disciplines* (pp. 1–24). American Psychological Association.
Mandy A. E. Van der Gaag, Naomi M. P. De Ruiter, Saskia E. Kunneman, and Harke Bosma	The researchers created the landscape of identity model, which combines qualitative and quantitative elements of identity formation. This framework conceptualizes identity as a network of commitments, each varying in strength and interconnectedness.	Van der Gaag, M. A. E., De Ruiter, N. M. P., Kunneman, S. E., & Bosma, H. (2020). The landscape of identity model: An integration of qualitative and quantitative aspects of identity development. *Identity: An International Journal of Theory and Research, 20*(4), 272–289. https://doi.org/10.1080/15283488.2020.1821154
Frank C. Worrell and colleagues	In 2000, Frank C. Worrell and colleagues created the Cross Racial Identity Scale (CRIS), which puts into practice William E. Cross Jr.'s expanded Nigrescence theory. The CRIS evaluates six attitudes related to racial identity: assimilation, miseducation, self-hatred, anti-White, Afrocentricity, and multiculturalist inclusive. These attitudes represent various ways in which individuals connect with their racial identity, spanning from a preference for identifying with a national label to a strong dedication to embracing multiple cultures.	Worrell, F. C., Vandiver, B. J., Cross Jr., W. E., Fhagen-Smith, P. E., Swim, J., & Caldwell, L. (2000). *Cross Racial Identity Scale (CRIS)* [Database record]. PsycTESTS. https://doi.org/10.1037/t01825-000
Seth J. Schwartz and colleagues	Schwartz was recognized for research on how identity influences the adaptation process of immigrants to new cultures. Studies investigate the ways in which individual and collective identities can provide stability for immigrants as they adjust to life in a different society.	Schwartz, S. J., Montgomery, M. J., & Briones, E. (2006). The role of identity in acculturation among immigrant people: Theoretical propositions, empirical questions, and applied recommendations. *Human Development, 49*(1), 1–30. https://www.jstor.org/stable/26763865

(continued)

TABLE 2.1 Key Scholars in Cultural Identity, Their Research on Development, and Further Exploration of Their Empirical and Conceptual Models *(continued)*

Cultural Identity Development Scholar	Topical Research on Cultural Identity Development	Further Reading on the Topic
Jürgen Baumert, Michael Becker, Malte Jansen, and Olaf Köller	These researchers have investigated the academic, psychologic, and social adaptation of youth from immigrant backgrounds	Baumert, J., Becker, M., Jansen, M., & Köller, O. (2024). Cultural identity and the academic, social, and psychological adjustment of adolescents with immigration background. *Journal of Youth and Adolescence, 53*, 294–315. https://doi.org/10.1007/s10964-023-01853-z
Anne C. Campbell, Jordyn Dezago, and Quintessence Townsend	Their research examines the driving forces, formation of self-concept, and collegiate experiences of LGBTQ+ students within the context of global tertiary education.	Campbell, A. C., Dezago, J., & Townsend, Q. (2024). Queer students in international higher education: A review of distinct motivations, considerations, and challenges. *Higher Education, 88*, 1567–1588. https://doi.org/10.1007/s10734-024-01183-4

Intersectionality

Intersectionality is a conceptual framework coined by Kimberlé Crenshaw in 1989. It refers to the way different forms of discrimination or disadvantages overlap and intersect, creating unique experiences for individuals. Among academics (Grzanka et al., 2020; Velez & Spencer, 2018), intersectionality is an analytic framework for understanding how multiple social identities (e.g., race, gender, class, sexuality) intersect at the microlevel of individual experience to reflect interlocking systems of privilege and oppression at the macro–social-structural level. Table 2.2 illustrates examples of the microlevel of experience and the macro–social-structural level in the context of intersectionality.

Intersectionality can be a powerful tool for explaining cultural identity development as it considers the multiple, overlapping social identities that individuals navigate. In application, it can be applicable to multiple identities or what I often refer to as pluralistic identity. Via being applied to pluralistic identity, intersectionality acknowledges that individuals possess multiple identities (e.g., race, gender, class, sexual orientation) that intersect and interact with each other. Understanding cultural identity development through this lens means recognizing that a person's cultural identity is shaped by the interplay of these various identities (Faissner et al., 2024). In relation to pluralistic identity, intersectionality may also be used to address contextual influences. In this way, it emphasizes the importance of context in shaping identity. Cultural identity development is influenced by

TABLE 2.2 Examples of the Microlevel of Experience and the Macro–Social-Structural Level

Microlevel (Note 1)	Concepts Applied	Macro-Socio-Structural Level (Note 2)	Concepts Applied
The day-to-day experiences of a Puerto Rican woman in the workplace. She might face unique challenges and discriminations that arise from both her racial and gender identities.	Microaggressions: Subtle, often unintentional, discriminatory comments or behaviors that undermine her confidence and sense of belonging. Often, this may be unique to a Puerto Rican woman because of the complexities around being "American," nationhood reflective of being from a United States colonized territory, and identifying as either White or Afro Latinx. Differential Treatment: Being overlooked for promotions or leadership roles because of biases against her race and gender. Stereotyping: Facing assumptions about her abilities or behavior based on racial and gender stereotypes.	The systemic policies and practices that disproportionately affect marginalized groups in the criminal justice system in the United States.	Racial Profiling and Discrimination: Structural racism in law enforcement and legal practices leads to higher arrest and incarceration rates for Black and Latinx populations compared with White individuals. Economic Disadvantage: Socioeconomic policies that limit access to quality education, healthcare, and employment opportunities for certain racial and ethnic groups exacerbate inequalities. Gendered Impact: Women of color may experience compounded disadvantages because of the intersection of race and gender, resulting in unique challenges such as higher rates of poverty and limited access to reproductive healthcare.

Note 1: These microlevel experiences are shaped by broader systemic and structural inequalities, illustrating how intersectionality operates at both individual and societal levels.

Note 2: These macrolevel factors illustrate how intersectionality helps to uncover the interconnected systems of power and oppression that shape the experiences of individuals at the societal level. Also, these macrolevel experiences provide the broader context within which individuals and communities operate, influencing their daily lives and long-term outcomes.

factors such as family, community, societal norms, and historical context. By considering these intersecting factors, educators can gain deeper insight into how they and their students form and navigate their cultural identities. (Johnson et al., 2022).

While taking into account contextual influences and pluralistic identity, intersectionality is also applied to an analysis of power dynamics and oppression (Azmitia & Mansfield, 2021). According to Azmitia and Mansfield, intersectionality highlights how power dynamics and systems of oppression impact identity development. In their editorial "Intersectionality and Identity Development: How Do We Conceptualize and Research Identity Intersectionalities in Youth Meaningfully?" they discuss how intersectionality serves as an analytic framework for understanding how social identities are configured by power and oppression. Emphasis is given to how intersectionality highlights the interconnected nature of various forms of discrimination and disadvantage, which cannot be fully understood in isolation. This approach helps to reveal the complex and overlapping experiences of individuals who navigate multiple social identities, such as race, gender, class, and sexuality. CES, whether faculty or in career contexts outside of the formal classroom, are encouraged to recognize these overlapping experiences and how they are being used to navigate cross-cultural encounters in the classroom, within the therapeutic relationships, and with colleagues.

Power in the context of intersectionality refers to the systems and structures that create, maintain, and occasionally disrupt social categories and hierarchies (Cole, 2023). It encompasses the ways in which various forms of oppression (e.g., racism, sexism, classism) intersect and reinforce one another to shape individuals' experiences and opportunities (Robinson, 2018). Power dynamics influence how individuals navigate their multiple identities and how they are perceived and treated by society (Wyatt et al., 2022). Oppression in the context of intersectionality refers to the systemic and structural disadvantages and injustices that individuals experience based on the overlapping and intersecting aspects of their social identities (e.g., race, gender, class, sexuality, ability Faissner et al., 2024). Oppression extends beyond individual acts of discrimination to encompass the broader societal forces that perpetuate inequality and marginalization.

Lastly, intersectionality serves as a framework for comprehending our complex experiences. Grzanka et al. (2020) examine this concept in relation to adulthood, demonstrating how intersectionality can be used as an analytical tool to examine and confront intricate social inequities at the convergence of various systems of oppression and privilege. These systems encompass race, gender, sexuality, social class, nation, age, religion, and ability. While this approach shares similarities with previously mentioned applications of the intersectionality framework, it specifically focuses on social justice and is investigated through the lens of psychology and related social sciences, such as counseling. Through this exploration, Grzanka et al. (2020) highlights the following concepts for understanding complex experiences. The following five key points summarize what was derived from their research:

1. Multidimensionality: There is significance in examining various aspects of identity, such as race, gender, and sexuality, and how their interplay influences individual experiences.
2. Dynamic Construction: Rather than being fixed, personal identities are continuously shaped and reshaped through ongoing interactions with societal structures and environments over time.
3. Structural Power: There is an impact of institutional power dynamics and systemic disparities on the development and manifestation of individual and group identities.
4. Outcomes of Systemic Disadvantage and Advantage: The overlap of various identity factors can result in different levels of systemic advantages and disadvantages, impacting individuals' ability to access resources and opportunities.

5. Translational Science for Social Justice: There is a call for the discipline of psychology (and related applied disciplines) to use intersectionality as a means to advance social justice, encouraging studies that tackle societal disparities and foster fairness.

Through this analysis of intersectionality and its application as a framework to explore cultural identity development, counselors, educators, and supervisors preparing for faculty positions are encouraged to engage in self-reflection regarding their personal cultural identity development through an intersectional lens. For this process to be initiated, there are actionable steps that can be taken to structure a transformational plan in preparation for implementing CRT approaches and pedagogy. Table 2.3 elucidates these action terms and their application to self-reflective work. The objective is to develop descriptive language that addresses the question of one's cultural identity and personal experiences, which can be confidently shared with colleagues, future students, and clients, as well as articulated in a teaching philosophy.

TABLE 2.3 Concepts for Forming the Journey of Communicating Personal Cultural Identity Development

Concept	Action
Introspection	Start by examining your personal experiences, principles, and convictions. Consider how your identity has been molded by cultural norms, traditions, and practices. Writing in a diary or conversing with loved ones can assist in uncovering these influences.
Knowledge and Understanding	Explore your cultural roots and history. This may involve researching your ethnic group's past, acknowledging the challenges and accomplishments of your forebears, and recognizing the impact of your heritage on your sense of self.
Involvement in Community	Participate actively in your cultural group. Attend cultural celebrations, festivals, and rituals. Interacting with individuals who share your background can reinforce your cultural identity.
Analytical Thinking	Evaluate and scrutinize your beliefs and values. Examine how societal expectations and stereotypes have shaped your perception of your own culture. This thorough analysis can lead to a more complex understanding of your identity.
Personal Connections	Engage in discussions about your cultural identity with others. Conversations with family members, mentors, or friends who share or appreciate your cultural background can offer valuable perspectives and support.
Cultural Manifestation	Discover ways to showcase your cultural identity through various forms of expression such as art, music, food, or other cultural practices. Engaging in these activities can strengthen your connection to your heritage.
Professional Counseling	If necessary, consult a counselor or therapist who specializes in cultural identity development. They can provide a supportive environment to explore and comprehend your cultural identity more thoroughly.

Learning From a Culturally Responsive Perspective

Culturally responsive pedagogy, when implemented effectively, yields substantial benefits for students by cultivating an inclusive and equitable educational milieu that acknowledges and esteems their diverse backgrounds. The integration of intersectionality into pedagogical practices enables educators to recognize and address the complex, multifaceted social identities of their students, encompassing factors such as race, gender, socioeconomic status, and ability. This approach facilitates the deconstruction of systemic biases and discriminatory practices, fostering an academic environment where all students experience validation, representation, and respect.

The implementation of CRT methodologies has been shown to enhance student engagement, participation, and sense of belonging, thereby positively impacting academic performance and personal development. Furthermore, as a pedagogical approach it promotes cultural identity formation by encouraging students to explore and affirm their cultural heritage and values. This process of self-discovery not only bolsters individual confidence but also cultivates an appreciation for the cultural identities of future clients with whom they will work within counseling practice.

Central to culturally responsive education are key concepts such as empathy, respect, and cross-cultural communication. These competencies are essential for navigating an increasingly diverse global landscape of the counseling discipline. By establishing a learning environment that supports cultural identity development, counselors, educators, and supervisors lay the groundwork for lifelong learning and personal growth, equipping students with the tools necessary to become culturally competent and socially responsible individuals across their careers as professional counselors.

The efficacy of culturally responsive pedagogy extends beyond immediate academic outcomes, influencing students' long-term personal and professional trajectories. This approach fosters critical thinking skills, encourages perspective-taking, and develops a nuanced understanding of complex social issues. As students engage with diverse viewpoints and experiences, they develop a more sophisticated worldview, better preparing them for leadership roles in a multicultural society, critical thinking, and global insights.

Fundamentally, CRT plays a crucial role in addressing educational disparities and promoting social justice. By acknowledging and valuing the cultural capital that students bring to the classroom, educators can bridge the gap between home and school cultures, making the educational experience more relevant and accessible to all learners. An alignment between students' lived experiences and academic content enhances cognitive engagement and facilitates deeper learning.

Essentially, the implementation of culturally responsive pedagogy represents a paradigm shift in education, moving beyond traditional, monocultural approaches to embrace a more inclusive, equitable, and dynamic learning environment. This approach not only enhances academic outcomes but also prepares students to become active, engaged citizens in an increasingly interconnected world.

MINDSET FOR CULTURALLY RESPONSIVE TEACHING IN COUNSELOR TRAINING PROGRAMS

Mindset encompasses an individual's established attitudes and mental predispositions that influence their perceptions, thoughts, and approaches to various situations (Dweck, 2006). It shapes behaviors, reactions, and overall life perspective, playing a crucial role in teaching preparation. Dweck, a Stanford University psychology professor, is renowned for her research on fixed and growth mindsets, demonstrating their impact on motivation, learning, and achievement. Her concept of growth mindset aligns well with preparing for CRT in counselor training programs, serving as a strategic tool with intentional and critical consciousness aspects. The adoption of a growth mindset by counselor educators is essential for implementing a CRT approach, and this importance stems from several key factors that I shape for counselor educators who are preparing to teach.

First, a growth mindset encourages the idea that one's capabilities and intellect can be enhanced through commitment, diligence, and ongoing education. This mindset can motivate counselor educators to continuously enhance their teaching techniques, reflect learning materials that increasingly integrate the sociocultural diversity of all students, and stay receptive to different viewpoints and cultural understandings. Recommendations to enhance a growth mindset include pursuing mentorship opportunities, engaging in peer supervision, observing classes in related disciplines taught by instructors who consider themselves practitioners of CRT, and developing a personal metric to track individual and professional growth in CES careers.

Adopting a growth mindset allows counselor educators to view challenges and setbacks as opportunities for development rather than insurmountable obstacles. For example, a student might challenge a faculty member over the Israel/Gaza conflict, questioning language choices, historical interpretations, or media portrayals. This can happen if the instructor is uncomfortable with the topic, struggles to communicate impartially, or lacks pedagogical strategies for framing such discussions, which are common among adult learners today. Faculty are encouraged to see these moments as opportunities to maintain a safe environment for healthy dialogue on contemporary and historical issues, leveraging our diverse identities. In counselor training programs, CRT methods are recommended to address the complexities and sensitivities involved, fostering resilience.

Counselor educators with a growth mindset are more likely to persist in creating inclusive classrooms, even amid difficult conversations or opposition. Preparing for such an inclusive, discourse-friendly environment involves developing more equitable learning spaces. Additionally, the counselor educator is to be secure in their personal and professional identity, not only possessing a growth mindset but also fostering it among students through critical thinking and awareness development.

Finally, embracing a growth mindset encourages change, which is essential for keeping up with evolving cultural dynamics both inside and outside the classroom and awareness of teaching methods that better meet the learning needs of diverse classrooms. By consistently enhancing personal and professional awareness, knowledge, and skills, counselor educators can more effectively comprehend and address the intricacies of students' diverse cultural backgrounds and the broader sociocultural-political contexts (both nationally and internationally). The growth mindset ultimately creates perceptual room for a more inclusive and equitable educational setting.

DEVELOPING INTUITIVE AWARENESS OF SOCIOCULTURAL CLIMATE ISSUES

Critical pedagogy (CP), which underpins CRT, provides a foundation for comprehending, tackling, and investigating sociocultural climate issues. These matters influence and manifest in the structured learning environment of classrooms, affecting the future counseling practices of students. Consequently, CES faculty must prepare for praxis that demonstrates an understanding of how individuals perceive global events and how this perception intertwines with curricular content. CP introduces various ways of knowing that contribute to developing an intuitive awareness of sociocultural climate issues, including emancipatory, transformative, experiential, dialogic, and critical approaches. This intuitive awareness reflects a deep-seated understanding of the complex interplay between societal norms, cultural dynamics, and environmental concerns, allowing educators and students to recognize and respond to these issues more effectively. These knowledge forms challenge conventional educational methods, offering CES faculty the tools that are helpful in preparing for instruction through a culturally responsive perspective, thereby fostering a more nuanced and empathetic approach to addressing sociocultural climate issues in both educational and counseling contexts. These ways of knowing or types of knowledge are described in the text that follows.

Emancipatory Knowledge

Emancipatory knowledge aims to free individuals from oppressive circumstances by understanding the fundamental causes of oppression and striving for social equity (Freire, 2000). Although it is connected to other forms of knowledge in CP, emancipatory knowledge specifically focuses on liberating people and groups from oppressive conditions. Rooted in CP, this form of understanding involves recognizing and challenging power structures and societal systems that sustain inequality and unfairness. It enables learners to critically examine their situations, develop a deep understanding of social injustices, and take action to change their reality. This transformative process not only enhances personal growth but also supports collective efforts to achieve social justice and equality. By embracing emancipatory knowledge, teachers and students can work together to create more inclusive and fair educational settings. This approach empowers individuals to analyze their circumstances critically, fosters awareness of societal inequities, and motivates them to take steps toward transforming their environment.

Dialogic Knowledge

Collaborative learning environments are fostered through dialogic knowledge, which involves the joint construction of understanding (Paul, 1987). In the context of CP, this approach underscores the significance of interaction and dialogue in learning. It serves as a means to promote inclusivity and equity, creating a collaborative setting where students and teachers jointly develop knowledge through meaningful discussions (Kibler et al., 2020). By challenging conventional hierarchical structures, dialogic pedagogy cultivates critical thinking and mutual respect. It prompts students to examine and contemplate their experiences, resulting in enhanced comprehension and empowerment. Current research demonstrates the efficacy of dialogic pedagogy in boosting critical thinking skills and democratic participation within educational settings. As a learning approach, the concept of dialogic will be further explained in Chapter 6 in the context of the CRT pedagogy descriptions.

Transformative Knowledge

Banks (2020) defines *transformative knowledge* as the process of critically evaluating and confronting established power dynamics, belief systems, and cultural norms to promote individual and collective change. This approach encourages students to scrutinize and contemplate their own convictions and presuppositions, resulting in a more profound comprehension and alteration of their worldviews. By doing so, individuals are empowered to become proactive catalysts for change, advocating for social equality and fairness. Current studies emphasize the significance of transformative knowledge in cultivating educational settings that are both inclusive and democratic.

Experiential Knowledge

In applications of CP in our teaching, hands-on learning and reflective practices are highly valued for their ability to impart knowledge. This approach, when applied in higher education settings, promotes active student participation, leading to enhanced comprehension and analytical abilities. By incorporating real-life scenarios into the curriculum, instructors can create a more vibrant and applicable learning atmosphere. This strategy aligns with CP's core principles, which aim to equip students with the tools to question and modify oppressive systems. Giroux (2020) underscores the importance of experiential education in advancing social equity and democratic learning practices.

Critical Knowledge

In the realm of CP in higher education, essential knowledge encompasses the examination and interrogation of societal and educational power structures, social frameworks, and ideological systems (Cooper, 2015). This approach encourages students to critically evaluate and confront oppressive mechanisms, cultivating a more profound understanding of social inequities and empowering them to become catalysts for change. By promoting a more egalitarian and inclusive learning environment, this pedagogical method motivates students to engage in critical thinking and participate in transformative educational experiences.

The types of knowledge in CP—experiential, critical, transformative, dialogic, and emancipatory—align seamlessly with a growth mindset by fostering continuous learning, critical reflection, and personal transformation. Experiential knowledge encourages learning through direct experience, while critical knowledge promotes questioning and analyzing power structures. Transformative knowledge focuses on personal and societal change, dialogic knowledge emphasizes collaborative learning, and emancipatory knowledge seeks to liberate individuals from oppressive conditions. Together, these forms of knowledge support the growth mindset's principles of embracing challenges, learning from feedback, and believing in the potential for development and improvement.

DEVELOPING TEACHING PHILOSOPHY FOR THE 21ST CENTURY

A teaching philosophy is expected for faculty positions across disciplines, serving as a reflective statement on personal and professional instructional methods, the meaning of teaching, and curriculum planning. Mary Bowne (2020), in "Developing a Teaching Philosophy," defines it as an articulation of an educator's beliefs, values, and teaching approaches, often with concrete classroom examples, guiding instructional practices and student interactions. Bowne (2020) highlights the importance of reflection and continuous development in crafting a teaching philosophy to enhance student learning.

Teaching philosophies are often specific to schools or disciplines, as search committees may seek details relevant to a particular major. For instance, in social sciences, a teaching philosophy might emphasize CP and professional development, especially if the instruction involves applied sciences. Sharmin and Chow (2020) and Baker (2021) highlight that modern teaching philosophies should reflect continuous growth, lifelong learning, and global awareness, which applies broadly across higher education. Baker (2021) notes that teaching philosophies facilitate critical reflection and professional development, while Sharmin and Chow (2020) argue that innovative approaches to these statements are crucial in today's sociocultural-political climate, especially for social sciences. For instance, they suggest that teaching philosophies shift in format and use innovative alternatives:

- exploring innovative approaches to replace conventional teaching philosophy statements
- emphasizing the influence of COVID-19 on educational methodologies and promoting the adoption of tech-integrated, remote, and blended learning strategies
- using introspective compositions or brief video presentations to serve as valuable tools for assessing instructional methods and objectives

To develop a CRT philosophy, begin by formulating content that shapes this approach. Strategically prepare content that articulates personal and professional positioning in teaching counselor curricula. While the statement will include common components, a teaching philosophy that is culturally responsive, tailored for higher education faculty, and distinct for counselor curricula is inherently more complex.

Table 2.4 presents an outline of content proposed to shape such a CES teaching philosophy. The three comparable columns are structured from general to more complex content. Content from each column creates a working paradigm that shapes a CRT philosophy.

TABLE 2.4 The Instructional Approach for Philosophy in Counselor Education Programs*

General (Least Complex)	Culturally Responsive Teaching (Moderately Complex)	Learning Needs of Graduate Students Entering the Counseling Profession (More Complex Content That Is to Blend Within Content of Columns 1 and 2)
Reflect on Your Beliefs and Values: Examine your perspective on the fundamental purpose of education and how you can make a meaningful impact. Analyze your past teaching experiences, accomplishments, and obstacles to uncover your fundamental principles and convictions regarding the processes of teaching and learning.	Commitment to Equity: Highlight the commitment to fostering a fair and inclusive educational setting that ensures every student, regarding their cultural heritage, feels esteemed and acknowledged.	Advanced Critical Thinking and Analysis: Foster advanced levels of analytical and critical thinking among graduate students. Emphasize the practical application of theoretical frameworks to real-life situations and the construction of complex arguments backed by data-driven evidence.
Define Your Goals: Articulate with precision your educational objectives for your students. What are the intended outcomes in your classroom? These may encompass the cultivation of critical thinking skills, the enhancement of student engagement, or the development of problem-solving abilities.	Cultural Competence: Emphasize the significance of cultivating cultural competence, which encompasses comprehending and valuing the diverse cultural backgrounds of students and integrating this awareness into pedagogical practices.	Research Proficiency: It is imperative to underscore the significance of research competencies, encompassing the design of studies, execution of advanced statistical analyses, and interpretation of data. Furthermore, it is essential to cultivate a research-oriented perspective that equips students for roles as practitioners that apply evidence-based interventions, comprehends academic and clinical research, and clearly communicates the use of clinical implications.
Describe Your Teaching Methods: Explain the methodologies and strategies used to attain your educational objectives. This may encompass interactive pedagogical techniques, collaborative learning approaches, or the integration of technological resources in the educational environment.	Inclusive Curriculum: Advocate for the incorporation of diverse perspectives and materials in the curriculum to ensure that students observe representations of themselves and their cultures in their educational content.	Ethical and Professional Development: Emphasize the importance of ethical practice and professional standards at an advanced level. Analyze complex ethical dilemmas and decision-making processes, preparing students for the nuanced challenges they may encounter in their professional careers. Be knowledgeable of the ACA Codes of Ethics and CACREP Standards for professional identity.
Assessment of Learning: Elaborate on the strategies implemented for assessing student comprehension and delivering constructive feedback. What evaluation approaches are used to measure academic progress, and how is this data used to refine instructional methodologies?	Student-Centered Approach: Implement an educational approach that positions learners at the forefront, emphasizing their unique aspirations, scholastic inclinations, and diverse backgrounds to establish an atmosphere conducive to academic engagement and social integration.	Cultural Humility and Competence: Emphasize the cultivation of cultural humility and competence, preparing students to engage effectively with diverse populations. Promote critical self-reflection regarding personal biases and facilitate the incorporation of multicultural perspectives into practice and research methodologies.

(continued)

TABLE 2.4 The Instructional Approach for Philosophy in Counselor Education Programs* *(continued)*

General (Least Complex)	Culturally Responsive Teaching (Moderately Complex)	Learning Needs of Graduate Students Entering the Counseling Profession (More Complex Content That Is to Blend Within Content of Columns 1 and 2)
Inclusivity and Diversity: Articulate the methodologies used to cultivate an inclusive and supportive scholastic atmosphere that caters to the needs of all students. Elaborate on the techniques used to integrate multifaceted perspectives and ensure each learner experiences a sense of validation and esteem within the academic context.	Critical Reflection: Promote sustained introspection regarding one's instructional methodologies and preconceptions, with the aim of continual refinement and modification to effectively cater to the diverse needs of a multifaceted student cohort.	Practical Application and Skills Development: Facilitate opportunities for the practical application of counseling and psychologic theories. Provide experiential learning through internships, practicums, and supervised clinical practice to enhance students' applied skills.
Continuous Improvement: Articulate your dedication to ongoing enhancement and professional growth. In what ways do you remain abreast of educational research and exemplary practices, and how do you integrate this expertise into your instructional methodologies?	Collaborative Learning: Facilitate collaborative learning environments wherein students can acquire knowledge from the diverse perspectives and experiences of their peers, thereby fostering mutual respect and understanding.	Leadership and Advocacy: Equip graduate students with the requisite skills to assume leadership and advocacy roles within their professional communities. Foster the development of competencies in team leadership, social justice advocacy, and policy influence.
Personal Anecdotes: To enhance the appeal and relatability of your teaching philosophy statement, incorporate real-life examples or personal experiences that demonstrate your pedagogical approach in practice. These narratives can serve to make your statement more compelling and accessible to readers.	Community Engagement: Highlight the critical role of fostering connections with the local community and using community-based insights and assets in the educational setting to enhance the pertinence and efficacy of the learning process.	Collaborative Learning and Professional Networking: Encourage graduate students to participate in interactive learning settings that facilitate engagement with their peers and industry professionals. Support the development of professional connections by advocating for involvement in academic conferences, training sessions, and discipline-specific organizations.

Note: *The progressions are from broad concepts to Intricate Ideas, developing a framework that offers insights Into educational methods and learning processes within the field.

ACA, American Counseling Association; CACREP, Council for Accreditation of Counseling and Related Educational Programs.

STRATEGIC PLANNING FOR SELF-CARE AND PREVENTION OF BURNOUT

For a culturally responsive counselor educator (CRCE), the maintenance of self-care practices and the prevention of burnout are essential for sustaining teaching careers and efficacy. Prioritizing self-care not only demonstrates healthful behaviors for counselors-in-training but also fosters emotional resilience and enhances empathy and compassion within the learning environment. It is an approach that is particularly critical when addressing complex topics pertaining to race, identity, and social justice.

Evidence-Based Practices of Self-Care and Burnout Prevention

Both self-care and burnout have been studied in relation to social justice (The Self-Care Institute, 2024; Wyatt et al., 2022), which much of the profession of counseling is predicated on when teaching about multiculturalism and cultural dynamics that impact and are impending in society. This is now more commonly addressed across the curricula, not just in one course. Wyatt et al. (2022) share clinical implications in the *Community Mental Health Journal* that self-care is a coping mechanism that may be used to deal with stressors of racism and discrimination. They further share that self-care is not just for the individual, but a form of resistance and preservation against oppressive systems (Wyatt et al., 2022). Similarly, research by The Self-Care Institute (2024) explores the intersections of burnout, self-care, and social justice. Outcomes of this research emphasize that self-care is a revolutionary act that supports well-being and the progress of social justice movements. Their study discusses how self-care can prevent burnout among activists and professionals working in social justice fields.

Another significant research project focuses on the intersection of self-care and community trauma. At the University of Denver, Danso (2024) conducted a study exploring how community trauma affects social justice workers and the restorative role of self-care practices. This research underscores the crucial role of self-care in fostering community resilience and mitigating the consequences of trauma.

Moreover, self-care practices support cognitive function and aid in the prevention of compassion fatigue, thereby enabling educators to provide optimal support for underserved and marginalized populations. Ultimately, self-care facilitates the preservation of educators' well-being while fostering a supportive and inclusive atmosphere conducive to learning. This is the case because there are going to be instances where institutional or systemic injustices are long-standing practices embedded in the cultures of colleges and universities that employ us.

When culturally responsive educators neglect to prioritize self-care and prevent burnout, they risk experiencing exhaustion, empathy fatigue, and diminished teaching efficacy. This can result in elevated stress levels, strained interpersonal relationships, and potential physical and psychologic health concerns. Furthermore, failure to model healthy practices may negatively impact the overall wellness culture within the educational environment, while increased staff turnover could disrupt student learning. It is imperative for educators to prioritize self-care to maintain their well-being and effectiveness, thereby ensuring they can provide optimal support and instruction to their students. In an effort to address what we can do to prevent burnout and increase or begin self-care strategically across careers as counselors, educators, and supervisors, scholars inform us of empirical evidence and modes that we can implement.

The National Association of School Psychologists (NASP; 2021) offers guidance on self-care and burnout prevention for professionals in mental healthcare. Their recommendations include evidence-based practices specifically designed for school mental health workers. The organization stresses the significance of self-care in preserving wellness and averting stress and burnout. NASP (2021) presents actionable techniques for incorporating self-care into everyday life, encompassing cognitive, spiritual, emotional, social, and physical aspects. By giving priority to these comprehensive self-care approaches, professionals in mental health can boost their overall well-being, strengthen their resilience, and maintain their efficacy in providing support to students. The practices that NASP (2021) esteems to help counselors maintain their well-being and resilience are:

1. Cognitive Self-Care: Participating in mentally stimulating pursuits, such as delving into books, solving brain teasers, and acquiring new abilities.
2. Emotional Self-Care: Engaging in mindfulness exercises, meditative practices, and other stress-reduction methods to regulate emotions and alleviate tension.
3. Physical Self-Care: Adopting a wholesome way of life through consistent physical activity, well-rounded diet, and sufficient rest.
4. Social Self-Care: Cultivating and nurturing positive connections with peers, loved ones, and professional contacts.
5. Spiritual Self-Care: Participating in pursuits that foster a feeling of meaning and belonging, such as practicing spiritual exercises, engaging in mindfulness techniques, or immersing oneself in the outdoors.
6. Professional Self-Care: Pursuing opportunities for professional growth, establishing clear limits, and efficiently handling one's workload.
7. Relaxation Techniques: Adopting stress-reduction methods like controlled breathing exercises, sequential muscle relaxation techniques, and practicing yoga postures.

A recent investigation explored the connections between resilience, self-care practices, and burnout among school counselors (Michael et al., 2024). The findings by Michael et al. (2024) indicated that school counselors who consistently engage in self-care and build resilience are less likely to experience burnout. Certain self-care activities were found to be particularly effective in reducing emotional exhaustion and improving feelings of professional accomplishment, including managing stress, fostering personal relationships, and promoting spiritual growth. These outcomes emphasize the importance of incorporating self-care techniques into professional development programs to improve the well-being and effectiveness of school counselors. The study's relevance stems from its depiction of authentic situations that counseling students aim to encounter and are encouraged to consider prior to fully entering their careers. A crucial lesson is that there is no better moment than the present to start implementing strategies for self-care and burnout prevention.

A model for counselor self-care and burnout prevention has been developed by Lee et al. (2023). In their research, Lee et al. (2023) used a serial mediation approach to examine counselor burnout. This approach identified crucial mediating factors between a negative work environment and the devaluation of clients, including personal life deterioration, exhaustion, and feelings of incompetence. The study's results highlight the necessity of tackling these elements to mitigate burnout among counselors. A summary of how Lee and colleagues describe these mediating factors is noted in the following list:

- Negative Work Environment: The framework initiates with an adverse workplace setting, which may encompass elements such as excessive workloads, insufficient assistance, and difficult interactions with clients.
- Deterioration in Personal Life: This negative work environment leads to deterioration in personal life, affecting the counselor's personal relationships and overall well-being.
- Exhaustion: The decline in one's personal life subsequently leads to mental and physical fatigue, making it challenging for counselors to sustain their enthusiasm and drive.
- Incompetence: In the end, when counselors reach a state of exhaustion, they may experience self-doubt, questioning their professional competence and the effectiveness of their work.
- Devaluing Clients: Counselors experiencing self-doubt may underestimate their clients' worth, potentially compromising their ability to empathize and engage effectively during therapeutic sessions.

Lee et al. (2023) offer valuable insights that CES professionals in leadership roles may adopt. Those in leadership roles who are considered in CES positions may include program directors, individuals who serve on boards connected to the counseling profession, and so on.

Lee's research also emphasizes three crucial aspects that all CES individuals are encouraged to practice: detecting burnout indicators early, adopting self-care techniques, and offering professional support. In terms of early detection, counselors can use the suggested model to spot initial burnout signs, such as disturbances in personal life and exhaustion, allowing them to establish preventive strategies before the situation escalates. Closely related to this is the focus on self-care methods, which the model deems essential for averting burnout. Counselors are encouraged to develop self-care strategies or seek assistance to preserve their mental well-being. Furthermore, the notion of professional support pertains to how supervisors and counseling center directors can use the model to cultivate supportive work settings that reduce negative conditions and improve counselor welfare.

As the elements of self-care and burnout prevention are imperative in the dynamic of preparing individuals for teaching counselor education curricula, it is important to adopt a perspective of lifelong learning. Lifelong learning will need to be about personal and other cultural identity development, as well as professional development, with these relating to sustaining a healthy CES career.

LIFELONG LEARNING IN COUNSELOR EDUCATION AND SUPERVISION

Theories and concepts of lifelong learning for faculty in higher education are explored by Thwe and Kálmán (2024), who review research from 2000 to 2022. Their review identifies key lifelong learning concepts and emphasizes its importance in educational research, highlighting essential skills and competencies. Findings indicate lifelong learning is vital for personal and professional development, with educational institutions playing a crucial role in fostering these skills in students and faculty. Complementing this, Harvard Graduate School of Education (HGSE; 2024) offers actionable strategies for faculty to engage in lifelong learning. A summary of the HGSE strategies is provided in the following list:

- Professional Development Programs: Engage in instructor-led initiatives aimed at enhancing your impact and improving your effectiveness as an educator and leader. These initiatives typically emphasize areas such as adult education, professional development, and long-term well-being.
- Networking and Collaboration: Participate in the HGSE community to expand your knowledge, work together, and form relationships with fellow professionals. Developing a robust professional network can offer assistance, facilitate information exchange, and create new avenues for professional advancement.
- Access to Resources: Use the HGSE's extensive education subject library and other key resources to stay updated with the latest research, theories, and practices in education.
- Career Services: Use career development resources to guide you through career-related decisions, procedures, and transitions. This encompasses planning a fulfilling and influential professional journey that goes beyond simply finding employment.
- Continuous Learning Opportunities: Seek out avenues for personal and professional advancement, including attending workshops, participating in seminars, and enrolling in online courses, to continually enhance your abilities and expand your knowledge base.

Continuous education is essential for counseling professors at the graduate level, as it enables them to stay up-to-date with the latest practices, theories, and ethical guidelines in their field. By actively pursuing ongoing professional growth, instructors can improve their expertise and abilities, which in turn enhances their teaching efficacy and the caliber of education they deliver to their students. Keeping abreast of current research and advancements allows faculty members to better equip their students for the intricacies of the counseling profession. Moreover, ongoing learning promotes personal development and flexibility, enabling instructors to adapt to shifts in the educational landscape and address the varied requirements of their students.

In the end, dedicating themselves to continuous learning helps faculty maintain their professional proficiency and contribute to the progress of the counseling discipline. As we conclude this discussion on the significance of ongoing education for faculty, it is worth noting its importance in preparing students who are training to become mental health practitioners.

CONCLUSION

This chapter focused on key factors that prepare individuals for teaching in the CES discipline. Critical preparatory areas include an advanced understanding of cultural identity development for oneself and others, formulating a strong teaching philosophy, adopting a growth mindset, and understanding the importance of self-care and being a lifelong learner. The benefits of preparing for teaching in each of these areas highlight the importance of fostering a more inclusive, empathetic, and effective educational environment. Collectively, the purpose and benefits of preparing for teaching in counselor training programs with a strong awareness of personal cultural identity development are noted in the following list:

- Enhanced Student Connections: Teachers who are aware of their own cultural backgrounds are more capable of forming genuine and supportive relationships with students from various cultures. This creates an environment of inclusion and confidence in the classroom.
- Culture-Informed Instruction: Awareness of one's cultural identity enables educators to adopt teaching methods that are sensitive to cultural differences. This approach acknowledges and appreciates students' diverse cultural heritages and incorporates them into lesson plans.
- Greater Compassion and Insight: Educators who delve into their own cultural identity development are better positioned to sympathize with students' unique experiences and obstacles. This deeper understanding can result in more supportive and efficient teaching techniques.
- Professional Growth: Self-reflection on cultural identity development can enhance educators' professional skills by promoting ongoing learning and adaptability to diverse educational environments.

CHAPTER RESOURCES

Culturally Responsive Counselor Educator Skills

CRCE Skills to Further Develop From This Chapter	
Cultural Identity Development	Cultural identity development is vital to self-awareness and other awareness skills that empower individuals to understand and appreciate their own cultural backgrounds and those of others. As an awareness skill, it fosters self-identity, empathy, and the ability to navigate multicultural environments effectively. It is an essential competency for CES working with diverse students, colleagues, and especially those in work environments across higher education and healthcare.
Intersectional Analysis	Intersectional analysis is a critical skill that involves understanding and examining how various social identities—such as race, gender, class, sexuality, and ability—intersect and interact to shape individuals' experiences and access to resources. This analytical framework helps individuals recognize and address complex forms of discrimination and privilege that arise from the interplay of these intersecting identities. Developing intersectional analysis as a skill is essential for fostering inclusive and equitable environments in both personal and professional contexts.

(continued)

CRCE Skills to Further Develop From This Chapter *(continued)*	
Growth Mindset	Developing a growth mindset is a crucial skill that involves embracing the belief that abilities and intelligence can be developed through dedication, effort, and continuous learning. It is encouraged to practice in order to be a CRCE. This mindset fosters resilience, adaptability, and a positive attitude toward challenges and setbacks. By cultivating a growth mindset, CRCE become more open to feedback, willing to take risks, and committed to personal and professional growth. As a skill, it not only enhances problem-solving and creativity but also promotes a lifelong love of learning, enabling individuals to thrive in an ever-changing multicultural world.
Culturally Responsive Teaching	Becoming a CRCE involves a commitment to continuous learning and self-reflection. Start by educating yourself about different cultures, histories, and perspectives through books, courses, and diverse media. Engage in self-reflection to understand your own cultural biases and how they influence your teaching practices. Foster an inclusive classroom environment by incorporating culturally diverse materials and perspectives into your curriculum. Actively listen to and value the experiences of your students, creating a safe space for open dialogue. Seek out professional development opportunities, such as workshops and conferences, focused on cultural competence. By taking these steps, you can develop the skills necessary to effectively support and engage all students.
Self-Care and Burnout Prevention	Developing self-care and burnout prevention as an educator involves cultivating a skill-set that includes emotional intelligence, time management, and stress management techniques. Emotional intelligence allows educators to recognize and regulate their own emotions and empathize with others, fostering a supportive and understanding environment. Effective time management skills help balance work responsibilities with personal time, ensuring educators have opportunities for rest and rejuvenation. Stress management techniques, such as mindfulness, exercise, and relaxation practices, are essential for maintaining mental and physical well-being. Additionally, seeking professional support, setting realistic goals, and maintaining a healthy work-life balance are crucial components of this skill-set, enabling educators to sustain their passion and effectiveness in their profession.
Teaching Philosophy	Developing a teaching philosophy in CES requires a blend of self-awareness, reflective practice, and a deep understanding of pedagogical theories. CES individuals must possess strong communication skills to articulate their values, beliefs, and teaching approaches clearly and coherently. Critical thinking is essential to evaluate and integrate various educational philosophies and methodologies effectively. Additionally, cultural competence and empathy are crucial for acknowledging and addressing the diverse needs of students, fostering an inclusive and supportive learning environment. Continuous professional development and a commitment to lifelong learning help educators stay updated with the latest trends and best practices in the field. By cultivating these skills, educators can create a well-rounded teaching philosophy that guides their practice and enhances the learning experiences of their students.
Lifelong Learning	Lifelong learning is an essential skill for educators, empowering them to continually enhance their knowledge, teaching methods, and professional competence. This commitment to ongoing education allows educators to stay current with the latest research, technologies, and pedagogical innovations, ensuring that they can effectively meet the diverse needs of their students. By embracing a mindset of continuous improvement and curiosity, educators model the value of learning for their students, fostering a culture of intellectual growth and adaptability. Lifelong learning also helps educators to remain passionate and engaged in their profession, preventing stagnation and promoting a dynamic, responsive teaching environment.

CES, counselor education and supervision; CRCE, culturally responsive counselor educator.

CONTENT SUMMARY

Cultural Identity Development

- Understanding Cultural Identity: Understand that a person's cultural identity plays a crucial role in their individual growth, encompassing customs, ancestral background, spoken tongue, and community frameworks.
- **Inclusive Curriculum:** Create educational programs that honor and incorporate the varied cultural heritages of the student body.
- For counselor educators dedicated to CRT, embracing a growth mindset is essential. It's a perceptual lens that fosters ongoing improvement, resilience, and a genuine commitment to understanding and appreciating diverse viewpoints that may be unfamiliar or contradictory to one's own.
- By adopting a growth mindset, counselor educators can better discern which learning materials are beneficial and which have been impeding progress in counselor preparation curricula. This understanding underscores the increasing efforts, evidenced by the publication of new learning resources, that teach to decolonize therapeutic practices in mental health counseling and that exist throughout counselor education programs.

Culturally Responsive Teaching Philosophy

- Know Your Students: Gather information about students' personal histories, hobbies, and difficulties to customize instructional approaches appropriately.
- Reflect on Personal Biases: Recognize and tackle personal prejudices to foster a fair and inclusive educational setting.
- Engage With Cultural References: Incorporate cultural references into educational practices to enhance student engagement and make the learning experience more meaningful.

Importance of Self-Care and Burnout Prevention

- Recognize Burnout Signs: Recognize the indicators of burnout, which may manifest as emotional fatigue and a pessimistic outlook.
- **Implement Self-Care Practices:** Regularly participate in activities that promote your physical, mental, and emotional health to sustain overall wellness.
- Seek Support: Leverage organizational resources and professional connections to cope with stress and avoid exhaustion.

Strategizing for Lifelong Learning

- Continuous Professional Development: Commit to ongoing learning and professional growth through workshops, conferences, and further education.
- Adaptability: Remain flexible and receptive to innovative instructional approaches and digital tools to support continuous learning throughout life.

Advanced Reflection Questions

1. How does your cultural background shape your teaching approach and student interactions?
2. What methods will you use to foster a classroom atmosphere that embraces and appreciates diverse cultural backgrounds?
3. What are your fundamental beliefs about education, and how do these principles influence your teaching methodology?
4. What key tenets direct your instructional practices and their impact on student engagement and curriculum development?
5. What techniques do you use to address your students' varied requirements, and how do you cultivate a learning environment that is both inclusive and encouraging?
6. What approaches will you implement to ensure all students feel respected and supported, taking into account their diverse backgrounds, capabilities, and learning preferences?
7. How do you intend to pursue ongoing professional growth to enhance your cultural awareness as an educator?
8. What resources and support networks will you use to continually improve your understanding of cultural identity and its educational implications?
9. What approaches will you adopt to maintain your resilience and well-being while fulfilling your role as a culturally responsive educator?

Further Reading

Borkoski, C., & Prosser, S. K. (2020). Developing faculty identity as a community engaged scholar: An unexamined barrier to promoting the public mission. In A. Papadimitriou & M. Boboc (Eds.), *Re-envisioning higher education's public mission* (pp. 77–95). Springer.

Pratt, D. D. (2020). *Five perspectives on teaching in adult and higher education* (3rd ed.). Krieger Publishing Company.

Radlauer-Doerfler, J., & VanDenBerg, J. E. (2020). *A practical guide to self-care for helping professionals.* CMH Network.

Skovholt, T. M., & Trotter-Mathison, M. (2011). *The resilient practitioner: Burnout prevention and self-care strategies for counselors, therapists, teachers, and health professionals* (2nd ed.). Routledge.

REFERENCES

Azmitia, M., & Mansfield, K. C. (2021). Editorial: Intersectionality and identity development: How do we conceptualize and research identity intersectionalities in youth meaningfully? *Frontiers in Psychology, 12*, 625765. https://doi.org/10.3389/fpsyg.2021.625765

Baker, L. A. (2021). Teaching philosophy statements as a vehicle for critical reflection. *Practitioner Research in Higher Education, 14*(1), 72–82. https://files.eric.ed.gov/fulltext/EJ1334141.pdf

Banks, J. A. (2020). *Diversity, transformative knowledge, and civic education: Selected essays* (1st ed.). Routledge. https://doi.org/10.4324/9781003018360

Bowne, M. (2020). Developing a teaching philosophy. *Journal of Effective Teaching, 20*(2), 1–15. https://files.eric.ed.gov/fulltext/EJ1175767.pdf

Cole, E. R. (2023). Beyond identity: Intersectionality and power. In E. L. Zurbriggen & R. Capdevila (Eds.), *The Palgrave handbook of power, gender, and psychology* (pp. 29–44). Palgrave Macmillan. https://doi.org/10.1007/978-3-031-41531-9_3

Cooper, C. (2015). Critical pedagogy in higher education. In C. Cooper, S. Gormally, & G. Hughes, *Socially just, radical alternatives for education and youth work practice* (pp. 39–64). Palgrave Macmillan. https://doi.org/10.1057/9781137393593_3

Cross Jr., W. E. (1971). The Negro-to-Black conversion experience: Toward a psychology of Black liberation. In R. L. Jones (Ed.), *Black psychology* (pp. 290–302). Cobb & Henry Publishers.

Cross, W. E., Parham, T. A., & Helms, J. E. (1991). The stages of Black identity development: Nigrescence models. In W. E. Cross Jr. (Ed.), *Shades of Black: Diversity in African American identity* (pp. 1–16). Temple University Press.

Danso, M. (2024). *Self-care or caring for?: Community trauma, social justice work, and the positioning of self-care*. University of Denver. https://www.du.edu/research/showcase/self-care-community-trauma-social-justice

Dweck, C. S. (2006). *Mindset: The new psychology of success*. Random House.

Faissner, M., Gaillard, A. S., Juckel, G., & Gather, J. (2024). Intersectionality and discriminatory practices within mental health care. *Philosophy, Ethics, and Humanities in Medicine, 19*, 9. https://doi.org/10.1186/s13010-024-00159-7

Freire, P. (2000). *Pedagogy of the oppressed* (30th anniversary ed.). Continuum.

Giroux, H. A. (2020). *On critical pedagogy* (2nd ed.). Bloomsbury Academic.

Grzanka, P. R., Flores, M. J., VanDaalen, R. A., & Velez, G. (2020). Intersectionality in psychology: Translational science for social justice [Editorial]. *Translational Issues in Psychological Science, 6*(4), 304–313. https://doi.org/10.1037/tps0000276

Harvard Graduate School of Education. (2024). *Career and lifelong learning*. Harvard Graduate School of Education Resources. Retrieved from https://www.gse.harvard.edu/

Helms, J. E. (1990). *Black and White racial identity: Theory, research, and practice*. Greenwood Press.

Johnson, D. J., Chuang, S. S., & Glozman, J. (Eds.). (2022). *Re/Formation and identity: The intersectionality of development, culture, and immigration*. Springer Nature.

Kibler, A., Valdés, G., & Walqui, A. (Eds.). (2020). *Reconceptualizing the role of critical dialogue in American classrooms: Promoting equity through dialogic education* (1st ed.). Routledge. https://doi.org/10.4324/9780429330667

Lee, D., Nam, S., Jeong, J., Na, G., & Lee, J. (2023). Developing and validating a process model of counselor burnout: A serial mediation model. *The Professional Counselor, 13*(3), 162–176. https://doi.org/10.15241/dl.13.3.162

Michael, K., Schujovitzky, D., & Karnieli-Miller, O. (2024). The associations between resilience, self-care, and burnout among school counselors. *PLoS ONE, 19*(9), e0309994. https://doi.org/10.1371/journal.pone.0309994

National Association of School Psychologists. (2021). *Evidence-based self-care practices to promote wellness and combat stress and burnout*. NASP Research and Policy Briefs. Retrieved from https://www.nasponline.org

Parham, T. A. (2020, August 27). Fundamental lessons for Black faculty and student success with Dr. Thomas A. Parham [Audio podcast episode]. In *Diverse: Issues In higher education*. https://www.diverseeducation.com/podcasts/podcast/15447480/fundamental-lessons-for-black-faculty-and-student-success-with-dr-thomas-a-parham

Paul, R. W. (1987). Dialogical thinking: Critical thought essential to the acquisition of rational knowledge and passions. In J. B. Baron & R. J. Sternberg (Eds.), *Teaching thinking skills: Theory and practice* (pp. 127–148). W. H. Freeman/Times Books/Henry Holt & Co.

Phinney, J. S. (1989). Stages of ethnic identity development in minority group adolescents. *The Journal of Early Adolescence, 9*(1–2), 34–49. https://doi.org/10.1177/0272431689091004

Robinson, Z. F. (2018). Intersectionality and gender theory. In B. Risman, C. Froyum, & W. Scarborough (Eds.), *Handbook of the sociology of gender. Handbooks of sociology and social research.* Springer. https://doi.org/10.1007/978-3-319-76333-0_5

The Self-Care Institute. (2024). The *intersections of burnout, self-care, and social justice* [Online course]. https://www.selfcareinstitute.com/courses/the-intersections-of-burnout-self-care-and-social-justice/

Sharmin, N., & Chow, A. K. (2020). Teaching philosophy statement: It is time to think outside the box. *McGill Journal of Education, 55*(1), 123–136. https://doi.org/10.26443/mje/rsem.v58i3.10283

Thwe, W. P., & Kálmán, A. (2024). Lifelong learning in the educational setting: A systematic literature review. *Asia-Pacific Journal of Education, 33,* 407–417. https://doi.org/10.1007/s40299-023-00738-w

Vedder, P., & van Geel, M. (2017). Cultural identity development as a developmental resource. In N. J. Cabrera & B. Leyendecker (Eds.), *Handbook on positive development of minority children and youth* (pp. 123–137). Springer Science + Business Media. https://doi.org/10.1007/978-3-319-43645-6_8

Velez, G., & Spencer, M. B. (2018). Phenomenology and intersectionality: Using PVEST as a frame for adolescent identity formation amid intersecting ecological systems of inequality. *New Directions for Child and Adolescent Development, 2018*(161), 75–90. https://doi.org/10.1002/cad.20247

Worrell, F. C., Vandiver, B. J., Cross Jr., W. E., Fhagen-Smith, P. E., Swim, J., & Caldwell, L. (2000). *Cross Racial Identity Scale (CRIS)* [Database record]. PsycTESTS. https://doi.org/10.1037/t01825-000

Wyatt, T. R., Johnson, M., & Zaidi, Z. (2022). Intersectionality: A means for centering power and oppression in research. *Advances in Health Science Education, 27,* 863–875. https://doi.org/10.1007/s10459-022-10110-0

PART II

ON BEING INFORMED, AWARE, AND READY TO APPLY CULTURALLY RESPONSIVE TEACHING IN COUNSELOR EDUCATION

CHAPTER 3

SHIFTING A CURRICULA PARADIGM: ADDRESSING A GROWING DIVERSITY IN COUNSELOR EDUCATION THROUGH THE FOUNDATIONS OF CULTURALLY RESPONSIVE TEACHING APPROACHES

Developing a philosophy of teaching in counselor education is a current issue steeped within the very roots of counselor education.

—Amy R. Broadwater, Cian L. Brown, & Meridith Moore

LEARNING OBJECTIVES After studying this chapter, you will be able to:

- Formulate conceptual frameworks derived from established culturally responsive pedagogical models to support the foundational elements of culturally responsive teaching (CRT) proposed for integration into counselor education curricula.
- Conduct a systematic review of CRT praxis to inform the development of metrics for evaluating the implementation of instruction, program design, and learning materials that are culturally responsive in counselor education programs.
- Incorporate multicultural competence into instructional practices that demonstrate proficiency as a culturally responsive counselor educator and supervisor.

SNAPSHOT: A counselor educator's career experience

Recent sociopolitical-cultural events have significantly impacted students and their educational experiences, as well as faculty in their teaching and relationship experiences with students and the learning materials. The COVID-19 pandemic exposed and exacerbated existing inequities, leading to a greater emphasis on mental health and academic support for students from diverse backgrounds. The Black Lives Matter movement and heightened awareness of systemic racism have compelled universities to prioritize diversity, equity, and inclusion in their curricula. Furthermore, cultural conflicts and political polarization have resulted in challenges in teaching about race, gender, and LGBTQ+ issues, with some universities, including counselor education programs, facing attempts to restrict access to inclusive materials. These sociopolitical-cultural factors have underscored the necessity for culturally responsive teaching (CRT) to create supportive and inclusive learning environments that address the complex realities faced by students in contemporary society.

Counselor education and supervision (CES) teaching during these times, predating the COVID-19 pandemic, included experiencing a novel form of apprehension in the classroom. This apprehension was a consequence of university shootings, mandatory participation in university-wide shooting drills, the permitting of White supremacist protests on campus, and students struggling to critically consider the events occurring in their environments and those relating to the learning materials across the counselor preparation curricula. It seemed as if students just started "chasing As," becoming more concrete in their knowledge acquisition and less conscious of the workforce they were planning to enter. A primary source of this apprehension was that during my doctoral studies, I was inadequately prepared for these circumstances, which became evident. While in my tenure-track faculty position and as program director, my particular department chair did not address any of the sociopolitical-cultural conflicts, incidents, and historic moments in faculty meetings. There was palpable tension in these meetings and in the classrooms between students, and frequently between faculty and students. I subsequently learned from colleagues at other universities that this apprehension was not unique but shared.

INTRODUCTION

In the past 8 years, scholarly literature on higher education has extensively examined the increasing diversity within academic institutions (Moses & Banh, 2018; Purdue Global, 2023; U.S. News & World Report, 2024). One significant contribution to this field is Bowman's (2010) article, "How Does Racial and Ethnic Diversity Affect the Classroom Environment?" In this article, Bowman explores the effects of racial and ethnic diversity on the classroom environment, finding that it leads to improved critical thinking and higher overall achievement levels for all students.

These findings align with contemporary research that highlights the positive impacts of diversity initiatives. For instance, recent studies indicate that promoting diversity benefits both historically marginalized communities and majoritized students—those placed in dominant positions by social or institutional structures—by enhancing intergroup relationships, increasing satisfaction with educational institutions, and fostering academic development (Dake et al., 2024).

Furthermore, studies emphasize the significance of establishing inclusive settings that encourage dialogue and cross-racial friendships. Such environments are crucial for promoting understanding and cooperation among diverse student populations. However, challenges persist, including addressing varied learning styles and ensuring fair representation across all sectors of higher education.

As academic institutions endeavor to cultivate inclusive environments, the growing diversity in higher education calls for flexible teaching approaches, especially in graduate programs. These programs are distinctive in catering to a varied group of students with diverse professional backgrounds and life experiences. Recognizing the crucial role of inclusivity in higher education, educators are now implementing innovative teaching methods and curricula that not only acknowledge but also capitalize on student diversity (Dake et al., 2024). This approach aims to create a more equitable and engaging learning experience, preparing graduate students for the intricacies of the global job market. Numerous counselor education and supervision (CES) individuals are demonstrating this objective by focusing more on pedagogical training that incorporates culturally responsive teaching (CRT) methods (Dorn-Medeiros et al., 2020; Hall et al., 2021; Irvine et al., 2021).

Counselor education programs are increasingly addressing diversity, both in the context of client populations and future counselors-in-training (CIT) who are in student cohorts matriculating across master's and doctoral programs. Current literature shares methods for educating and supporting students with diverse cultural backgrounds. Using qualitative grounded theory research, a study by Ju et al. (2020) in *The Professional Counselor* examined approaches for attracting, retaining, and assisting students from underrepresented racial minority groups in doctoral counselor education programs. The study involved 15 faculty members who discussed their experiences and successes in meeting diverse students' needs. The results highlight three main areas: characteristics of institutions and programs, recruitment tactics, and strategies for support and retention. Ju et al. (2020) stress the importance of awareness, understanding, proactive measures, and faculty engagement in fostering an inclusive and supportive environment for students from diverse backgrounds.

Expanding on Ju et al.'s (2020) findings, it is essential to continue enhancing and refining strategies to support underrepresented racial minority students in doctoral counselor education programs. Future studies should assess the long-term effects of these strategies on student retention and achievement. Moreover, investigating the impact of mentorship programs and CRT methods can provide valuable insights into creating an inclusive and supportive academic setting. By focusing on these areas, counselor education programs can better equip future professional counselors and CES individuals to effectively serve diverse populations.

Recent attention to increasing student and faculty diversity, and the need for this diversity to be reflected in counselor education materials (Chun et al., 2020), underscores that creating an inclusive and supportive environment extends beyond recruitment and retention (Thacker & Barrio Minton, 2021). It also involves implementing effective teaching strategies that resonate with diverse student groups. This realization prompts a crucial examination of CRT within counselor education programs. By integrating CRT, educators can develop curricula that acknowledge and value the cultural backgrounds of all students, thereby enriching their learning experiences and professional growth. This chapter delves into advanced principles of CRT in terms of its roots in pedagogy and its implementation in counselor education. Emphasis is situated on its influence on teaching in counselor education, academic achievement around the forms of knowledge acquisition, and the evaluating efficacy of training programs, which are necessary in determining how to prepare for teaching in today's sociopolitical-cultural era of the 21st century.

TEACHING IN COUNSELOR EDUCATION

In recent years, the significance of teaching in counselor education programs has increased substantially. This importance is evident in various domains, but three areas are frequently emphasized in counseling literature: multicultural competence, evidence-based teaching methods, and reflective practice and supervision. These three aspects correspond to the tripartite nature of CES—encompassing the roles of counselor, educator, and supervisor. Traditionally, these areas have been approached from a broad, introductory perspective in doctoral curricula, providing general knowledge rather than in-depth exploration of specific pedagogical approaches that consider skill development, purpose, and nuanced understanding necessary for teaching in the current sociocultural-political environment. Consequently, for those preparing to become CES faculty, it is crucial to thoroughly investigate, apply, and practice each of these areas.

Teaching within counselor education programs requires a nuanced approach to ensure that future counselors are well-prepared for the diverse and dynamic environments they will encounter. Effective teaching strategies in counselor education emphasize the development of both foundational knowledge and practical skills, fostering professional and personal growth.

Theoretical Foundations

Understanding the theoretical underpinnings of counseling remains crucial, but there is now a significant shift toward incorporating cultural diversity into the teaching of these foundations (Flynn & Castleberry, 2023). CES individuals are increasingly embedding cultural competence and awareness into the curriculum, ensuring that CIT are well-versed in various counseling theories while simultaneously developing a deep understanding of cultural diversity. This integrated approach covers psychodynamic, humanistic, cognitive-behavioral, and systemic approaches but now within a framework of culturally responsive pedagogy. This practice is encouraged yet not consistently implemented across the profession. It also frequently encounters resistance or opposition by students and CES individuals who are faculty.

By interweaving cultural diversity throughout the theoretical foundations, educators ensure that these foundational elements not only resonate with students from diverse backgrounds but also prepare future counselors to provide culturally sensitive and effective care to a wide range of clients. This approach recognizes that understanding cultural contexts is not a separate skill but an integral part of applying counseling theories effectively in practice.

Practical Application

Counselor education has traditionally focused on equipping future counselors with theoretical knowledge and practical skills necessary for effective client interactions. However, the profession is evolving to address the growing need for cultural competence and social justice advocacy. This is especially true during the clinical experiential courses such as practicum and internship.

While maintaining its core emphasis on counseling techniques and theories, the clinical experiences in counselor education programs are increasingly incorporating curricula that promote cultural awareness, sensitivity to diverse populations, and the ability to recognize and address systemic inequities. The shift reflects a broader understanding that effective counseling must consider the sociocultural contexts of clients and the impact of social structures on mental health and well-being. As a result, counselor education is now moving toward a more holistic approach that not only prepares counselors for individual client work but also empowers them to be agents of change in promoting cultural understanding and social justice within their communities and the broader society.

Push to Use Greater Culturally Responsive Instructional Approaches

Scholar counselor educators and educator pedagogists are increasingly addressing this topic in the literature, recognizing its significance in shaping the future of counselor education and practice (Mitulsky et al., 2014; Samuels, 2018). Corresponding themes in multidisciplinary literature on the topic imply that integration of CRT into higher education, including counselor education programs, is imperative for fostering inclusive and effective learning environments. The push is to develop flexible and ongoing curricula that honor and incorporate the diverse cultural backgrounds of all students and that captures events happening in society. By doing this, counselor educators can create a more engaging and enriching classroom experience that encourages critical thinking, being more conscious in reflections shared in classroom discussion and discourse, and possibly feeling more seen not just by faculty but across what they are learning. Counselor education is progressing toward enhancing student engagement and academic achievement to equip future counselors with the requisite skills to serve diverse client populations effectively and with cultural humility. In the instances where this is not happening (Gleason et al., 2024), the profession needs to formally address discrimination experiences to better support students (doctoral and master's level). Hence, there is a need for a framework that CES individuals may demonstrate and be evaluated upon, which originates in formal preparation for teaching and establishing professional relationships with students who will often become future colleagues.

Embracing CRT in counselor education would be to deem it a cornerstone of multicultural education, which seeks to ensure that the unique cultural perspectives of each student are recognized, respected, and integrated into the learning process. This pedagogical shift is crucial for preparing culturally competent counselors who can navigate the complexities of an increasingly diverse society that show up as presenting problems of our clients.

Continuous Teaching Development Among Faculty

Continuous teaching development is crucial for faculty teaching CIT it directly impacts the quality of education and preparation these future professionals receive. By engaging in ongoing learning, CES individuals stay abreast of cutting-edge research, emerging best practices, and evolving ethical standards in the counseling field. There is also encouragement to be aware of ongoing events happening in greater society that impact how all are having to navigate life in and outside of the classroom. As a commitment to professional growth, it enables CES faculty to provide more relevant, effective, and contemporary instruction, ultimately enhancing the competence of graduating counselors—licensed professional counselors who feel prepared to address presenting problems of clients that include dilemmas related to sociocultural and political dynamics, which we know impact mental health and overall well-being (American Psychological Association [APA], 2022).

Moreover, in an increasingly diverse society, continuous development allows CES individuals to refine their CRT methods, ensuring they can effectively prepare counselors to work with clients from various backgrounds that are similar and different from their own. Ongoing improvement in teaching practices not only benefits students but also contributes to the advancement of the counseling profession as a whole as better-trained counselors enter the workforce equipped to address complex societal needs.

The responsibilities of CES faculty have evolved, shifting toward more concrete and evaluative approaches to instruction. It is now imperative to dismantle outdated pedagogical methods that were not designed for contemporary societal needs. Instead, contemporary approaches, such as CRT, are encouraged to enhance teaching practices and effectively reach all students. As the nature of instruction in higher education continues to change, it is crucial to examine the pedagogical foundations of culturally responsive pedagogy, which offers concrete and evaluative methods to effectively engage diverse student populations. The following section provides a greater depth of CRT from a pedagogical lens, in terms of where it stems and practical implications.

PEDAGOGY THAT GROUNDS THE CULTURALLY RESPONSIVE TEACHING APPROACH

The pedagogies in here are what ground the CRT approach and can be considered frameworks that guide and allow for examination of historic and more contemporary evidence-based pedagogical models that support practical applications of CRT. They serve to provide a comprehensive set of components for a systematic CRT approach in the preparation of counselor education curricula.

Culturally Relevant Pedagogy

The conceptual foundation of culturally relevant pedagogy (CRP) emphasizes the importance of educators incorporating students' cultural heritage into their pedagogical approaches. It underscores the positive impact of culturally-aligned instruction on students' academic performance and cultural competence. According to Gloria Ladson-Billings (1995), CRP is defined as a pedagogical strategy that actively acknowledges and uses students' cultural backgrounds and identities as valuable assets in the educational context.

The CRP pedagogy aims to cultivate academic excellence, cultural proficiency, and critical consciousness among learners. Specifically, Ladson-Billings outlines three core components of CRP (Ladson-Billings, 1995):

- Student Learning: This element prioritizes academic excellence and cognitive development, aiming to support students in their scholastic achievements while nurturing their abilities to think critically and tackle complex problems.
- Cultural Competence: This element focuses on assisting students to cultivate a positive sense of self and gain a comprehensive understanding of their own cultural heritage as well as that of others. It aims to foster an environment where diversity is valued and respected.
- Critical Consciousness: This element aims to foster students' critical understanding of societal disparities and unfairness, motivating them to become catalysts for change within their local communities.

Geneva Gay's Culturally Responsive Teaching Model

Gay's framework offers a comprehensive approach to educating students from various backgrounds. It stresses the significance of incorporating students' cultural heritage into every aspect of their educational experience, with the intention of fostering their social, intellectual, political, and emotional growth. The model serves as a holistic strategy for supporting the learning needs of a diverse student body. Components of Gay's revised CRT model include the following (Gay, 2002, 2010):

- Knowledge Base of Diverse Cultures: Educators should develop a comprehensive grasp of the cultural attributes and accomplishments of various ethnic communities. This entails studying the cultural heritage, beliefs, and customs of their students to develop a more encompassing and pertinent educational program.
- Culturally Relevant Curriculum: Educators should create or implement educational programs that honor and embrace the diverse cultural heritage of students. This involves integrating culturally appropriate resources, illustrations, and viewpoints into the instructional material.
- Cultural Caring and Learning Community: Educators should foster an inclusive and encouraging classroom environment that makes students feel valued and respected. This involves building strong relationships with students and developing a classroom culture that encourages a feeling of community and inclusion.
- Intercultural Communication: Educators should implement communication techniques that acknowledge cultural diversity. This involves using culturally sensitive language, body language, and instructional approaches that connect with students from various cultural backgrounds.
- Cultural Congruity in Instruction: Educators should align educational approaches and classroom strategies with the cultural backgrounds of students.

This encompasses modifying instructional techniques to skillfully approach contemporary and historic sociocultural-political issues that impact what is being taught and where change is necessary.

With regard to Gay's (2010) revisions of her CRT model, she augmented the content to address the quality of life for students of color in institutions of higher education, emphasizing the significance of fostering supportive environments across all educational levels, inside and outside of the classroom. Furthermore, Gay included corroborating research on the validity of CRT as a model that extends beyond Black adult learners, asserting that CRT is applicable to all students and supports the learning needs of diverse racially minoritized cultural groups (Gay, 2010). Through the implementation of these components, educators can cultivate a more engaging and effective learning experience for all students, thereby promoting equity and social justice in education (Gay, 2010).

Culturally Sustaining Pedagogy

Django Paris and H. Samy Alim (2017) introduced the concept of culturally sustaining pedagogy (CSP) as an extension and critique of previous pedagogical models such as CRP. Their framework emphasizes the necessity of sustaining and fostering linguistic, literate, and cultural pluralism as an integral component of the democratic project of schooling. Paris and Alim underscore the significance of CSP in graduate programs as a means to prepare future educators for effective practice in diverse educational settings. They advocate for the integration of CSP into teacher education curricula to facilitate the development of educators' skills necessary for sustaining and nurturing the cultural and linguistic diversity of their students (Paris & Alim, 2017). This approach encompasses fostering critical reflection, establishing authentic relationships with students, and promoting social justice and equity within the classroom environment. CSP purports to do the following (Paris & Alim, 2017):

- Perpetuate and Foster Pluralism: Educators promote and maintain the diverse cultural, linguistic, and literate practices of students.
- Dynamic and Critical Approach: Educators address the evolving nature of youth identity and cultural practices, while maintaining a critical perspective on systemic inequalities.
- Counterhegemonic Potential: Educators acknowledge and support the capacity of youth culture to challenge and transform systemic inequalities.

Paris and Alim posit that CSP transcends mere relevance or responsiveness to students' cultures; it actively endeavors to sustain and nurture the cultural and linguistic diversity of students in a dynamic global context. Graduate programs that implement CSP aim to foster a more inclusive and equitable educational environment by equipping educators with the requisite knowledge and tools to support students from diverse cultural backgrounds. This approach serves to ensure that students' unique cultural identities are respected and valued, thereby promoting a more holistic and empowering learning experience (Paris & Alim, 2017).

Motivational Framework for Culturally Responsive Teaching

This framework is designed to enhance intrinsic motivation in both educators and learners by focusing on four key motivational conditions: establishing inclusion, developing attitudes, enhancing meaning, and engendering competence. Through the creation of a supportive and inclusive learning environment, fostering positive attitudes, making learning meaningful, and facilitating students' development of a sense of competence, educators can more effectively engage students from diverse cultural backgrounds. The framework emphasizes the significance of understanding students as unique individuals and valuing their cultural identities, which consequently promotes deeper learning and motivation. Descriptions of the four motivational conditions formulated by Ginsberg and Wlodkowski (2017) are as follows:

- Establishing Inclusion: This condition emphasizes the importance of creating a respectful and secure learning environment where students experience a sense of connection and value. Strategies include initiating with introductions, inviting students to disclose their preferred pronouns, and collaboratively developing course ground rules that reflect students' objectives, concerns, and expectations.
- Developing Attitudes: This involves facilitating students' development of a positive disposition toward learning and course content. Educators can provide options for participation, demonstrate the application of material to real-world contexts, and foster a growth mindset by encouraging students to perceive challenges as opportunities for development.
- Enhancing Meaning: This condition focuses on rendering learning engaging and relevant to students' values and perspectives. Strategies include using reflective assignments, broadening perspectives through activities such as role-play or debates, and establishing connections between course content and students' personal and cultural experiences.
- Engendering Competence: This involves facilitating students' effective demonstration of their skills and knowledge. Educators can provide opportunities for students to select assignment formats that align with their strengths, apply knowledge in real-world scenarios, and offer constructive feedback that promotes improvement.

The framework aims to create a welcoming and all-encompassing educational setting that promotes greater participation and enthusiasm among students with varied cultural identities by emphasizing these four conditions (Ginsberg & Wlodkowski, 2017). It strives to foster an environment conducive to learning for a diverse student population.

In review, the various pedagogical frameworks described here ground CRT and give it practical relevance for use in preparing for teaching counselor education. In summary, they include the following:

1. CRP by Ladson-Billings focuses on student learning, cultural competence, and critical consciousness.

2. Gay's CRT model, emphasizes diverse cultural knowledge, relevant curriculum, cultural caring, intercultural communication, and instructional congruity.
3. CSP by Paris and Alim aims to foster linguistic, literate, and cultural pluralism.
4. Motivational framework for CRT by Ginsberg and Wlodkowski focuses on inclusion, attitudes, meaning, and competence.

These pedagogical frameworks serve as historical premises that provide a comprehensive overview of how we might better understand the principles of CRT for use in and across counselor education curricula. Next, we go into teaching in counselor education programs with intentionality for this era of the 21st century.

PRINCIPLES OF CULTURALLY RESPONSIVE TEACHING

The principles presented here are specifically designed for adult education and aim to connect with the preparation of faculty for instructional and leadership roles in counselor education programs. It is essential to recognize adult learning as a distinct pedagogical theory within the broader educational framework and study of teaching (i.e., pedagogy). Implementing teaching methods that correspond to how adults process and internalize complex, unfamiliar content is vital. Additionally, these principles are shaped from the history of (a) educational reform toward a shift to multicultural education and (b) culturally responsive pedagogy. They are to encourage educators and learners to incorporate their personal experiences into the taught material, using worldviews as navigational tools (which may require occasional adjustments and conflict with what is being taught).

- Principle 1—Creating a Welcoming and Affirming Environment: This principle underscores the significance of establishing a classroom atmosphere wherein all students experience a sense of safety, respect, and value. It entails recognizing and affirming students' cultural identities and ensuring that their backgrounds are represented in the learning environment.
- Principle 2—High Expectations and Rigorous Instruction: CRT encompasses setting elevated academic standards and providing rigorous instruction that challenges students while considering their diverse learning needs. This principle encourages educators to cultivate a growth mindset and support students in undertaking academic risks.
- Principle 3—Inclusive Curriculum and Assessment: An inclusive curriculum incorporates diverse perspectives and materials that reflect the cultural backgrounds of all students. It also involves using assessment methods that are equitable and impartial, enabling students to demonstrate their knowledge and skills in culturally relevant ways.
- Principle 4—Ongoing Professional Learning: Educators must engage in continuous professional development to enhance their cultural competence and remain informed about best practices for teaching diverse student populations. This principle

emphasizes the importance of lifelong learning and reflective practice in becoming effective culturally responsive educators.

Understanding the principles of CRT is essential for counselor educators in preparing future counselors. Through the implementation of these principles, counselor educators can develop inclusive curricula that reflect diverse cultural perspectives and incorporate culturally relevant materials, thereby facilitating students' identification with the content they are studying. This reflection is tied to the concept of encouraging students to use their social and cultural capital in learning.

According to Samuels (2018), social capital in the context of culturally responsive pedagogy is defined as the value derived from social networks, relationships, and community connections that can provide support and resources for individuals. Cultural capital, on the other hand, refers to the knowledge, skills, and cultural competencies that individuals acquire, which have cultural value and can enhance their social standing and integration into society (Samuels, 2018).

These forms of capital are crucial for creating equitable and inclusive classrooms, as they help students connect their learning to their own cultural backgrounds and leverage their social networks for academic and personal growth. These forms of capital influence educational processes and outcomes in higher education settings. Research that supports attending to social and cultural capital reflects central elements regarding the purpose of counselor educators when selecting instructional materials that intersectional identities are limitedly represented in research, in terms of who is considered an expert and who makes the notable "who's who" lists in textbooks. This importance is grounded in what Samuels (2018) considers:

- Enhanced Engagement: Engaging students in education becomes more effective when leveraging their social and cultural resources. By linking learning to students' personal cultural contexts and life experiences, educators can create a more engaging and impactful educational environment.
- Building Confidence: Incorporating students' cultural backgrounds and personal identities into the educational content enhances their self-assurance and fosters a greater sense of inclusion within the learning environment.
- Promoting Inclusivity: Creating an environment that embraces various cultural viewpoints promotes inclusivity, ensuring every student feels appreciated and honored.
- Improving Academic Outcomes: Leveraging social and cultural capital can lead to better academic outcomes by providing students with the tools and resources they need to succeed.
- Encouraging Critical Thinking: Exposure to diverse cultural viewpoints encourages critical thinking and helps students develop a more comprehensive understanding of the world.

Furthermore, educators can cultivate a supportive learning environment that encourages students to share their own cultural experiences, thus promoting empathy and understanding among peers. This approach also encompasses the incorporation of reflective practices, enabling students to critically evaluate their own biases and assumptions.

By mastering these principles, future counselors are better equipped to establish rapport with clients from various cultural backgrounds, apply culturally sensitive interventions, and address the unique needs of diverse populations effectively, ultimately promoting equity and social justice within the counseling profession.

21ST CENTURY TEACHING

In the 21st century, the relevance of CRT approaches is magnified by the rapid changes in technology, societal norms, and global interconnectedness. The increasing diversity in student populations and the evolving nature of the counseling profession demand that educators remain adaptable and forward-thinking. By integrating multicultural competence, evidence-based teaching methods, and reflective practice into their pedagogy, CES individuals can better prepare students to meet the challenges that they and many of their clients will face. Embracing innovative teaching strategies and continuously enhancing their skills ensures that educators are not only imparting knowledge but also modeling the adaptability and critical thinking skills necessary for success in the 21st century.

Multicultural Competence in Teaching

Multicultural competence plays a pivotal role in shaping CRT approaches, which are a set of strategies designed to address the diverse needs of students in counselor education. As society becomes increasingly diverse, it is imperative for CES individuals to develop and refine their ability to understand, respect, and effectively address the unique needs of students from various cultural backgrounds. This competence extends beyond mere awareness of cultural differences; it encompasses the knowledge, skills, and attitudes necessary to create inclusive learning environments that foster the growth and development of all students.

The article "Multicultural and Social Justice Counseling Competencies" by Ratts et al. (2015) provides a comprehensive framework for using the Multicultural and Social Justice Counseling Competencies (MSJCC) as a praxis in teaching CIT. The MSJCC framework emphasizes four key developmental domains: counselor self-awareness, client worldview, counseling relationship, and counseling and advocacy interventions. By integrating these competencies into counselor education, programs can help trainees develop the necessary attitudes, knowledge, skills, and actions to effectively work with diverse clients and address issues of power, privilege, and oppression.

Integrating MSJCC across the counselor education curriculum is both feasible and beneficial. This can be achieved by embedding the MSJCC framework into various courses, assignments, and activities. For example, courses on counseling theories can include discussions on how different theories address or neglect issues of power, privilege, and oppression. Practicum and internship experiences can be designed to place students in diverse settings where they can apply these competencies in real-world counseling situations. Additionally, faculty can incorporate case studies, role-plays, and reflective journals that prompt students to critically analyze their own cultural identities and biases. By consistently integrating these competencies throughout the curriculum, counselor education programs can ensure that students develop the necessary skills to become culturally responsive and socially just practitioners.

For CES individuals, it is vital to cultivate multicultural competence, as this ensures that aspiring counselors can successfully interact with clients from various backgrounds. Ratts et al. (2016) emphasize that proficiencies in multicultural awareness and social justice are fundamental for maintaining ethical standards in the counseling profession.

In giving multicultural competency a practical sense, CES academics are formulating contemporary frameworks that allow for conceptual understanding to come to life through instruction. One such framework is the interaction for learning framework (ILF; Chun et al., 2020).

The ILF is a tool designed to explore bias and promote multicultural competence in counselor education programs. It provides a structured method for planning and implementing multicultural interactions in instructional settings. It includes six dimensions, such as planning interactions, creating environments for interaction, and assessing learning outcomes. By using the ILF, counselor education programs can better prepare future counselors to work effectively with diverse populations. The framework helps students develop cultural competence, self-awareness, and the ability to engage in meaningful interactions with clients from various cultural backgrounds. Chun et al. (2020) emphasize that integrating the ILF into counselor education can lead to more inclusive and effective counseling practices, ultimately benefiting both students and clients.

As counselor education programs continue to evolve, it is equally important to embrace evidence-based teaching practices to enhance educational outcomes and ensure that students receive the highest quality of instruction.

Evidence-Based Teaching Practices

The incorporation of research-supported teaching methods in counselor education curricula significantly enhances the overall quality of training and prepares students to effectively implement these approaches in their future careers. Minton et al. (2014) highlight the importance of integrating evidence-based strategies into counselor education programs to improve student learning outcomes. By embedding these methods into the curriculum, counselor educators can ensure that their students are well-equipped with the skills and knowledge necessary to succeed in diverse and dynamic professional environments.

Furthermore, Minton et al. (2018) provide an update on pedagogical practices in counselor education from 2011 to 2015. These CES scholars conducted a content analysis of 133 peer-reviewed articles published in journals of the American Counseling Association (ACA) and its divisions. The focus was on teaching and learning, teaching content, teaching techniques, and overall pedagogical practices. From this analysis, there were several key factors to highlight. The first was the focus areas of the analysis, whereby the analysis revealed clear trends toward publishing about specific content areas, with extensive attention given to social and cultural diversity. A second key highlight of this analysis centered upon pedagogical foundations, which offered that much of the CES literature focused on pedagogical foundations and methodologies used in counselor education programs, emphasizing the importance of integrating core knowledge and skills. And lastly, Minton et al. (2018) highlighted the impact of the 2016 CACREP Standards, which placed greater emphasis on workplace demands for entry-level counselors and doctoral-level counselor educators and supervisors.

In alignment with the purpose of this book, Barrio Minton and colleagues offer clinical implications that concern: (a) doctoral preparation, which should begin to increase emphasis on the need for rigorous training in pedagogy for doctoral students, ensuring they are well-prepared to teach future counselors; (b) cultural competence, emphasizing the need to focus more on social and cultural diversity in the literature because it underscores the importance of developing culturally competent counselors who can effectively work with diverse populations; and (c) instructional strategies, suggesting that counselor education programs should continue to innovate and adapt their instructional strategies to meet the evolving needs of the profession and the diverse student populations they serve (Barrio Minton et al., 2018).

It is noteworthy that the Council for Accreditation of Counseling and Related Educational Programs (CACREP) has revised its Standards, having now published the 2024 Standards. The 2024 CACREP Standards encompass several key revisions aimed at simplifying and clarifying accreditation requirements while promoting a unified counseling profession. According to CACREP (2023), here is a summary of main revisions:

- Simplification and Clarification: The accreditation standards have been modified to enhance clarity and reduce complexity, thus facilitating a more straightforward interpretation and implementation of the criteria by educational programs.
- Learning Environment Standards: New standards have been introduced pertaining to the institution, academic unit, and program faculty and staff.
- Doctoral Standards: The requirement for a practicum at the doctoral level has been removed to accommodate the diversity of individuals entering doctoral programs. However, programs can choose to retain the practicum requirement if desired.
- Professional Identity: Counselor educators are now required to possess a valid counseling license as part of a recently implemented regulation.
- Professional Practice: Emphasis is on supervised experiences in counseling and the assessment of doctoral students' counseling skills to ensure preparedness for doctoral internships.

According to CACREP, these revisions are designed to enhance the quality of counselor education programs and ensure that they are well-equipped to meet the evolving needs of the profession and the diverse student populations they serve (CACREP, 2023).

Reflective Practice and Supervision

Effective counselor education relies heavily on promoting self-reflection and offering comprehensive supervision. The supervisory process aids students in blending theoretical concepts with hands-on skills, thus enhancing their professional development. Bernard and Goodyear (2018) assert that supervision plays a vital role in shaping competent and ethical counseling professionals.

The significance of reflective practice and supervision is further explored in Miller's (2023) article titled "Supervision to Support Reflective Practices." Miller's research revealed three key findings:

1. The significance of an official leadership position and the perspective applied when examining evaluative and non-evaluative feedback
2. The implementation of reflective methods to initiate changes in teaching practices
3. The relationship between reflective practices and the school environment, professional growth, and student involvement

These discoveries are valuable because of their practical applicability in educational settings and their potential to guide policy changes in the United States education system, promoting more formative approaches aimed at enhancing instructional quality (Miller, 2023).

By emphasizing the importance of reflective practice and comprehensive supervision, counselor education programs can foster a culture of continuous learning and self-improvement. This approach not only benefits the students in their professional development but also enhances the quality of counseling services provided to diverse client populations.

Moreover, Miller highlights strategies such as structured reflection tools, regular supervision sessions, peer reflection, and the use of reflective models to help supervisees systematically examine their experiences and improve their teaching practices. A comprehensive description of these strategies that are adapted for counselor education is offered in Table 3.1.

TABLE 3.1 Miller's Five Evidence-Based Strategies for Teaching Reflective Practice and Supervision That Have Been Adapted for Counselor Educators

Strategy	Description
Structured reflection tools	These tools help supervisees systematically examine their experiences and identify areas for improvement. Examples include reflective journals, self-assessment questionnaires, and guided reflection prompts.
Regular supervision sessions	Consistent and scheduled supervision sessions provide a safe space for supervisees to discuss their experiences, challenges, and successes. These sessions encourage ongoing reflection and professional growth.
Peer reflection	Encouraging peer reflection allows supervisees to gain different perspectives and insights from their colleagues. This collaborative approach fosters a supportive learning environment and promotes shared learning.
Reflective models	Using established reflective models, such as Gibbs' reflective cycle or Schön's reflective practitioner, helps supervisees structure their reflections and deepen their understanding of their practice.
Feedback mechanisms	Implementing effective feedback mechanisms ensures that supervisees receive constructive and actionable feedback on their performance. This feedback is crucial for their development and helps them refine their counseling skills.

PRAXIS FOR COUNSELOR EDUCATION

In the context of graduate studies, praxis refers to the process of applying theoretical knowledge and research to practical action. It encompasses a continuous cycle of reflection and action, wherein students integrate academic learning with real-world practice. The APA also defines praxis, providing a definition that closely reflects the content of this book because of its meaning and reference to applying what is learned via "practice." They say that praxis refers to the process of applying a theory or concept in a practical, real-world context. It involves the enactment, embodiment, or realization of ideas through action (APA, n.d.). Moreso among social science educational settings, praxis often emphasizes the connection between theoretical knowledge and practical application, aiming to bridge the gap between what is learned and how it is practiced (APA, n.d.). This concept is particularly significant in fields such as psychology, education, social work, and counseling, where theoretical frameworks are to be effectively translated into practice to address complex societal issues from a human-centered approach. In applied graduate programs within social sciences, praxis typically encompasses the following:

- Fieldwork and Internships: These involve practical experiences in which students apply their academic knowledge in professional settings, thereby acquiring hands-on experience and developing professional competencies.
- Action Research: This refers to a form of inquiry wherein students conduct research aimed at addressing practical problems within their own professional contexts, often involving iterative cycles of planning, implementation, observation, and reflection.
- Reflective Practice: This involves encouraging students to engage in critical reflection on their experiences, challenges, and successes and to use these reflections to inform their subsequent actions and decision-making processes.
- Community Engagement: This refers to involving students in projects that address community needs and promote social justice, thus bridging the gap between academic learning and societal impact.

By emphasizing praxis, graduate programs aim to prepare students not only to comprehend theoretical concepts but also to effectively implement them in their professional and personal endeavors.

Praxis is highly pertinent to CRT because it bridges the gap between theoretical knowledge and practical application. In the context of CRT, praxis involves educators actively engaging in critical reflection on their pedagogical practices, evaluating their cultural biases, and implementing strategies that acknowledge and incorporate students' diverse cultural backgrounds into the learning environment. By engaging in praxis, CES individuals implement the following:

- Student Engagement in Critical Self-Reflection Regarding Cultural Biases: This facilitates an understanding of how personal perspectives may influence pedagogical approaches and student interactions.

- Structure and Prepare Culturally Responsive Pedagogical Methods: Educators can use specific techniques and methodologies that are inclusive and respectful of students' cultural identities.
- Ongoing Evaluation and Adjustment of Praxis: Continuous reflection and assessment enable educators to refine their approaches to better address the needs of their diverse student populations.
- Inclusive Learning Environments: Through the application of theoretical principles, educators can establish a classroom atmosphere that values and respects cultural diversity, thereby promoting equity and social justice.

Praxis essentially ensures that the principles of CRT are not merely theoretical concepts but are actively implemented and integrated into pedagogical practices, leading to more effective and equitable educational outcomes. When systematically applied, a praxis of CRT is most effective when its impact is quantified and evaluated.

Metrics for Measuring Outcomes of Culturally Responsive Teaching in Counselor Education Classrooms

The culturally responsive classroom assessment framework (Evans, 2023) serves as a guide for designing and evaluating classroom assessments that align with CRT principles. It builds on Stembridge's (2020) six themes of culturally responsive education—engagement, cultural identity, relationships, vulnerability, assets, and rigor—to establish a conceptual foundation for culturally responsive classroom assessments. The framework aims to assist educators in designing assessments that reflect and respect the diverse cultural backgrounds of their students, thereby promoting equity and inclusivity in the classroom.

Counselor education programs may also seek to evaluate the entire program if it was designed to be culturally responsive. To implement this, the Culturally Responsive Higher Education Curriculum Assessment Tool is suggested for use. Developed by Allan Hancock College in collaboration with the Metropolitan Center for Research on Equity and the Transformation of Schools, this tool assists faculty members in assessing the extent to which their curriculum is culturally responsive and sustaining (McNulty et al., 2002). It provides a framework for faculty to evaluate whether their curriculum reflects and respects the diverse cultural backgrounds of their students. The tool encourages educators to consider multiple cultural perspectives and integrate them into their teaching practices, with the objective of creating a more inclusive and equitable learning environment (McNulty et al., 2002). By using this metric, faculty can identify areas for improvement and implement necessary modifications to enhance the cultural responsiveness of their curriculum.

The implementation of the Culturally Responsive Higher Education Curriculum Assessment Tool presents a potentially efficacious approach to ensuring curricular inclusivity and equity. The following list provides a systematic guide for the use of this instrument:

- Initial Reflection: Educators commence by engaging in introspection regarding their own cultural biases and comprehending how these may influence their pedagogical practices. This process will facilitate approaching the assessment procedure with an objective and analytical mindset.

- Curriculum Review: Educators then undertake a comprehensive evaluation of the current curriculum, identifying areas where diverse cultural perspectives are incorporated and where they may be deficient. They should give careful consideration to the content, materials, and instructional methodologies used.
- Assessment Application: Educators use the assessment instrument to evaluate the cultural responsiveness of their curriculum. This instrument provides specific criteria and inquiries to guide the educator's evaluation. They should consider the following aspects of their curriculum:
    - representation of the cultural diversity of their student population
    - incorporation of multiple cultural perspectives and voices
    - use of culturally relevant materials and examples
    - promotion of cultural competence and critical consciousness
- Identify Strengths and Areas for Improvement: On the basis of the assessment, educators should identify the strengths of the curriculum and areas where enhancements can be implemented. This will facilitate the prioritization of modifications and focus on the most critical aspects initially.
- Action Plan Development: Educators will formulate an action plan to address the areas for improvement identified in the assessment. This plan should encompass specific steps, required resources, and an implementation timeline. Educators should consider professional development opportunities to enhance cultural competence and pedagogical practices.
- Implementation and Monitoring: Educators should execute the changes outlined in the action plan and monitor their impact on students' learning experiences. They should solicit feedback from students and colleagues to evaluate the effectiveness of the modifications and make necessary adjustments.
- Continuous Reflection and Adjustment: Educators should engage in ongoing reflection and refinement of the curriculum to ensure it remains culturally responsive and relevant. They must regularly revisit the assessment tool to evaluate progress and identify new areas for enhancement.

By adhering to these flexible guidelines, CES individuals can develop a more inclusive and equitable curriculum that acknowledges and respects the diverse cultural backgrounds of students, thereby fostering a more supportive and effective learning environment.

To ensure that various selected metrics are being used effectively and to achieve the desired outcomes, CRT models may provide exploratory frameworks to initiate this process. These approaches are particularly advantageous for CES faculty members who are striving to advance in their leadership within the program and in roles across counseling associations (e.g., ACA and Association for Counselor Educators and

Supervisors [ACES]) and even support faculty in the role of CACREP reaccreditation liaison.

CHALLENGES THAT SURFACE IN SHIFTING TO CULTURALLY RESPONSIVE TEACHING IN COUNSELOR EDUCATION

In transitioning to CRT within counselor education, several contextual challenges may arise. These challenges must be addressed to ensure the successful implementation of CRT practices, thereby creating a more inclusive and effective educational environment.

Resistance to Change

One significant challenge is resistance to change, both at the institutional and individual levels. Faculty members and administrators may be accustomed to traditional teaching methods and may resist adopting new approaches. Overcoming this resistance requires effective leadership, clear communication of the benefits of CRT, and ongoing professional development to support educators in making the transition.

Lack of Resources

Implementing CRT often requires additional resources, such as training materials, workshops, and ongoing support. Institutions may face budget constraints that limit the availability of these resources. Securing funding and prioritizing investment in CRT initiatives are essential steps in overcoming this barrier.

Varying Levels of Cultural Awareness

Faculty members and students may have differing levels of cultural awareness and competence. This disparity can lead to inconsistencies in the implementation of CRT. Providing comprehensive training and fostering an environment that encourages continuous learning and self-reflection can help bridge this gap.

Curriculum and Instructional Design

Redesigning curricula to incorporate culturally responsive elements can be a complex process. Educators must thoughtfully integrate multicultural perspectives into course content, learning activities, and assessments. Collaborating with experts in CRT and using existing frameworks, such as the ILF, can guide this process.

Evaluation and Assessment

Assessing the effectiveness of CRT practices can be challenging. Traditional evaluation methods may not fully capture the impact of these approaches on student learning and engagement. Developing new assessment tools and incorporating qualitative feedback from students can provide a more comprehensive understanding of the effectiveness of CRT.

Misconstruing Cultural Norms

Although CES faculty teach the aforementioned three areas (evaluation and assessment, curriculum and instructional design, and varying levels of cultural awareness), obstacles remain in implementing practices that foster greater transformative learning in counselor training programs. One notable challenge is the potential for misconstruing cultural norms and beliefs that are explored and differentiated in course textbooks (e.g., ones used in multicultural counseling courses), which may result in ineffective counseling approaches (Sue & Sue, 2016). Counselors might require more extensive training to effectively navigate these intricacies.

Language Barriers

Another hurdle is the presence of language barriers. Clear communication is essential in counseling, and linguistic differences can pose significant challenges. Counselors may find it difficult to grasp their clients' viewpoints and experiences when they don't share a common language, leading to complications in delivering appropriate care (Constantine & Sue, 2006; Summers & Nelson, 2020). Addressing this future difficulty begins with it being addressed in and across counselor education curricula. Hence, the question arises: How can CES develop teaching strategies that equip CIT to mitigate the potential of a linguistic diversity struggle?

ADVOCACY-FOCUSED TEACHING STRATEGIES TO COMBAT CULTURALLY RESPONSIVE TEACHING BARRIERS

For barriers to CRT to be avoided in counselor education, several advocacy-focused teaching strategies can be implemented:

1. Empowerment Workshops: Organize workshops that empower students to become advocates for culturally responsive practices in their future roles.
2. Policy Analysis Projects: Assign students to analyze and critique existing policies that impact diverse communities, encouraging them to propose culturally responsive alternatives.
3. Community Advocacy Initiatives: Engage students in real-world advocacy projects addressing cultural issues in local communities.
4. Cultural Immersion Experiences: Facilitate immersive experiences in diverse communities, followed by reflection and action planning sessions.
5. Guest Speaker Series: Invite diverse practitioners and community leaders to share their experiences and strategies for cultural advocacy.
6. Case Study Debates: Present complex cultural scenarios and have students debate and advocate for culturally responsive solutions.
7. Advocacy Skill-Building Workshops: Provide training on effective communication, lobbying, and grassroots organizing techniques for cultural advocacy.

8. Cross-Cultural Dialogue Forums: Create safe spaces for open discussions on cultural issues, encouraging students to practice advocacy skills.
9. Media Literacy Projects: Teach students to critically analyze media representations of diverse cultures and create advocacy campaigns to address misrepresentations.
10. Legislative Engagement: Guide students in contacting local representatives about culturally relevant issues in counseling and education.
11. Cultural Competence Self-Advocacy: Encourage students to develop personal action plans for ongoing cultural competence development and self-advocacy.
12. Intersectionality Awareness Campaigns: Task students with creating awareness campaigns that highlight the complexities of intersecting cultural identities.

CONCLUSION

This chapter examines several key concepts pertaining to culturally responsive and sustaining pedagogies. It explores Gloria Ladson-Billings' CRP, which emphasizes student learning, cultural competence, and critical consciousness to promote academic success and social awareness. Geneva Gay's CRT is also discussed, highlighting the integration of students' cultural backgrounds into teaching practices through a culturally relevant curriculum, intercultural communication, and cultural caring. The chapter then examines Django Paris and H. Samy Alim's CSP, which aims to sustain cultural and linguistic diversity in education by addressing systemic inequalities and embracing student/learner culture.

Additionally, the chapter covers various assessments designed to measure the cultural responsiveness of teaching practices, such as the Culturally Responsive Higher Education Curriculum Assessment Tool and the culturally responsive classroom assessment framework. Also included is a discussion on the concept of praxis in relation to the CRT approaches, which involves applying theoretical knowledge to practical action. By understanding and implementing these frameworks and theories, counselor educators can skillfully create more inclusive, equitable, and empowering educational experiences for CIT from diverse cultural backgrounds.

CHAPTER RESOURCES

Culturally Responsive Counselor Educator Skills

CRCE Skills to Further Develop From This Chapter

Skill	Implementation
Inclusive Curriculum	The educational program incorporates materials that showcase a range of cultural viewpoints and backgrounds. This approach involves incorporating diverse readings, examples, and case studies that represent various cultural contexts, ensuring students can see their own communities and identities reflected in their learning materials.

(continued)

CRCE Skills to Further Develop From This Chapter *(continued)*	
Development of Cultural Competence Training	CES faculty are advised to go beyond merely teaching cultural competence to actively training students in integrating it into their counseling skill set. This approach involves offering prompt feedback, guidance, and opportunities for hands-on learning experiences. Such methods support students in developing the ability to address issues faced by clients from various cultural backgrounds, while also honing their skills in cross-cultural communication and intervention strategies. This may be in the form of a workshop styled class as opposed to lecture or teaching from a PPT for class or delivery of learning materials.
Reflective Practice	Educators promote self-reflection among students, urging them to analyze their own cultural backgrounds, prejudices, and preconceptions. This introspection enables students to recognize how their personal histories shape their interactions with clients, ultimately improving their capacity to deliver culturally appropriate counseling services.
Experiential Learning	Curricula feature hands-on learning experiences, including diverse field placements, community service initiatives, and immersive activities. These practical opportunities enable students to implement their theoretical knowledge and enhance their real-world skills in authentic environments.
Supportive Learning Environment	Establishing an environment that supports and embraces all learners is essential. Teachers cultivate a climate of mutual respect and acceptance, encouraging students to express their viewpoints freely and feel appreciated. This approach involves adopting diverse instructional strategies that cater to various learning preferences and cultural backgrounds.
Mentoring and Support	Initiatives offer guidance and assistance to students from diverse backgrounds that are typically underrepresented. These programs facilitate connections between students and academic or industry mentors who can provide advice, encouragement, and professional contacts, aiding students in successfully navigating their academic and career paths.

CES, counselor education and supervision; CRCE, culturally responsive counselor educator; PPT, PowerPoint.

CONTENT SUMMARY

Scholars in Culturally Responsive Pedagogy

- Gloria Ladson-Billings' CRP: This framework emphasizes three core components: student learning, cultural competence, and critical consciousness. It promotes academic success, positive cultural identity, and social awareness among students.
- Geneva Gay's CRT: This model highlights the importance of integrating students' cultural backgrounds into teaching practices. It includes components like a knowledge base of diverse cultures, culturally relevant curriculum, cultural caring, intercultural communication, and cultural congruity in instruction.
- Django Paris and H. Samy Alim's CSP: This pedagogy aims to sustain and foster cultural and linguistic diversity in education. It emphasizes the dynamic nature of culture and identity, and the potential of youth culture to challenge systemic inequalities.

Assessment and Praxis

- Assessments for Measuring Cultural Responsiveness: We discussed several tools, including the Culturally Responsive Higher Education Curriculum Assessment Tool, culturally responsive classroom assessment framework, and Culturally Responsive Education and Assessments Inventory, which help educators evaluate and improve the cultural responsiveness of their teaching practices.
- Praxis in Graduate Studies: We explored the concept of praxis, which involves applying theoretical knowledge to practical action, and its relevance to CRT. Praxis helps educators reflect on their practices, implement culturally responsive strategies, and create inclusive learning environments.

Advanced Reflection Questions

1. How can one develop a graduate-level curriculum that effectively incorporates CRT practices while simultaneously challenging students to critically engage with and expand upon these concepts in their scholarly work?
2. In what manner can one facilitate substantive collaboration and discourse among graduate students, ensuring that diverse cultural perspectives are not only recognized but also valued and used to enhance the academic environment?
3. Critically examine one's own positionality and cultural biases as an educator. How might these factors influence one's approach to teaching graduate students, and what strategies can be used to mitigate potential biases?
4. How can one design and implement assessment methods that accurately evaluate the cultural responsiveness of graduate students' academic work and their ability to apply these principles in professional practice?
5. What continuous professional development opportunities can one pursue to enhance understanding of CRT at the graduate level, and how can one encourage students to engage in similar reflective and growth-oriented practices?

Further Reading

Budhai, S. S., & Lewis Grant, K. S. (2022). *Culturally responsive teaching online and in person: An action planner for dynamic equitable learning environments*. Corwin.

Davis, J. M., & Arroyo, P. (2023). Teaching multicultural competence in counselor education: A review of the literature. *Journal of Counselor Education and Supervision, 62*(3), 215–230.

Gonzalez, M., & Smith, L. (2022). Integrating social justice into counselor education: A pedagogical approach. *Journal of Counselor Education and Supervision, 61*(4), 301–318. https://doi.org/10.1002/ceas.12145

Johnson, S., & Brown, E. (2023). Counselor educators' perspectives on teaching cultural humility: A qualitative study. *Journal of Counselor Education and Supervision, 62*(2), 145–160.

Lee, D., & Chen, A. (2021). Culturally responsive supervision: A framework for training counselors. *Journal of Counselor Education and Supervision, 60*(2), 145–162.

Summers, L. M., & Nelson, L. (2020). *Multicultural counseling: Responding with cultural humility, empathy, and advocacy*. Springer Publishing Company.

REFERENCES

American Psychological Association. (2022). *Stress in America 2022: Concerned for the future, beset by inflation*. https://www.apa.org/news/press/releases/stress/2022/concerned-future-inflation

American Psychological Association. (n.d.). Praxis. *APA dictionary of psychology*. Retrieved September 16, 2024, from https://dictionary.apa.org/praxis

Bernard, J. M., & Goodyear, R. K. (2018). *Fundamentals of clinical supervision* (6th ed.). Pearson.

Bowman, N. A. (2010). How does racial and ethnic diversity affect the classroom environment? *Journal of Higher Education, 81*(3), 316–343.

Chun, J., Connor, A., Alsaman, M., Urkmez, B., & Kosciulek, J. F. (2020). Capitalizing on diversity in counselor education: An application of the interaction for learning framework. *Journal of Multicultural Counseling and Development, 48*(3), 161–175. https://doi.org/10.1002/jmcd.12175

Constantine, M. G., & Sue, D. W. (2006). Factors contributing to optimal multicultural counseling and therapy. *Journal of Counseling Psychology, 53*(1), 127–136. https://doi.org/10.1177/0011000005281318

Council for Accreditation of Counseling and Related Educational Programs. (2023). *CACREP 2024 standards*. Retrieved from https://www.cacrep.org/section-2-cacrep-standards-2024

Dake, D. A., Bukari, M., Opoku-Asare, N. A., Kquofi, S., & Brewu, J. K. (2024). Diversity in higher education: A review of the literature. *International Journal of Academic Multidisciplinary Research, 8*(11), 164–174. Retrieved from http://ijeais.org/wp-content/uploads/2024/11/abs/IJAMR241123.html

Dorn-Medeiros, C. M., Christensen, J. K., Lértora, I. M., & Croffie, A. L. (2020). Relational strategies for teaching multicultural courses in counselor education. *Journal of Multicultural Counseling and Development, 48*(3), 149–160. https://doi.org/10.1002/jmcd.12174

Evans, C. M. (2023). Applying a culturally responsive pedagogical framework to design and evaluate classroom performance-based assessments in Hawai'i. *Applied Measurement in Education, 36*(3), 269–285. https://doi.org/10.1080/08957347.2023.2214655

Flynn, S. V., & Castleberry, J. J. (Eds.). (2023). *Counseling theories and case conceptualization: A practice-based approach*. Springer Publishing.

Gay, G. (2002). *Culturally responsive teaching: Theory, research, and practice*. Teachers College Press.

Gay, G. (2010). *Culturally responsive teaching: Theory, research, and practice* (2nd ed.). Teachers College Press.

Ginsberg, M. B., & Wlodkowski, R. J. (2017). Motivational framework for culturally responsive teaching. In J. N. Rhodes (Ed.), *Inclusive teaching: Strategies for promoting equity in the college classroom* (pp. 29–46). Jossey-Bass.

Gleason, B. K., Clark, M., Salpietro, L., & Jacoby, R. (2024). Wellness and discrimination in counselor education. *Teaching and Supervision in Counseling, 6*(3), 6–18. https://doi.org/10.7290/tsc06omhy

Hall, K. G., Barden, S., & Conley, A. (2021). A relational-cultural framework: Emphasizing relational dynamics and multicultural skill development. *The Professional Counselor, 4*(1), 1–12. https://doi.org/10.15241/kgh.4.1.71

Irvine, T., Labarta, A., & Emelianchik-Key, K. (2021). Using a relational-cultural and Adlerian framework to enhance multicultural pedagogy. *The Professional Counselor, 11*(2), 233–247. https://doi.org/10.15241/ti.11.2.233

Ju, S., Martinez, R., & Smith, D. (2020). Attracting, retaining, and supporting underrepresented racial minority students in doctoral counselor education programs: A grounded theory study. *The Professional Counselor, 10*(4), 445–457.

Ladson-Billings, G. (1995). *Toward a theory of culturally relevant pedagogy.* American Educational Research Journal, 32(3), 465–491.

McNulty, L., Rantz, R., & Guttman, B. (2002). *Culturally responsive curriculum scorecard.* Metropolitan Center for Research on Equity and the Transformation of Schools, New York University.

Miller, L. S. (2023). Supervision to support reflective practices. *Journal of Educational Supervision, 6*(1), 1–18. https://doi.org/10.31045/jes.6.1.1

Minton, C. A. B., Morris, C. A. W., & Bruner, S. L. (2018). Pedagogy in counselor education: 2011–2015 update. *Counselor Education and Supervision, 57*(3), 227–236. https://doi.org/10.1002/ceas.12112

Minton, C. A. B., Morris, C. A. W., & Yaites, L. D. (2014). Pedagogy in counselor education: A 10-year content analysis of journals. *Counselor Education and Supervision, 53*(3), 162–177. https://doi.org/10.1002/j.1556-6978.2014.00055.x

Mitulsky, L., Gilbert, M., & Bogo, M. (2014). Professional identity and social work: An exploratory study of the experience of students in a social work program. *Social Work Education, 33*(3), 343–356.

Moses, Y. T., & Banh, J. (2018). Diversity literature review in higher education; the next research agenda. *eScholarship*. Retrieved from https://escholarship.org/content/qt1s4679q5/qt1s4679q5_noSplash_ab571975de7fd93a7cf9451ad6bc8771.pdf?t=nsmzp8

Paris, D., & Alim, H. S. (Eds.). (2017). *Culturally sustaining pedagogies: Teaching and learning for justice in a changing world.* Teachers College Press.

Purdue University Global. (2023, March 29). *Why diversity in colleges & universities matters.* https://www.purdueglobal.edu/blog/student-life/why-diversity-in-colleges-universities-matters/#:~:text=When%20you%20interact%20with%20people,become%20more%20innovative%20through%20collaboration

Ratts, M. J., Singh, A. A., Nassar-McMillan, S., Butler, S. K., & McCullough, J. R. (2015). *Multicultural and social justice counseling competencies.* American Counseling Association.

Ratts, M. J., Singh, A. A., Nassar-McMillan, S., Butler, S. K., & McCullough, J. R. (2016, January). Multicultural and social justice counseling competencies: Practical applications in counseling. *Counseling Today*. https://www.counseling.org/publications/counseling-today-magazine/article-archive/article/legacy/multicultural-and-social-justice-counseling-competencies-practical-applications-in-counseling

REL Appalachia at SRI International. (n.d.). *Instruments for measuring the cultural responsiveness of students' educational experiences*. Institute of Education Sciences. https://ies.ed.gov/ncee/edlabs/regions/appalachia/resources/pdfs/handout1_instruments-measuring-responsiveness_acc.pdf

Samuels, A. J. (2018). *Exploring culturally responsive pedagogy: Teachers' perspectives on fostering equitable and inclusive classrooms*. SRATE Journal, 27(1), 22-30.

Samuels, A. J. (2018). Exploring culturally responsive pedagogy: Teachers' perspectives on fostering equitable and inclusive classrooms. *SRATE Journal, 27*(1), 22–30. https://files.eric.ed.gov/fulltext/EJ1166706.pdf

Stembridge, A. (2020). *Culturally responsive education in the classroom: An equity framework for pedagogy*. Routledge.

Sue, D. W., & Sue, D. (2016). *Counseling the culturally diverse: Theory and practice* (7th ed.). Wiley.

Summers, L. M., & Nelson, L. (Eds.). (2020). *Multicultural counseling: Responding with cultural humility, empathy, and advocacy*. Kendall Hunt Publishing.

Thacker, N., & Barrio Minton, C. A. (2021). Minoritized professionals' experiences in counselor education: A review of research. *Counselor Education & Supervision, 60*(3), 35–50. https://doi.org/10.1002/ceas.12195

U..S. News & World Report. (2024). *Best colleges 2024: National university rankings*. https://www.usnews.com/best-colleges/rankings/national-universities

CHAPTER 4

CULTURALLY RESPONSIVE COUNSELOR EDUCATION: TOOLS FOR TEACHING

Culturally responsive teaching is a student-centered approach that invites students to bring their expertise to the table by identifying and harnessing the assets of students who have historically been underserved in schools.

—Flemming

LEARNING OBJECTIVES After studying this chapter, you will be able to:

- Critically analyze and evaluate the sociocultural complexities that influence teaching practices and learning outcomes in counselor education. This evaluation explores how these complexities influence the effectiveness of culturally responsive teaching (CRT) and identifies strategies to address them in diverse educational contexts.
- Develop and execute teaching methods that are sensitive to cultural differences, taking into account the unspoken norms, sociocultural advantages, and respectful cultural understanding. You will gain resources to develop comprehensive teaching plans and educational activities that align with multicultural education best practices and successfully engage students from various cultural backgrounds.
- Encourage students to examine their own cultural awareness and biases through self-reflection. This involves demonstrating the ability to integrate compassion, support, and introspective practices into their instructional and supervisory approaches. Furthermore, students will create teaching methods focused on advocacy to tackle systemic racial challenges and enhance social equity within counselor training programs.

SNAPSHOT: A counselor educator's career experience

In the process of preparing for an evening of instruction, it is customary to plan a lecture, incorporate several discussion questions, and design an activity intended to facilitate transformative learning among students. However, there have been instances (over the past 12 years) when discourse regarding campus activities takes precedence over planned curricula because of protests by external groups occurring on campus earlier in the day. Consequently, one may modify the class structure to commence with an assessment of students' well-being and potential impact from the off-campus protesters who were legally permitted to demonstrate against Black and LGBTQIA+ groups, while being protected by state police in the exercise of their First Amendment rights. When there is minimal response to this established safe space, one may begin to contemplate the unspoken thoughts and unexpressed sentiments. What course of action should be taken? What emotional response is appropriate? Are there pedagogical tools that could have been used to elicit more open dialogue in this scenario or in similar circumstances?

INTRODUCTION

The introductory quotation of Chapter 4 encapsulates the fundamental principle of culturally responsive teaching (CRT) as a student-centered approach. According to Flemming (2019), it is imperative to use instructional methodologies that demonstrate the action-oriented nature of CRT, thereby substantiating its historical significance within the American educational system. In this chapter, the conceptual tools and frameworks essential for fostering CRT in counselor education are examined. Exploration of how these tools can help educators address the diverse needs of their students is offered as a way to create a more inclusive and equitable learning environment.

The conceptual tools covered in this chapter have been introduced in Chapter 3. However, in this chapter they are explored via descriptions and guides that counselor education and supervision (CES) faculty are encouraged to apply within CRT approaches. They are

- awareness of sociocultural complexities
- hidden curriculum
- social and cultural capital
- cultural humility
- empathy and advocacy
- reflective practice
- multicultural counseling and teaching competence
- pedagogical strategies
- advocacy-focused teaching strategies
- language barriers
- technology in counselor education

AWARENESS OF SOCIOCULTURAL COMPLEXITIES

For CES educators committed to cultural responsiveness, it is essential to grasp the intricate social and cultural factors that shape teaching methods. Okech and Rubel (2018) assert that by acknowledging these influences, instructors can foster an inclusive learning environment that honors and appreciates the diverse cultural backgrounds of their students. The following are some ways an educator can develop the use of this conceptual tool:

1. *Contextual Analysis*

   To begin, CES educators can perform a comprehensive assessment of their classroom setting and the wider educational landscape. This assessment should encompass an examination of student demographics, cultural heritage, and economic backgrounds. Through this process, educators can pinpoint potential obstacles to effective learning and formulate approaches to overcome them.

2. *Inclusive Curriculum Design*

   Creating a curriculum that embraces and represents the varied cultural backgrounds and viewpoints of students is essential. This can be accomplished by integrating diverse content, featuring authors from different backgrounds, and using a wide range of educational resources that showcase various cultures and perspectives. Teachers should also strive to develop a curriculum that is adaptable and can be tailored to accommodate the diverse needs of their student body.

3. *Professional Development*

   For CES educators, ongoing professional growth is crucial to remain up-to-date with societal complexities and innovative teaching methods. Attending educational events such as workshops, seminars, and courses focused on cultural awareness, equity in education, and inclusive teaching practices can enhance educators' knowledge and abilities. Additionally, engaging with peers and specialists in the educational field can offer valuable perspectives and assistance.

4. *Reflective Practice*

   The implementation of reflective practices can significantly enhance the pedagogical approaches of CES educators. This process involves a critical examination of one's own beliefs, biases, and instructional methods. By engaging in systematic reflection on classroom experiences and interactions with students, educators can pinpoint areas that require improvement and develop teaching strategies that are more culturally responsive. Various mechanisms can facilitate this reflective process, such as keeping a reflective journal, seeking input from peers, and participating in supervisory discussions.

5. *Classroom Environment*

   Establishing a classroom environment that is inclusive and welcoming is essential. Educators can accomplish this objective by exhibiting cultural artifacts, commemorating diverse cultural events, and cultivating a sense of community among students. Facilitating open dialogue and respecting diverse perspectives contributes to the creation of a secure environment where students feel valued and supported.

6. *Student Engagement*

   Active student engagement is essential for comprehending and addressing sociocultural complexities. Educators should use interactive pedagogical approaches, such as group discussions, role-playing exercises, and project-based learning methodologies, to facilitate student involvement in the learning process. Encouraging students to share their cultural experiences and perspectives can enhance the classroom environment and foster mutual understanding.

7. *Culturally Responsive Assessment*

   Assessment practices should be culturally responsive and equitable. Educators can use a diverse range of assessment methodologies, including portfolios, presentations, and self-assessments, to evaluate students' varied abilities and strengths. It is imperative to avoid biased assessment instruments that may disadvantage specific student populations.

Through the implementation of these strategies, educators can cultivate a more comprehensive understanding of sociocultural complexities and establish a more inclusive and efficacious learning environment. This approach not only enhances the educational experience for students but also prepares them to become culturally competent counselors capable of effectively serving diverse populations.

HIDDEN CURRICULUM

The hidden curriculum refers to the implicit messages and values transmitted through the educational environment and practices, beyond the formal curriculum. The concept of the hidden curriculum within the context of critical pedagogy refers to the implicit lessons that students learn through the culture, organization, and practices of their educational environment, which are not explicitly included in the formal curriculum (Darder et al., 2017). These lessons often reinforce societal norms, values, and power structures, and can perpetuate inequalities. Critical pedagogy has a continuing aim to uncover and challenge these hidden curricula to promote social justice and empower students to become critical thinkers and agents of change (Florence, 1998). The following are some ways an educator can develop the use of this conceptual tool:

1. *Identifying Hidden Curriculum Elements*

   CES educators are suggested to demonstrate knowledge and awareness of this concept by identifying the elements of the hidden curriculum present in their classroom and institution. This encompasses recognizing implicit biases, power dynamics, and social norms that are conveyed through interactions, classroom policies, and institutional practices. Reflective practice and student feedback can facilitate educators' awareness of these latent elements.

2. *Promoting Inclusivity*

   To mitigate the potential adverse effects of the hidden curriculum, educators should actively promote inclusivity within their classroom environment. This entails creating an atmosphere wherein all students feel valued and respected. The implementation of inclusive pedagogical practices, such as using diverse materials, encouraging multiple perspectives, and fostering a culture of respect, serves to ameliorate the impact of the hidden curriculum.

3. *Critical Discussions*

   Facilitating critical discussions regarding the hidden curriculum with students can enhance awareness and promote analytical thinking. Educators may use case studies, empirical examples, and reflective inquiries to engage students in discourse about implicit messages and social norms. This approach facilitates students' development of a more comprehensive understanding of the hidden curriculum and its influence on their educational experiences.

4. *Modeling Inclusive Behavior*

   CES educators play a pivotal role in exemplifying inclusive behavior and attitudes. Demonstrating respect for diversity, using inclusive language, and addressing biases and stereotypes in real time constitute effective methods to positively influence the hidden curriculum. Through the modeling of these behaviors, educators establish the foundation for an inclusive and equitable learning environment.

5. *Reflective Practice*

   The practice of reflection enables educators to critically examine their own assumptions, biases, and pedagogical approaches. Consistent reflective practices facilitate the identification and address of implicit curricula within the classroom environment. Methodologies such as journaling, peer evaluation, and supervisory feedback serve as efficacious tools for cultivating reflective practice and fostering continuous professional development.

6. *Student Feedback*

   The acquisition and integration of student feedback is imperative for comprehending the implications of the hidden curriculum. Educational practitioners can use surveys, focus groups, and structured discussions to gather insights from students regarding their learning experiences and perceptions. This feedback facilitates educators in identifying areas for improvement and developing strategies to cultivate a more inclusive learning environment.

7. *Institutional Policies and Practices*

   Educators should advocate for institutional policies and practices that promote inclusivity and equity. This necessitates collaboration with colleagues and administrators to address systemic issues and foster a culture that values diversity. By influencing institutional change, educators can contribute to the creation of a more supportive environment that mitigates the negative effects of the hidden curriculum.

By addressing the hidden curriculum, CES educators can establish a more inclusive and equitable learning environment that accommodates the diverse needs of all students.

This approach not only enhances the educational experience but also prepares students to become culturally competent counselors who can effectively serve diverse populations. Via the application, CES educators encourage counselors-in-training to use what they know about themselves and any aspect of their cultural identity. This can be informed with a deeper understanding of social and cultural capital, as described in the text that follows.

SOCIAL AND CULTURAL CAPITAL

Social and cultural capital are fundamental concepts in elucidating students' educational experiences and outcomes. Bourdieu (1986) emphasizes the significance of social networks and cultural competencies in enhancing students' learning experiences and facilitating equitable opportunities for academic success. Moreover, social and cultural capital are essential concepts in understanding educational inequalities and student outcomes.

Social capital refers to the networks, relationships, and social interactions that provide individuals with support, access to resources, and opportunities. This encompasses familial connections, peer relationships, and community affiliations that facilitate academic and professional achievement. Cultural capital, conversely, comprises the knowledge, skills, education, and cultural competencies that individuals possess, which can influence their ability to navigate and succeed within various social and institutional contexts. This includes familiarity with the dominant culture's norms, values, and practices, which can confer advantages in educational settings.

Collectively, social and cultural capital underscore the importance of both social relationships and cultural knowledge in shaping educational experiences and outcomes, thereby emphasizing the necessity for educators to recognize and leverage these assets to create more equitable learning environments.

The following are some ways an educator can develop the use of this conceptual tool:

1. *Recognizing Students' Assets*

   It is imperative for educators to initially recognize and appreciate the social and cultural capital that students bring to the academic setting. This approach necessitates a comprehensive understanding of students' diverse backgrounds, life experiences, and the unique competencies they contribute to the learning environment. By acknowledging these inherent assets, educators can foster a more inclusive and empowering educational atmosphere.

2. *Incorporating Diverse Perspectives*

   The integration of diverse cultural perspectives into the curriculum enhances students' learning experiences and promotes cultural competence. Educators can incorporate readings, case studies, and examples that reflect the diversity of students' backgrounds. This approach facilitates students' identification with the course content and fosters a deeper connection to the material.

3. *Building Relationships*

   Establishing robust relationships with students is essential for comprehending and using their social and cultural capital. Educators should allocate time to familiarize themselves with their students, cultivate trust, and foster an open and supportive classroom environment. This objective can be achieved through regular assessments, individual consultations, and the creation of opportunities for students to articulate their experiences and perspectives.

4. *Collaborative Learning*

   Collaborative learning activities, such as group projects and peer teaching, enable students to share their knowledge and skills with one another. This approach uses the social and cultural capital of the entire class and fosters a sense of community. Furthermore, collaborative learning facilitates the development of teamwork and communication skills among students.

5. *Community Engagement*

   Facilitating student engagement with their communities has the potential to enhance their social and cultural capital. Educational practitioners can incorporate community-based projects, service learning initiatives, and collaborations with local organizations into the curriculum. These experiential learning opportunities provide students with practical applications of their academic knowledge and foster stronger connections to their communities.

6. *Mentorship Programs*

   Mentorship programs can provide students with supplementary support and resources to facilitate their academic progress. Pairing students with mentors who share similar cultural backgrounds or experiences can assist them in navigating challenges and developing their social and cultural capital. Educators can facilitate these connections and provide guidance throughout the mentorship process.

7. *Reflective Practice*

   CES educators are encouraged to engage in reflective practice to examine their own cultural competence and potential biases. Reflecting on their pedagogical approaches and interactions with students assists educators in identifying methods to more effectively leverage students' social and cultural capital. Journaling, peer feedback, and professional development opportunities serve as efficacious tools for fostering reflective practice.

8. *Inclusive Assessment*

   Assessment practices should recognize and value the diverse abilities and strengths of students. Educators can use a range of assessment methodologies, including portfolios, presentations, and self-assessments to capture students' achievements. This approach ensures that assessments are equitable and inclusive and that they acknowledge the social and cultural capital that students bring to their educational experience. Table 4.1 includes examples of inclusive assessment strategies that harness the ideas relating to demonstrating knowledge of how to highlight social and cultural capital in CRT in counselor education:

TABLE 4.1 Examples of Inclusive Assessment Strategies for Use Across Counselor Preparation Curricula That Are Described as Culturally Responsive

Diverse assessment methods	Use a variety of assessment methods, such as written exams, oral presentations, role-plays, and portfolios, to accommodate different learning styles and strengths.
Rubrics with clear criteria	Develop rubrics with clear, specific criteria that outline expectations for each assessment task. Such rubrics ensure consistency and transparency in grading.
Formative assessments	Incorporate formative assessments, such as quizzes, reflections, and feedback sessions, to provide ongoing opportunities for students to improve and demonstrate their understanding.
UDL	Apply UDL principles to create flexible assessments that can be accessed and understood by all students, regardless of their abilities or backgrounds.
Self-assessment and peer assessment	Encourage self-assessment and peer assessment to promote reflection and critical thinking. These assessments also help students develop a deeper understanding of the material and their own learning processes.
Culturally relevant assessments	Design assessments that are culturally relevant and sensitive to the diverse backgrounds of students. These assessments can include incorporating culturally relevant content and examples in assessment tasks.
Accommodations for disabilities	Provide appropriate accommodations for students with disabilities, such as extended time, alternative formats, or assistive technology, to ensure they can fully demonstrate their knowledge and skills.
Feedback and reflection	Offer constructive feedback and opportunities for reflection after assessments. This helps students understand their strengths and areas for improvement, fostering continuous learning and growth.

UDL, Universal Design for Learning.

Through the implementation of these strategies, educators can effectively use social and cultural capital to foster a more inclusive and supportive learning environment. This approach not only enhances the educational experience for students but also prepares them to become culturally competent counselors capable of effectively serving diverse populations.

CULTURAL HUMILITY

Cultural humility encompasses the recognition and mitigation of power differentials within the counselor–client relationship and maintains receptiveness to clients' cultural experiences. Tervalon and Murray-García (1998) advocate for cultural humility as a critical component of CRT.

The following are some ways an educator can develop the use of this conceptual tool:

1. *Self-Reflection*

   It is imperative for educators to undertake ongoing introspection to gain insight into their personal cultural prejudices, presuppositions, and convictions. This endeavor requires systematic scrutiny of their perspectives and conduct toward various cultural cohorts. The cultivation of heightened self-awareness among educators can be facilitated through practices such as contemplative writing, exercises in present-moment awareness, and the solicitation of constructive input from both peers and students.

2. *Openness to Learning*

   Cultural humility necessitates a receptiveness to acquiring knowledge from students and colleagues regarding their cultural experiences. Educators should establish opportunities for discourse and actively engage with the perspectives of others. This may involve inviting guest speakers from diverse backgrounds, facilitating cultural exchange activities, and encouraging students to share their cultural narratives.

3. *Addressing Power Imbalances*

   It is crucial for teachers to recognize and tackle power disparities within their classrooms. This includes acknowledging their own authoritative role and implementing measures to foster a more balanced learning atmosphere. Effective approaches involve using language that is inclusive, encouraging group-based decision processes, and guaranteeing that every student's perspective is acknowledged and valued during class discussions.

4. *Cultural Competence Training*

   Engaging in cultural competence education can improve teachers' knowledge of diverse cultural customs and viewpoints. These educational initiatives typically involve workshops, seminars, and e-learning courses that address subjects like cultural awareness, sensitivity, and intercultural communication. Continuous professional growth in this field is crucial for sustaining cultural humility.

5. *Openness to Culturally Responsive Pedagogy*

   Adopting CRT strategies enables educators to more effectively address the diverse needs of their student population. This approach involves tailoring instructional techniques to accommodate various cultural learning preferences and offering materials that are culturally appropriate. Additionally, teachers should weave cultural humility into their lessons by emphasizing its significance and showcasing its practical application in counseling scenarios.

6. *Being Mindful in Relationships With Students and Colleagues*

   Cultivating healthy and respectful connections with students and colleagues is essential for demonstrating cultural humility. CES educators are encouraged to display intentional and sincere curiosity about students' cultural heritage and life experiences, while creating a classroom atmosphere where learners feel secure and appreciated. Relative to colleagues, such building of relationships is important because of many instances where junior or more culturally diverse faculty are often left out. The goal is to equitably support all faculty to enhance their careers, as well as their place and role in the program, across the university setting, and in the profession. Both relationships can be accomplished through consistent check-ins, individual conversations, and learning activities that embrace diverse cultures.

7. *Advocacy and Allyship*

   Cultural humility encompasses a commitment to social justice and standing in solidarity with marginalized groups. Educators can exemplify this commitment by endorsing initiatives that promote equality and inclusiveness, opposing discriminatory actions, and using their position to highlight underrepresented perspectives. By instructing students about advocacy and allyship, educators can motivate them to initiate positive changes within their local communities (American Counseling Association [ACA], 2015).

Implementing these approaches allows teachers to cultivate cultural sensitivity and establish a more welcoming and accommodating educational setting. This method not only improves the learning experience for students but also equips them to become culturally adept counselors capable of effectively working with diverse client populations.

EMPATHY AND ADVOCACY

Developing empathy and advocacy skills is essential in counselor education to prepare students for working with diverse client populations. According to Ratts et al. (2015), integrating these competencies into teaching methods is vital for equipping future counselors with the necessary tools to tackle social justice concerns and promote their clients' overall welfare.

The following are some ways an educator can develop the use of this conceptual tool:

1. *Case Studies*

   Incorporating case studies that showcase a range of cultural backgrounds and experiences can enhance students' ability to empathize. Instructors may use authentic scenarios or construct fictional cases that challenge students to examine the viewpoints and difficulties encountered by clients from various cultural settings. By analyzing these case studies in the classroom, students can hone their empathy skills and cultivate culturally sensitive counseling techniques.

2. *Role-Playing*

   Engaging in role-play exercises proves to be an effective strategy for cultivating empathy and refining communication abilities. Instructors can craft scenarios where students alternate between portraying clients and counselors, with a specific focus on addressing cultural complexities and obstacles. This immersive learning technique enables students to gain a more comprehensive understanding of their clients' situations by figuratively experiencing their perspectives.

3. *Discussions and Debates*

   Engaging students in dialogues and discussions about cultural diversity and social justice issues helps develop their critical thinking and empathy skills. Teachers can use thought-provoking questions that push students to examine various perspectives and consider the effects of institutional inequities. These in-depth conversations can enhance students' comprehension of the vital role advocacy plays in the counseling profession.

4. *Service Learning*

   Integrating service-learning initiatives into educational programs offers students the chance to interact with varied communities and develop empathy and advocacy skills in practical contexts. These initiatives may include collaborations with neighborhood organizations, volunteer work, or campaigns for social change. By participating in service learning, students can apply classroom concepts to real-world situations and cultivate a dedication to social equity.

5. *Guest Speakers*

   The educational experience can be enhanced by welcoming speakers from various cultural backgrounds and advocacy groups. These guests can offer personal anecdotes about their experiences, obstacles, and achievements in championing their communities' causes. Such interactions provide students with valuable perspectives and can motivate them to pursue advocacy roles in their future professions.

6. *Empathy Mapping*

   Empathy mapping serves as a technique for visualizing and comprehending the experiences, requirements, and feelings of clients. In educational settings, instructors can incorporate this method into classroom exercises, encouraging students to develop empathy maps for various client situations. This activity enables students to gain a more sophisticated insight into their clients' viewpoints and promotes empathetic approaches to counseling.

7. *Advocacy Training*

   For students to be equipped with the necessary skills for promoting social justice in their future careers, it is crucial to offer training in advocacy techniques. Educational institutions can incorporate lessons on advocacy methods, policy evaluation, and grassroots organization into their programs. Practical exercises, such as creating advocacy strategies or participating in policy-related role-playing scenarios, can effectively improve students' ability to advocate for social causes.

8. *Reflective Practice*

   Developing empathy and advocacy skills relies heavily on the practice of reflection. To foster this, teachers can prompt students to participate in activities such as reflective writing, peer evaluations, and guided discussions. These exercises enable students to critically analyze their own prejudices, perspectives, and actions. Through this process of reflection, students enhance their self-awareness and develop a dedication to ongoing personal and professional improvement.

By incorporating these strategies, educators can develop empathy and advocacy in their students, preparing them to be effective and compassionate counselors who are committed to social justice. This approach not only enhances the educational experience but also equips students with the skills needed to support and advocate for their clients from diverse backgrounds.

REFLECTIVE PRACTICE

Reflective practice entails the continuous examination of one's beliefs, biases, and practices to enhance cultural competence. Schön (1983) emphasizes the significance of reflective practice in improving educators' cultural competence and their capacity to adapt counseling approaches to address the needs of diverse clients.

The following are some ways an educator can develop the use of this conceptual tool:

1. *Journaling*

   Reflective journaling is a powerful tool for fostering self-reflection among students. These personal logs offer a confidential outlet for learners to delve into their ideas, responses, and educational experiences. Teachers can enhance this process by providing specific cultural competence-related prompts and advocating for consistent entries, enabling students to monitor their personal development throughout the course.

2. *Supervision and Peer Feedback*

   Students can enhance their counseling skills through regular oversight and peer evaluation sessions, which provide chances for self-reflection and receiving valuable feedback. A collaborative learning atmosphere can be cultivated through group supervision and peer assessment activities, enabling students to exchange insights and benefit from each other's practical experiences.

3. *Self-Assessment Tools*

   Students can benefit from using self-evaluation instruments to recognize their strengths and identify areas needing improvement. Tools such as the Multicultural Counseling Inventory (MCI) or cultural competence self-assessment checklists offer a framework for students to evaluate their cultural awareness, knowledge, and skills. These instruments provide a methodical approach to self-reflection.

4. *Critical Incidents*

   Examining significant events that occur during counseling sessions, known as critical incidents, can enhance reflective practices. Instructors may request students to record and contemplate these incidents, with a particular emphasis on cultural aspects and their own reactions. This process of examination allows students to extract valuable lessons from their experiences and formulate improved approaches for future interactions.

5. *Reflective Discussions*

   In the classroom, promoting reflective discussions enables students to express and explore their viewpoints. Teachers can use various techniques such as open-ended inquiries, scenario analyses, and simulations to foster contemplation and conversation. By prompting students to explore their cultural preconceptions and prejudices, educators can enhance self-reflection and broaden understanding among learners.

6. *Mindfulness Practices*

   Integrating mindfulness exercises into the educational program can improve reflective learning. Methods like meditation, controlled breathing, and body awareness exercises assist students in becoming more focused on the present moment and conscious of their mental and emotional states. By cultivating mindfulness, students can develop a stronger sense of self-awareness and interpersonal understanding, which supports their reflective development.

7. *Reflective Writing Assignments*

   Incorporating reflective writing assignments, such as essays and papers, helps students engage in critical evaluation of their educational experiences and progress in cultural competence. Instructors can provide specific prompts for students to contemplate, including their own cultural background, encounters with diverse populations, or responses to course materials. Through this process of reflection, students are better able to express their personal growth and insights gained.

MULTICULTURAL COUNSELING AND TEACHING COMPETENCE

Multicultural counseling competence is the ability to understand, communicate with, and effectively interact with people across cultures (Holcomb-McCoy, 2004). The ACA's Multicultural and Social Justice Counseling Competencies (MSJCC) provide a comprehensive framework for integrating multicultural and social justice principles into counseling practice. The following are some key components of the MSJCC:

1. *Counselor Self-Awareness*

   To effectively serve their clients, counselors need to cultivate a deep understanding of their own cultural background, prejudices, and values. This process involves introspection on personal life experiences and recognizing how these elements shape their client interactions. The MSJCC underscore the necessity of self-awareness for counselors, regardless of their privileged or marginalized status.

2. *Client and Student Worldview*

   Grasping the worldviews of clients and students plays a crucial role in delivering effective counseling services. Practitioners should delve into the cultural contexts, belief systems, and life experiences of their clients to offer support that is culturally appropriate. This aspect of the MSJCC prompt counselors to take into account their clients' viewpoints and modify their therapeutic strategies accordingly.

3. *Counseling and Student Relationships*

   Developing a robust and respectful educational and therapeutic alliance is essential for cultural competency in counseling and for learning. The MSJCC emphasize the importance for counselors to cultivate trust and connection with clients from various cultural backgrounds. This process involves demonstrating empathy, maintaining an open mindset, and adapting to the cultural requirements of clients. Reflect back to the Ratts et al. (2015) article on use of the MSJCC praxis to delve deeper into the relevance for building these relationships.

4. *Counseling and Advocacy Interventions*

   Mental health professionals should implement strategies that target both personal and broader societal concerns. The MSJCC recommend approaches that enhance equity and confront power disparities. These encompass defending clients' entitlements, tackling prejudice, and striving for fair outcomes.

PEDAGOGICAL STRATEGIES

CRT uses several effective instructional approaches, including group-based learning, hands-on activities, and issue-centered education. According to Kolb (1984), these methods encourage student participation, enhance analytical thinking, and facilitate the practical application of knowledge to real-life situations.

The following are some specific strategies for adult students at master's and doctoral level instruction:

1. *Activate Prior Knowledge*

   Prompt students to use their personal cultural backgrounds and existing knowledge when interacting with unfamiliar content. This approach facilitates the connection of new information to their current understanding, enhancing the relevance and significance of the learning process.

2. *Contextualize Learning*

   Connect educational content to students' sociocultural backgrounds. This approach involves establishing links between the subject matter and the learners' local environments, demonstrating how classroom knowledge applies to real-life situations in their communities.

3. *Leverage Cultural Capital*

   Identify and leverage the cultural assets and resources that students contribute to the learning environment. This process may involve integrating diverse viewpoints, content, and illustrations that are representative of the students' cultural backgrounds and life experiences.

4. *Build Relationships*

   Establish meaningful and respectful connections with students by fostering a welcoming and inclusive learning atmosphere where students feel appreciated and listened to. Cultivating these relationships can be achieved through consistent check-ins, individual conversations, and collaborative activities.

5. *Use Diverse Teaching Methods*

   Use diverse instructional techniques to cater to various learning preferences and cultural contexts. Such techniques may encompass group discussions, simulations, real-world scenarios, and audiovisual presentations. By offering multiple avenues for students to interact with the subject matter, educators can ensure that all learners have the opportunity to actively participate and achieve success.

6. *Encourage Reflective Practice*

   Foster self-reflection in students by encouraging them to regularly examine their learning experiences, prejudices, and cultural preconceptions. This can be achieved through various methods such as keeping a journal, receiving feedback from peers, and engaging in classroom discussions. The practice of self-reflection aids students in developing self-awareness and enhancing their cultural competence.

7. *Foster Critical Thinking*

   Promote critical thinking among students regarding cultural and social justice issues. This includes challenging them to examine preconceptions, evaluate power structures, and reflect on the consequences of systemic disparities. The ability to think critically is crucial for effective counseling practices.

8. *Provide Supportive Feedback*

   Provide students with productive and culturally appropriate feedback that promotes their development and enhances their skills. Comments should be precise, implementable, and mindful of students' diverse cultural contexts and life experiences.

9. *Create Inclusive Assessments*

   Create evaluations that ensure fairness and inclusivity for the entire student body. These evaluations may involve implementing diverse assessment techniques, including portfolio submissions, oral presentations, and self-evaluations, to effectively measure the wide range of student capabilities and talents.

10. *Advocate for Equity*

    Demonstrate leadership in promoting social justice and equality within the classroom environment. Such leadership encompasses tackling discrimination, fostering inclusivity, and empowering students to stand up for themselves and their peers.

11. *Technology Integration*

    The incorporation of technological tools into educational curricula can improve learning outcomes and broaden access to education. Teachers can use various digital resources, such as online educational platforms, remote video sessions, virtual reality (VR)–based simulations, and other electronic aids to develop captivating and interactive learning environments. Additionally, technology enables students from diverse backgrounds to collaborate and communicate more effectively.

12. *Interactive Lectures*

    Blending traditional lecturing techniques with engaging elements like group discussions, audience surveys, and visual aids, interactive lectures aim to captivate students and promote active involvement. This approach allows educators to deliver new content, spark conversations on culturally significant subjects, and showcase a range of viewpoints. By using interactive lectures, instructors can effectively convey information while fostering student engagement and participation.

13. *Problem-Based Learning*

    An educational approach known as problem-based learning (PBL) involves students acquiring knowledge through the resolution of complex, real-world challenges. This method fosters the development of critical thinking abilities, problem-solving skills, and self-directed learning. Instructors can create PBL exercises that focus on culturally pertinent issues and obstacles, enabling students to acquire the necessary competencies for handling diverse counseling situations.

14. *Collaborative Learning*

    Group-based learning is a method in which students collaborate to tackle challenges, finish assignments, or explore subjects together. This approach enhances active participation, interpersonal skills, and the ability to work as a team. Educators can foster a lively and participatory classroom setting that appreciates various viewpoints by implementing team projects, peer assessment activities, and group learning exercises.

15. *Experiential Learning*

    Learning through direct experience and subsequent reflection is the cornerstone of experiential learning. This educational approach enables students to put theoretical knowledge into practice in real-world contexts. To foster the development of practical skills and provide hands-on experience in counseling, educators can incorporate various experiential learning activities. These may include internships, practical placements, simulations, and role-playing exercises.

Implementing these culturally sensitive teaching methods allows instructors to foster a more welcoming and productive learning atmosphere for graduate-level adult students pursuing careers in counseling. This strategy not only improves the quality of education but also equips students with the skills to become culturally aware and socially conscious counselors.

ADVOCACY-FOCUSED TEACHING STRATEGIES

Integrating the advocacy competencies developed by the ACA into educational methods is crucial for equipping future counselors with the ability to effectively advocate for their clients and communities. These competencies, as outlined by the ACA, define the necessary abilities, expertise, and conduct required for counselors to engage in advocacy across various levels (Toporek et al., 2010). The following are some strategies for integrating these competencies into the curriculum:

1. *Client/Student Empowerment*

   Teachers should prioritize equipping students with the ability to stand up for themselves and their future clients. This process encompasses instructing students on how to recognize their own strengths and available resources, understand systemic obstacles, and cultivate self-advocacy abilities (Toporek et al., 2010). Practical exercises such as simulations, real-world scenarios, and strategic planning can assist students in honing these skills within a nurturing learning environment.

2. *Client/Student Advocacy*

   It is essential to train students in client advocacy skills. Such training involves instructing them on how to assist clients in obtaining necessary resources, interact with service providers, and create strategies to overcome obstacles. To provide practical experience in advocating for clients, instructors can use role-playing exercises, community-based initiatives, and presentations by field experts.

3. *Community Collaboration*

   A crucial component of advocacy involves promoting student engagement with community organizations and stakeholders. Teachers can establish connections with local agencies, nonprofit organizations, and advocacy groups to create opportunities for students to participate in community-oriented projects. This approach helps students grasp the significance of collaborative efforts in bringing about change.

4. *Systems Advocacy*

   Equipping students with the skills to advocate for systemic changes is vital in addressing the broader issues that affect clients. This approach entails instructing students about the societal, political, economic, and cultural elements that impact individuals and communities. To cultivate systems-level advocacy abilities in students, instructors can weave discussions on policy evaluation, legislative action, and social equity into their course content.

5. *Reflective Practice*

   Integrating reflective practices into educational methods enables students to analyze their advocacy work critically and recognize areas that need enhancement. Teachers can facilitate student reflection on their experiences and promote learning through the use of reflective writing exercises, feedback from peers, and collaborative discussions.

6. *Professional Development*

   It is essential to offer continuous professional growth opportunities to students to improve their advocacy abilities. These can encompass advocacy and social justice-focused workshops, seminars, and conferences. Additionally, teachers can motivate students to join professional organizations and advocacy groups to remain knowledgeable and involved.

By integrating these advocacy-focused teaching strategies, educators can prepare students to become effective advocates for their clients and communities. This approach not only enhances the educational experience but also equips students with the skills needed to promote social justice and equity in their professional practice.

LANGUAGE BARRIERS

Overcoming language obstacles is essential for successful communication in counseling environments. Linguistic differences can create substantial hurdles in comprehending clients' perspectives and life experiences, potentially resulting in difficulties providing suitable treatment (Summers & Nelson, 2020). The following are some strategies for overcoming language barriers in counselor education:

1. *Language Support Resources*

   It is central to offer language assistance tools to help counselors-in-training address linguistic challenges. These resources may include translation services, dictionaries for multiple languages, and software designed for language acquisition. Additionally, instructors can motivate students to enroll in language classes or participate in workshops aimed at enhancing their skills in languages commonly used by their client populations.

2. *Cultural and Linguistic Training*

   Integrating cultural and linguistic education into the curriculum enables students to acquire the necessary competencies for effectively collaborating with clients from various language backgrounds. This educational approach can encompass subjects such as intercultural communication, language-specific cultural subtleties, and techniques for collaborating with translators. To offer hands-on experience, instructors may use methods such as simulations, real-world scenarios, and presentations by visiting experts.

3. *Use of Interpreters*

   Equipping students with skills to effectively collaborate with interpreters is essential for addressing language obstacles. Instructors can offer guidance on choosing and working alongside interpreters, safeguarding privacy, and preserving the therapeutic relationship. The training curriculum should incorporate hands-on sessions with interpreters to enhance students' self-assurance and proficiency in this domain.

4. *Visual and Nonverbal Communication*

   Encouraging the use of visual aids and nonverbal communication can enhance understanding when language barriers exist. Educators can teach students to use diagrams, drawings, and other visual tools to convey information. Additionally, training in nonverbal communication skills, such as body language, facial expressions, and gestures, can help bridge language gaps.

5. *Culturally Relevant Communication Techniques*

   It is important for CES educators to emphasize the significance of culturally relevant communication techniques. This entails comprehending and respecting cultural variations in communication styles, including directness, formality, and the utilization of silence. Students should be instructed to adapt their communication approaches to align with their clients' cultural norms and preferences.

6. *Building Language Proficiency*

   Promoting the enhancement of students' language proficiency in the languages used by their client populations constitutes a valuable pedagogical strategy. Educational institutions can facilitate this process by incorporating language acquisition opportunities into the curriculum, including language exchange programs, immersion experiences, and language practice groups.

7. *Reflective Practice*

   The mitigation of language barriers is significantly influenced by reflective practice. It is incumbent on educators to promote student engagement in introspective analysis of their communicative interactions with linguistically diverse clientele, facilitating the identification of obstacles and the formulation of ameliorative strategies. The implementation of reflective journaling, supervisory guidance, and peer-based evaluative feedback serves as efficacious mechanisms for cultivating this essential practice.

8. *Technology Integration*

   Using technology can aid in overcoming language barriers. Educators can introduce students to translation apps, speech-to-text software, and online communication tools that facilitate multilingual interactions. Incorporating technology into counseling practice can enhance accessibility and communication with clients who speak different languages.

   Through the incorporation of these strategies into counselor education curricula, educators can effectively prepare students to navigate linguistic barriers and provide culturally appropriate care to diverse populations. This approach not only enhances the educational experience but also equips future counselors with the requisite skills to communicate effectively with clients from varied linguistic backgrounds.

This discussion revisits the previously introduced work of teacher educator Zaretta Hammond, whose book, *Culturally Responsive Teaching and the Brain* (2015), offers substantive guidance on addressing linguistic diversity and promoting CRT. Hammond proposes the ready for rigor framework, which integrates CRT with academic rigor. This framework aims to facilitate students' development into independent learners by providing appropriate support and challenges (Hammond, 2015). Educators may implement this framework through the establishment of high expectations, provision of scaffolding, and encouragement of student ownership in the learning process.

By incorporating these insights from Zaretta Hammond's work, educators can effectively address linguistic diversity and promote CRT in their classrooms. This approach not only enhances students' learning experiences but also fosters a more inclusive and equitable educational environment (Constantine & Sue, 2006).

Graduate-level faculty can implement this framework with counseling students to enhance their learning experiences and cultural competence. The following list indicates how:

1. *Awareness: Faculty need to cultivate self-awareness and cultural awareness in their students. This involves:*
    - Self-Reflection: Encouraging students to reflect on their own cultural backgrounds, biases, and assumptions through journaling, discussions, and reflective essays.
    - Cultural Awareness: Integrating content that explores diverse cultural perspectives and histories. Using case studies that reflect the experiences of various cultural groups can help students understand different worldviews.
2. *Learning Partnerships: Building strong, respectful relationships between faculty and students is crucial:*
    - Trust and Rapport: Faculty should establish a supportive and trusting environment. This includes showing genuine interest in students' experiences and being approachable and empathetic.
    - Collaboration: Encouraging collaborative learning through group projects, peer review sessions, and study groups. This fosters a sense of community and shared learning.
3. *Information Processing: Engaging students in deep, meaningful learning experiences:*
    - Culturally Relevant Content: Incorporate readings, case studies, and examples that reflect the cultural diversity of the student body and the populations they will serve as counselors.
    - Active Learning: Use interactive teaching methods such as role-playing, simulations, and problem-based learning to engage students in applying their knowledge to real-world counseling scenarios.
4. *Community Building: Creating a supportive and inclusive classroom environment:*
    - Inclusive Practices: Promoting inclusivity by respecting and valuing all cultural perspectives in classroom discussions and activities.
    - Safe Space: Ensuring the classroom is a safe space for students to express their cultural identities and experiences without fear of judgment.

Table 4.2 shows the ready for rigor framework in action.

TABLE 4.2 Hammond's Ready for Rigor Framework in Action

Action Construct	Description
Cultural autobiographies	Have students write and share their cultural autobiographies to foster self-awareness and cultural understanding among peers.
Cultural immersion projects	Assign projects that require students to engage with diverse communities, such as volunteering, attending cultural events, or interviewing individuals from different cultural backgrounds.
Case study analysis	Use diverse case studies that highlight different cultural contexts and challenges in counseling practice. Facilitate discussions on how to approach these cases with cultural competence.
Role-playing scenarios	Conduct role-playing exercises where students practice counseling clients from various cultural backgrounds, emphasizing empathy, cultural humility, and effective communication strategies.

Source: Adapted from Hammond, Z. (2015). *Culturally Responsive Teaching and the Brain: Promoting authentic engagement and rigor among culturally and linguistically diverse students.* Corwin Press.

By integrating the ready for rigor framework into their teaching practices, graduate-level faculty can create a culturally responsive and academically rigorous learning environment. This approach not only enhances the educational experience for counseling students but also prepares them to be culturally competent and effective counselors.

TECHNOLOGY IN COUNSELOR EDUCATION

The integration of technological advancements in counselor education offers both advantages and obstacles. These innovative tools can improve teaching methods, making learning more accessible, interactive, and efficient. Online platforms provide flexibility, enabling both synchronous and asynchronous learning from diverse locations, although dependable internet access is essential for fair participation. Digital resources such as video calls, virtual simulations, and VR technology enhance the educational experience by offering hands-on training and replicating authentic situations, thereby improving students' abilities and self-assurance. Educators must remain current with technological developments and implement them judiciously.

Analytics tools track student advancement, pinpoint areas for improvement, and personalize instruction. By examining performance and engagement data, instructors can make well-informed choices and offer targeted assistance. Nevertheless, the implementation of technology raises ethical issues regarding privacy and confidentiality, requiring strict adherence to ethical standards to safeguard sensitive information. Incorporating cutting-edge technology into counselor education curricula can significantly enhance learning, especially from a culturally responsive standpoint. Here are some applications:

1. *Virtual Reality and Simulations*

   VR systems can generate lifelike scenarios that enable students to hone their counseling abilities in a regulated, simulated setting. This approach includes engaging in simulations with clients from various cultural backgrounds, thereby fostering the development of cultural sensitivity and understanding among students.

2. *Teletherapy Platforms*

   Remote counseling sessions are made possible through online therapy platforms; these offer a valuable means to reach populations with limited access to mental health services. These digital tools also create opportunities for students to engage in multicultural counseling, allowing them to interact with clients from diverse cultural and linguistic backgrounds.

3. *Online Learning Management Systems*

   A learning management system (LMS) offers a unified platform where students can access course content, turn in assignments, and engage in online discussions. Educators can foster a more inclusive educational setting by integrating culturally diverse materials and resources, thereby acknowledging and appreciating the varied cultural heritage of their students. Canvas, Brightspace, and Blackboard are examples of LMS. Consequently, such platforms may be of particular significance for CES faculty members who hold leadership positions within academic departments. Nevertheless, numerous instances exist where both students and faculty members lack proficiency in navigating the LMS. It is proposed that external consultants be engaged to facilitate program-wide training sessions on optimal utilization and maximization of benefits derived from the LMS.

4. *Mobile Apps and Digital Tools*

   Students can enhance their learning and practice beyond the classroom through digital tools and smartphone applications. Various apps offering mental health assistance, language interpretation, and training in cultural awareness can assist students in acquiring the necessary skills for effective collaboration with a diverse clientele. Examples are mood mobile apps such as MoodPanda and MoodKit.

5. *Collaborative Technologies*

   Tools like Google Hangouts, Microsoft Teams, Zoom, and other collaborative platforms can facilitate communication and collaboration among students from different cultural backgrounds. These technologies can also be used to connect students with international peers and experts, broadening their cultural perspectives.

6. *Interactive Multimedia*

   Incorporating diverse media formats like video content, audio broadcasts, and hands-on digital experiences can enhance student engagement and make learning more culturally relevant. These multimedia tools can effectively showcase various counseling situations and demonstrate culturally sensitive approaches in practice. Gamification and screen recording software (e.g., ScreenPal and other newer artificial intelligence [AI] programs) are examples of interactive multimedia that may be used in counselor training programs. They work well for online instruction.

7. *Data Analytics and Feedback Systems*

   CES educators can use data analytics to monitor student performance and pinpoint areas requiring extra assistance. Additionally, feedback mechanisms can offer tailored guidance to students, aiding in the enhancement of their counseling abilities and cultural awareness. An example of this is M-Powering Teachers, a new AI-generated feedback tool for educators that supports students. More details on AI programs for use across counselor education curricula are explored in Chapter 6 of this book.

8. *Culturally Responsive Instructional Design*

   Technology can be leveraged by instructors to develop culturally sensitive and all-encompassing teaching methods. This involves crafting educational exercises that honor students' cultural heritage, incorporating culturally appropriate illustrations, and offering resources in various languages.

By incorporating these technological tools into counselor training curricula, instructors can foster a more welcoming and productive learning atmosphere that readies students for working with diverse client groups (Chun et al., 2020). This strategy not only improves the quality of education but also arms future counselors with the necessary abilities to deliver culturally adept services.

CONCLUSION

This chapter has presented a series of CRT strategies that can be implemented across counselor education curricula. The objective of these conceptual tools is to integrate them into teaching preparation for counselor educators who aspire to faculty positions and who develop and facilitate trainings, as well as to introduce instructional methodologies that can be framed within a culturally responsive approach. Collectively, the concepts explored are intended to shape and guide practices in preparation for becoming and serving as a CES professional in the contemporary context of the 21st century.

CHAPTER RESOURCES

Culturally Responsive Counselor Educator Skills

CRCE Skills to Further Develop From This Chapter	
Teaching Tool	Key Skills Needed
Awareness of sociocultural complexities in teaching	Cultural competence, empathy, active listening, critical thinking
Hidden curriculum	Awareness of implicit biases, reflective practice, cultural sensitivity
Social and cultural capital	Networking, community engagement, cultural literacy

(continued)

CRCE Skills to Further Develop From This Chapter *(continued)*	
Cultural humility, empathy and advocacy	Self-reflection, empathy, advocacy skills, emotional intelligence
Reflective practice	Self-awareness, critical reflection, continuous learning
Multicultural competence	Cultural knowledge, communication skills, adaptability
Pedagogical strategies	Instructional design, inclusive teaching strategies, flexibility
Language barriers	Multilingual abilities, patience, clear communication, creative problem-solving
Technology use in counselor education	Digital literacy, tech integration, adaptability, innovative thinking
Advocacy-focused teaching	Leadership, advocacy skills, policy knowledge, strategic planning

CRCE, culturally response counselor educator.

CONTENT SUMMARY

- Awareness of Sociocultural Complexities: Educators need to understand and address the various cultural, social, and political dynamics influencing students' learning experiences to create a supportive and inclusive educational environment.
- Hidden Curriculum: Recognizing and addressing the implicit messages and values conveyed through the educational environment beyond the formal curriculum ensures that all students feel valued and respected.
- Social and Cultural Capital: Leveraging students' networks, relationships, knowledge, and cultural competencies enhances their learning experiences and provides equitable opportunities for success.
- Cultural Humility: Involves recognizing power imbalances in the counselor–client relationship, encouraging self-reflection, and being open to learning from clients about their cultural experiences.
- Empathy and Advocacy: Incorporating empathy and advocacy into teaching practices prepares counselors to work effectively with diverse populations and address social justice issues.
- Reflective Practice and Multicultural Counseling Competence: Encouraging continuous self-examination and incorporating multicultural theories and practices into the curriculum helps students develop cultural competence and adaptability in counseling.
- A diverse array of pedagogical instruments can be adapted to form CRT methodologies. This necessitates a comprehensive understanding of these tools and further investigation to acquire more detailed knowledge regarding their potential application in counselor preparation program curricula.

Advanced Reflection Questions

1. How do the sociocultural complexities within your own teaching environment influence your ability to implement CRT practices? Provide specific examples and discuss strategies you have used or could use to address these complexities.
2. What elements of the hidden curriculum exist within your current educational setting, and how do they impact student experiences and learning outcomes? Discuss how you can identify and modify these elements to create a more inclusive and equitable learning environment.
3. Reflect on how you currently recognize and use the social and cultural capital of your students. What challenges have you faced in leveraging these assets, and what steps can you take to better integrate students' cultural backgrounds and experiences into your teaching practices?
4. Consider your role as an advocate for social justice within counselor education. How do you incorporate empathy and advocacy into your teaching and supervision methods? Provide examples of specific strategies or activities you use to foster these qualities in your students, and evaluate their effectiveness.

Further Reading

An, W., & Western, B. (2019). Social capital in the creation of cultural capital: Family structure, neighborhood cohesion, and extracurricular participation. *Social Science Research, 81*, 192–208. https://doi.org/10.1016/j.ssresearch.2019.03.015

Kärner, T., & Schneider, G. (2024). A scoping review on the hidden curriculum in education: Mapping definitory elements for educational theory building. *Research in Education Curriculum and Pedagogy: Global Perspectives, 1*(1), 1–23. https://doi.org/10.56395/recap.v1i1.1

Lee, S., Cha, Y.-K., & Ham, S.-H. (2023). The global institutionalization of multicultural education as an academic discourse. *Societies, 13*(8), 191. https://doi.org/10.3390/soc13080191

Nykyporets, S. (2023). Exploring the dynamics of foreign language education within socio-cultural transformations: A comprehensive analysis. *Logos: Scientific Research and Methods of Their Implementation, 29*(9), 48. https://doi.org/10.36074/logos-29.09.2023.48

Pope-Davis, D. B., Coleman, H. L. K., Liu, W. M., & Toporek, R. L. (Eds.). (2004). *Handbook of multicultural competencies in counseling and psychology*. Sage Publications.

REFERENCES

American Counseling Association. (2015). *ACA advocacy competencies*. https://www.counseling.org/docs/default-source/competencies/aca-advocacy-competencies-updated-may-2020.pdf?sfvrsn=f410212c_4

Bourdieu, P. (1986). The forms of capital. In J. Richardson (Ed.), *Handbook of theory and research for the sociology of education* (pp. 241–258). Greenwood.

Chun, J., Connor, A., Alsaman, M., Urkmez, B., & Kosciulek, J. F. (2020). Capitalizing on diversity in counselor education: An application of the interaction for learning framework. *Journal of Multicultural Counseling and Development, 48*(3), 161–175. https://doi.org/10.1002/jmcd.12175

Constantine, M. G., & Sue, D. W. (2006). Addressing linguistic diversity in counseling. In M. G. Constantine & D. W. Sue (Eds.), *Addressing racism: Facilitating cultural competence in mental health and educational settings* (pp. 165–176). Wiley.

Darder, A., Torres, R. D., & Baltodano, M. (Eds.). (2017). *The critical pedagogy reader* (3rd ed.). Routledge.

Flemming, V. O., & Lyons, M. L. (2019). Counseling Latinx and men. In D. W. Sue & D. Sue (Eds.), Multicultural issues in counseling: New approaches to diversity (5th ed., Chapters 7 & 11). American Counseling Association.

Florence, N. (1998). *Bell Hooks' engaged pedagogy: A transgressive education for critical consciousness*. Bergin & Garve.

Hammond, Z. (2015). *Culturally responsive teaching and the brain: Promoting authentic engagement and rigor among culturally and linguistically diverse students*. Corwin Press.

Holcomb-McCoy, C. (2004). Multicultural counseling competencies: Assessment, education, training, and supervision. In D. B. Pope-Davis, H. L. K. Coleman, W. M. Liu, & R. L. Toporek (Eds.), *Handbook of multicultural competencies in counseling and psychology* (pp. 393–403). Sage Publications.

Kolb, D. A. (1984). *Experiential learning: Experience as the source of learning and development*. Prentice-Hall.

Okech, J. E. A., & Rubel, D. J. (Eds.). (2018). *Counselor education in the 21st century: Issues and experiences*. American Counseling Association.

Ratts, M. J., Singh, A. A., Nassar-McMillan, S., Butler, S. K., & McCullough, J. R. (2015). Multicultural and Social Justice Counseling Competencies: Guidelines for the counseling profession. *Journal of Multicultural Counseling and Development, 44*(1), 28–48. https://doi.org/10.1002/jmcd.12035

Schön, D. A. (1983). *The reflective practitioner: How professionals think in action*. Basic Books.

Summers, M., & Nelson, M. (2020). Overcoming language barriers in counseling. In D. W. Sue & D. Sue (Eds.), *Counseling the culturally diverse: Theory and practice* (8th ed.). Wiley.

Tervalon, M., & Murray-García, J. (1998). Cultural humility versus cultural competence: A critical distinction in defining physician training outcomes in multicultural education. *Journal of Health Care for the Poor and Underserved, 9*(2), 117–125. https://doi.org/10.1353/hpu.2010.0233

Toporek, R. L., Lewis, J. A., & Ratts, M. J. (2010). The ACA advocacy competencies: An overview. In M. J. Ratts, R. L. Toporek, & J. A. Lewis (Eds.), *ACA advocacy competencies: A social justice framework for counselors* (pp. 11–20). American Counseling Association.

PART III

EVALUATING CULTURALLY RESPONSIVE TEACHING THROUGH THE COUNSELOR EDUCATION PROGRAMMING: SYSTEMS, METRICS, AND ARTIFICIAL INTELLIGENCE

CHAPTER 5

CULTURALLY RESPONSIVE TEACHING ACROSS THE REQUIRED COURSEWORK

Since the 1980s, scholars have called on the counseling field to be more culturally responsive and have readily identified methods and relational strategies that can be integrated into the counseling relationship to ensure culturally responsive practice.

—Natoya H. Haskins and Colleagues

LEARNING OBJECTIVES After studying this chapter, you will be able to:

- Create course descriptions that acknowledge and respect diverse cultural backgrounds.
- Formulate assignments that reflect and address the cultural contexts of students and clients.
- Design evaluation rubrics that are fair, unbiased, and inclusive of diverse perspectives and experiences.

SNAPSHOT: A counselor educator's career experience

The majority of new or junior counselor education and supervision (CES) faculty are assigned to teach courses within the counselor education (CE) curricula that have been previously designed. Consequently, the course syllabus is typically provided to them by the previous instructor, complete with course description, assignments, required textbook, and learning objectives. Furthermore, junior faculty often maintain the existing course structure during their initial teaching experience in their new position. However, if a course has not undergone revision for more than 5 years, it may be necessary to update its design. This need for modification frequently becomes apparent when preformatted PowerPoint presentations from the textbook contain outdated material that conflicts with contemporary developments in society, the profession, or the mental healthcare system. Although such instances may facilitate impromptu discussions in class, they may also create the impression that junior faculty are inadequately prepared or adhering to the principle of maintaining established practices. It is important to consider how one will approach the task of teaching a set of courses as a new faculty member in the CE program.

INTRODUCTION

This chapter provides illustrations of how culturally responsive teaching (CRT) is practiced across the counselor education curriculum. The required courses in counselor preparation and training programs are used to describe how CRT in counselor education may be applied. The chapter is sectioned according to these courses. Each section details what doctoral students preparing to teach are suggested to practice in the course, from textbook selection and design of course syllabi to providing feedback. Essentially, this chapter rounds out the strategy to practice affirming and equitable teaching practices offered as integrative prescriptions for teaching counselor educators how to teach and prepare for multicultural learners and instruction.

Table 5.1 provides content to follow along and use as a guide that distinguishes each of the courses according to core courses, specialization courses, and clinical experience courses.

CORE COURSES

Foundations in Counseling (Culturally Responsive Version)

This course introduces students to the profession of counseling with a focus on understanding and valuing diverse cultural backgrounds. Through scholarly research and writing, students will examine the role and function of counselors in various settings,

TABLE 5.1 Required Courses

Core Courses	Specialization Courses	Clinical Experience Courses
Foundations in Counseling	Psychopathology	Practicum
Counseling Theories and Techniques	Addictions Counseling	Clinical Internship
Ethics and Professional Issues in Counseling	Family and Couples Counseling	
Counseling Across the Life Span	Human Sexuality and Counseling	
Career Development in Counseling	Counseling in Community Settings	
Assessment and Diagnosing in Counseling		
Research Methods in Counseling		
Multicultural Counseling Practices		
Group Counseling		

Note: General core courses are commonly required to obtain the credential for licensed professional counselor. Some requirements differ from state board to state board (e.g., Florida Board of Examiner's in Counseling requires a human sexuality course to obtain the LPC). A suggestion will be to cross-reference the required courses to obtain the professional counselor licensed in your state. The names of courses also differ per counseling program; hence, the basic topic of the courses is listed.

LPC, licensed professional counselor.

emphasizing the importance of cultural competence in effective counseling practice. Current trends and issues in counseling, including the impact of cultural, social, and political factors on mental health, are addressed. Students will develop an awareness of their own cultural identities and biases and learn strategies for working with clients from diverse backgrounds. The course also covers ethical and legal considerations, with a particular emphasis on advocating for equity and access to mental health services for all clients.

Course Learning Objectives

- Develop Cultural Competence: Students will demonstrate an understanding of the cultural, social, and political factors that impact mental health and learn strategies to provide culturally responsive counseling.
- Understand Ethical and Legal Considerations: Students will analyze ethical standards and legal considerations in the counseling profession, with a focus on advocating for equity and access to mental health services for all clients.
- Enhance Self-Awareness: Students will reflect on their own cultural identities and biases, developing self-awareness and strategies for working effectively with clients from diverse backgrounds.
- Explore Counselor Roles and Functions: Students will examine the roles and functions of counselors in various settings, emphasizing the importance of cultural competence in effective counseling practice.

CACREP (2024) Standards That Align With This Course

In Section 3 of the Council for Accreditation of Counseling and Related Educational Programs (CACREP) 2024 *Standards*, the section that aligns with this course is "A. PROFESSIONAL COUNSELING ORIENTATION AND ETHICAL PRACTICE" (p. 12). This subheading in this section of the *Standards* is the primary section to refer to for this course. However, other subheadings, such as "B. SOCIAL AND CULTURAL IDENTITIES AND EXPERIENCES" (p. 13), are also applicable. Hence, the direction for counselor education and supervision (CES) faculty will be to go through Section 3 and reference the aligned *Standards* for each course and any other imperative areas that are expected to be reflected in the course.

For the subsequent course applications in the chapter, the primary *Standard* area in Section 3 will highlight the primary subheading to pull course reflections from for that application (e.g., content within the *Standard* that will be addressed in the course). A best way to do this is during course preparations, specifically when developing the course learning objectives and expectations for assignment outcomes.

Example Assignment: Cultural Identity Reflection Paper

Assignment Directions: Write a reflective paper on your own cultural identity and how it influences your approach to counseling. Include the following elements:

- Cultural Background: Describe your cultural background, including factors such as race, ethnicity, gender, sexual orientation, socioeconomic status, religion, and ability. Discuss how these aspects of your identity have shaped your worldview.

- Personal Experiences: Reflect on significant personal experiences that have impacted your cultural identity and perspective on mental health and counseling.
- Biases and Assumptions: Identify any biases and assumptions you hold and discuss how they may influence your interactions with clients from diverse cultural backgrounds.
- Culturally Responsive Counseling: Explain how you plan to integrate cultural competence into your counseling practice, including specific strategies for working with clients from different cultural backgrounds.

Length: Five to seven pages, double-spaced, APA format

Culturally Responsive Rubric

Criteria	Excellent (4)	Good (3)	Fair (2)	Needs Improvement (1)
Cultural Background	Thorough and insightful description of cultural background	Clear description of cultural background	Basic description of cultural background	Minimal or unclear description of cultural background
Personal Experiences	In-depth reflection on personal experiences	Clear reflection on personal experiences	Basic reflection on personal experiences	Minimal reflection on personal experiences
Biases and Assumptions	Comprehensive identification and analysis of biases	Clear identification and analysis of biases	Basic identification and analysis of biases	Minimal identification and analysis of biases
Culturally Responsive Counseling	Detailed and specific strategies for culturally responsive counseling	Clear strategies for culturally responsive counseling	Basic strategies for culturally responsive counseling	Minimal or unclear strategies for culturally responsive counseling
Writing Quality	Clear, well-organized, and free of errors	Clear and organized, with few errors	Somewhat clear and organized, with several errors	Unclear or disorganized, with many errors
APA Format	Correct and consistent use of APA format	Mostly correct use of APA format	Some errors in APA format	Many errors in APA format

Counseling Theories and Techniques (Culturally Responsive Version)

This course provides an in-depth exploration of major counseling theories and their applications, with a strong emphasis on cultural competence and sensitivity. Students will learn to integrate a variety of theoretical approaches, including psychodynamic, cognitive-behavioral, humanistic, and systemic models, into culturally responsive counseling practice. The course highlights the importance of understanding clients' cultural backgrounds, values, and experiences in shaping their mental health and therapeutic needs. Techniques for building rapport and fostering a therapeutic alliance with clients from diverse cultural groups will be discussed. Students will also examine how cultural biases and systemic inequities impact mental health and access to care. Through role-playing, case studies, and interactive discussions, students will develop practical skills in applying culturally informed counseling techniques in real-world scenarios.

Course Learning Objectives

- Integrate Theoretical Approaches: Students will demonstrate the ability to integrate a variety of counseling theories, including psychodynamic, cognitive-behavioral, humanistic, and systemic models, into culturally responsive counseling practice.
- Build Culturally Responsive Rapport: Students will develop techniques for building rapport and fostering therapeutic alliances with clients from diverse cultural backgrounds.
- Understand Cultural Biases: Students will critically examine how cultural biases and systemic inequities impact mental health and access to care, and learn strategies for mitigating these biases in counseling.
- Apply Culturally Informed Techniques: Students will practice and refine counseling techniques that are culturally informed and relevant to the unique needs of clients from diverse cultural groups.

CACREP (2024) Standards That Align With This Course

The primary set of *Standards* that reflect course content for *Theories* is located in Section 3, subheading "E. COUNSELING PRACTICE AND RELATIONSHIPS" (p. 14). However, theories are diverse within the counseling profession and across the curricula. For example, theories are addressed in multicultural counseling, life span and development, career, and in research and assessment in counseling practice. It is advisable to review these sections if the course design will extend beyond the introductory level of theories of counseling and psychotherapy, as these may be interconnected with theories in other subject matter across the curricula.

Example Assignment: Culturally Responsive Counseling Case Study

Assignment Directions: Choose a counseling theory and apply it to a case study involving a client from a diverse cultural background. Your case study should include the following elements:

- Client Description: Provide a detailed description of the client's cultural background, presenting problem, and relevant personal history.
- Theory Selection: Explain why you chose the particular counseling theory and how it aligns with the client's cultural context and presenting issues.
- Application of Theory: Demonstrate how you would apply the chosen theory in your work with the client, including specific techniques and interventions that are culturally responsive.

- Ethical Considerations: Identify any ethical considerations related to the client's cultural background and discuss how you would address them in your counseling practice.
- Outcome and Reflection: Reflect on the potential outcomes of your counseling approach and any insights you gained from this exercise about culturally responsive counseling.

Length: Eight to 10 pages, double-spaced, APA format

Culturally Responsive Rubric

Criteria	Excellent (4)	Good (3)	Fair (2)	Needs Improvement (1)
Client Description	Comprehensive and insightful description of the client	Clear and detailed description of the client	Basic description of the client	Minimal or unclear description of the client
Theory Selection	Thorough explanation of theory selection and cultural alignment	Clear explanation of theory selection and cultural alignment	Basic explanation of theory selection and cultural alignment	Minimal or unclear explanation of theory selection
Application of Theory	Detailed and specific application of theory with culturally responsive techniques	Clear application of theory with culturally responsive techniques	Basic application of theory with some culturally responsive techniques	Minimal application of theory with few or no culturally responsive techniques
Ethical Considerations	Comprehensive identification and analysis of ethical considerations	Clear identification and analysis of ethical considerations	Basic identification and analysis of ethical considerations	Minimal identification and analysis of ethical considerations
Outcome and Reflection	In-depth reflection on potential outcomes and insights gained	Clear reflection on potential outcomes and insights gained	Basic reflection on potential outcomes and insights gained	Minimal reflection on potential outcomes and insights gained
Writing Quality	Clear, well-organized, and free of errors	Clear and organized, with few errors	Somewhat clear and organized, with several errors	Unclear or disorganized, with many errors
APA Format	Correct and consistent use of APA format	Mostly correct use of APA format	Some errors in APA format	Many errors in APA format

Ethics and Professional Issues in Counseling (Culturally Responsive Version)

This course explores the ethical and professional issues faced by counselors, with a special focus on cultural competence and advocacy for diverse populations. Students will examine the ethical standards and codes of conduct established by professional counseling organizations, including the American Counseling Association (ACA) Code of Ethics. The course addresses the complexities of ethical decision-making in multicultural contexts, emphasizing the importance of understanding and respecting clients' cultural values and beliefs. Topics such as confidentiality, informed consent, dual relationships, and professional boundaries are discussed through the lens of cultural sensitivity. Students will learn strategies for advocating for equitable access to mental health services and combating systemic barriers that impact marginalized communities. Case studies and real-world scenarios are used to illustrate ethical dilemmas and foster critical thinking skills.

Course Learning Objectives

- Analyze Ethical Standards: Students will examine the ethical standards and codes of conduct established by professional counseling organizations, with a focus on understanding and applying these standards in culturally diverse contexts.
- Navigate Ethical Dilemmas: Students will develop skills to identify and navigate ethical dilemmas that arise in multicultural counseling settings, ensuring that their practices are respectful and inclusive of clients' cultural values and beliefs.
- Advocate for Equity and Access: Students will learn strategies for advocating for equitable access to mental health services and combating systemic barriers that impact marginalized communities.
- Reflect on Cultural Biases: Students will engage in self-reflection to understand their own cultural identities and biases, and learn how to address these biases in their professional practice to provide culturally competent counseling.

CACREP (2024) Standards That Align With This Course

The *Standards* pertinent to this course are located within Section 3, under the subheading "A. PROFESSIONAL COUNSELING ORIENTATION AND ETHICAL PRACTICE" (p. 12). Each of the *Standards* outlined in Section 3 corresponds in some manner to the ethical responsibilities expected of professional counselors. All ethical practices are to be addressed in this course, while other *Standard*s are to be acknowledged and applied through the use of the ACA Code of Ethics. In my instruction, I also incorporate the various competencies that can be found on the ACA website: www.counseling.org.

Example Assignment: Ethical Case Analysis and Reflection Paper

Assignment Directions: Students will select a real-world case or scenario related to ethical and professional issues in counseling. They will analyze the case, identify the relevant ethical standards and legal considerations, and propose appropriate actions and interventions. Additionally, students will reflect on their own values and biases and consider how these might impact their decision-making process.

Instructions:

1. Choose a case or scenario that involves ethical and professional issues in counseling.
2. Identify and explain the relevant ethical standards and legal considerations.
3. Propose appropriate actions and interventions based on the case analysis.

4. Reflect on your own values, biases, and cultural background and discuss how these might influence your decision-making process.
5. Write a five- to seven-page paper that includes your analysis, proposed actions, and reflection.

Culturally Responsive Rubric

Criteria	Excellent (90-100)	Good (80-89)	Satisfactory (70-79)	Needs Improvement (Below 70)
Case Analysis	Thorough analysis with clear identification of ethical standards and legal considerations	Good analysis with clear identification of most ethical standards and legal considerations	Adequate analysis with identification of some ethical standards and legal considerations	Limited analysis with insufficient identification of ethical standards and legal considerations
Proposed Actions and Interventions	Proposed actions are well-reasoned, ethical, and culturally responsive	Proposed actions are ethical and culturally responsive with minor gaps	Proposed actions are somewhat ethical and culturally responsive with several gaps	Proposed actions lack ethical considerations and cultural responsiveness
Reflection on Values and Biases	Insightful and thorough reflection on personal values, biases, and cultural background	Good reflection on personal values, biases, and cultural background	Satisfactory reflection on personal values, biases, and cultural background	Limited reflection on personal values, biases, and cultural background
Writing Quality	Clear, well-organized, and free of errors	Mostly clear and well-organized with minor errors	Somewhat clear with several errors	Unclear and disorganized with numerous errors
Cultural Competence	Demonstrates high cultural competence in analysis and proposed actions	Demonstrates good cultural competence with minor gaps	Demonstrates some cultural competence with several gaps	Lacks cultural competence in analysis and proposed actions
APA Format	Correct and consistent use of APA format	Mostly correct use of APA format	Some errors in APA format	Many errors in APA format

Counseling Across the Life Span (Culturally Responsive Version)

This course explores the developmental stages and transitions that individuals experience from infancy to late adulthood, with a focus on culturally responsive counseling practices. Students will examine the physical, cognitive, emotional, and social development across the life span, recognizing the influence of cultural, social, and environmental factors. The course emphasizes the importance of understanding and respecting clients' cultural backgrounds, family structures, and community contexts when providing counseling services. Students will learn to apply culturally sensitive interventions tailored to the unique developmental needs of clients at different life stages. Topics such as multicultural family dynamics, culturally influenced life transitions, and cross-cultural perspectives on aging will be discussed. Through case studies, role-playing, and interactive discussions, students will develop skills in delivering effective, culturally informed counseling across diverse populations and life-span stages.

Course Learning Objectives

- Understand Developmental Stages: Students will demonstrate an understanding of physical, cognitive, emotional, and social development across the life span, with an emphasis on how cultural, social, and environmental factors influence these stages.
- Develop Culturally Responsive Interventions: Students will learn to apply culturally sensitive counseling interventions tailored to the unique developmental needs of clients at different life stages.
- Analyze Multicultural Family Dynamics: Students will examine multicultural family structures and dynamics, and how these factors impact clients' development and mental health across the life span.
- Promote Cultural Awareness and Sensitivity: Students will enhance their cultural awareness and sensitivity, developing strategies to respect and integrate clients' cultural backgrounds, values, and experiences in counseling practice.

CACREP (2024) Standards That Align With This Course

The primary set of *Standards* is located in Section 3, subheading "C. LIFESPAN DEVELOPMENT" (p. 13). As with previous courses, this course encompasses theories and ethical practices within the learning material. Therefore, it is necessary to review the section and identify the *Standards* in other subheadings that correspond to the learning objectives and outcomes (e.g., assignment and course).

Example Assignment: Life-Span Development Case Study

- Assignment Directions: Select an individual (real or hypothetical) from a specific developmental stage (e.g., infancy, childhood, adolescence, adulthood, or older adulthood). Write a case study that includes the following elements:
  - Individual Description: Provide a detailed description of the individual's cultural background, developmental stage, and relevant personal history.
  - Developmental Milestones: Identify and discuss the key developmental milestones for the selected stage, considering the cultural, social, and environmental factors that influence these milestones.
  - Culturally Responsive Interventions: Propose counseling interventions that are culturally relevant and tailored to the individual's developmental needs and cultural context.

- Ethical Considerations: Identify any ethical considerations related to the individual's cultural background and developmental stage, and discuss how you would address them in your counseling practice.
- Reflection: Reflect on the insights gained from this exercise about culturally responsive counseling across the life span.

Length: Eight to 10 pages, double-spaced, APA format

Culturally Responsive Rubric

Criteria	Excellent (4)	Good (3)	Fair (2)	Needs Improvement (1)
Individual Description	Comprehensive and insightful description of the individual	Clear and detailed description of the individual	Basic description of the individual	Minimal or unclear description of the individual
Developmental Milestones	Thorough discussion of developmental milestones with cultural context	Clear discussion of developmental milestones with cultural context	Basic discussion of developmental milestones with some cultural context	Minimal discussion of developmental milestones with little or no cultural context
Culturally Responsive Interventions	Detailed and specific culturally relevant interventions	Clear culturally relevant interventions	Basic culturally relevant interventions	Minimal or unclear culturally relevant interventions
Ethical Considerations	Comprehensive identification and analysis of ethical considerations	Clear identification and analysis of ethical considerations	Basic identification and analysis of ethical considerations	Minimal identification and analysis of ethical considerations
Reflection	In-depth reflection on insights gained	Clear reflection on insights gained	Basic reflection on insights gained	Minimal reflection on insights gained
Writing Quality	Clear, well-organized, and free of errors	Clear and organized, with few errors	Somewhat clear and organized, with several errors	Unclear or disorganized, with many errors
APA Format	Correct and consistent use of APA format	Mostly correct use of APA format	Some errors in APA format	Many errors in APA format

Career Development in Counseling (Culturally Responsive Version)

This course provides an in-depth examination of career development theories and practices, emphasizing the importance of culturally responsive counseling in supporting clients' career aspirations. Students will explore traditional and contemporary career development theories, considering how cultural, social, and economic factors influence career choices and opportunities. The course highlights the significance of understanding clients' cultural backgrounds, values, and life experiences in career counseling. Students will learn techniques for conducting culturally sensitive career assessments, helping clients set realistic career goals, and developing individualized career plans. Topics such as addressing systemic barriers, promoting equity in career opportunities, and advocating for underrepresented groups in the workforce are covered. Through case studies, role-playing, and interactive discussions, students will develop skills in providing effective, culturally informed career counseling to diverse populations.

Course Learning Objectives

- Integrate Career Development Theories: Students will demonstrate an understanding of traditional and contemporary career development theories, considering the influence of cultural, social, and economic factors on career choices and opportunities.
- Conduct Culturally Sensitive Assessments: Students will develop techniques for conducting career assessments that are respectful and inclusive of clients' cultural backgrounds and life experiences.
- Address Systemic Barriers: Students will learn strategies for identifying and addressing systemic barriers that impact career development, promoting equity in career opportunities for clients from diverse backgrounds.
- Develop Individualized Career Plans: Students will create individualized career plans that are culturally relevant and tailored to the unique needs and aspirations of clients from diverse cultural groups.

CACREP (2024) Standards That Align With This Course

The primary set of *Standards* is located in Section 3, subheading "D. CAREER DEVELOPMENT" (p. 14). Given the numerous advancements in career counseling, contemporary research explores issues such as discrimination, racism in hiring practices, and workplace problems related to political and societal factors. Such issues are more frequently addressed in the therapeutic process and are incorporated into treatment and intervention planning. In my clinical practice, approximately 35% of clients present with career-related concerns that are interconnected with their mental health and overall well-being. Career counseling serves as a core course, a specialization, and integrates topics from other courses within the counselor education curricula. Consequently, it is essential to review additional course *Standards* that are relevant for inclusion in this course.

Example Assignment: Career Development Plan and Presentation

Assignment Directions: Develop a comprehensive career development plan for a client from a diverse cultural background. Prepare a presentation that includes the following elements:

- Client Description: Provide a detailed description of the client's cultural background, career goals, and relevant personal history.
- Career Assessment: Conduct a culturally sensitive career assessment, discussing the tools and methods used.

- Career Development Theories: Apply relevant career development theories to the client's situation, explaining how these theories guide your approach.
- Individualized Career Plan: Develop an individualized career plan that is culturally relevant and tailored to the client's unique needs and aspirations.
- Addressing Barriers: Identify and discuss any systemic barriers the client may face and propose strategies to overcome these barriers.
- Presentation: Prepare a 10-minute presentation summarizing your findings and recommendations. Use visual aids to enhance your presentation.

Length: Eight to 10 pages, double-spaced, APA format (for the written portion)

Culturally Responsive Rubric

Criteria	Excellent (4)	Good (3)	Fair (2)	Needs Improvement (1)
Client Description	Comprehensive and insightful description of the client	Clear and detailed description of the client	Basic description of the client	Minimal or unclear description of the client
Career Assessment	Thorough and culturally sensitive career assessment	Clear and culturally sensitive career assessment	Basic career assessment with some cultural sensitivity	Minimal career assessment with little or no cultural sensitivity
Career Development Theories	In-depth application of relevant career development theories	Clear application of relevant career development theories	Basic application of relevant career development theories	Minimal or unclear application of relevant career development theories
Individualized Career Plan	Detailed and specific culturally relevant career plan	Clear and culturally relevant career plan	Basic culturally relevant career plan	Minimal or unclear culturally relevant career plan
Addressing Barriers	Comprehensive identification and strategies to overcome barriers	Clear identification and strategies to overcome barriers	Basic identification and strategies to overcome barriers	Minimal identification and strategies to overcome barriers
Presentation	Clear, engaging, and well-organized presentation	Clear and organized presentation	Somewhat clear and organized presentation	Unclear or disorganized presentation
Writing Quality	Clear, well-organized, and free of errors	Clear and organized, with few errors	Somewhat clear and organized, with several errors	Unclear or disorganized, with many errors
APA Format	Correct and consistent use of APA format	Mostly correct use of APA format	Some errors in APA format	Many errors in APA format

Assessment and Diagnosing in Counseling (Culturally Responsive Version)

This course focuses on the principles and practices of assessment and diagnosis in counseling, with an emphasis on cultural competence and sensitivity. Students will learn to administer, interpret, and apply a variety of assessment tools and techniques, taking into account the cultural context of each client. The course will cover standardized tests, behavioral observations, clinical interviews, and other diagnostic methods, highlighting the importance of using culturally appropriate and validated instruments. Students will explore the impact of cultural biases on assessment and diagnosis, and learn strategies for mitigating these biases to ensure fair and accurate evaluations. Topics such as understanding cultural expressions of distress, considering cultural factors in diagnostic formulation, and collaborating with clients from diverse backgrounds in the assessment process are discussed. Through case studies and practical exercises, students will develop skills in conducting culturally responsive assessments and making accurate, culturally informed diagnoses.

Course Learning Objectives

- Conduct Culturally Informed Assessments: Students will demonstrate the ability to administer, interpret, and apply a variety of assessment tools and techniques, taking into account the cultural context of each client.
- Mitigate Cultural Biases in Diagnosis: Students will learn strategies for identifying and mitigating cultural biases in the assessment and diagnosis process, ensuring fair and accurate evaluations of clients from diverse backgrounds.
- Develop Culturally Responsive Diagnostic Skills: Students will enhance their skills in understanding cultural variations in the manifestation of mental health disorders and integrate this knowledge into their diagnostic practices.
- Collaborate With Diverse Clients: Students will develop techniques for collaborating with clients from diverse cultural backgrounds throughout the assessment and diagnosis process, ensuring that their perspectives and experiences are respected and incorporated into treatment planning.

CACREP (2024) Standards That Align With This Course

The primary *Standards* for this course are located in Section 3, subheading "G. ASSESSMENT AND DIAGNOSTIC PROCESS" (p. 15). As this set of *Standards* also encompasses course material for the *Psychopathology* course, it is essential to address *Standards* that pertain to ethical diagnostic practices, the sociocultural implications associated with diagnosis, and the systemic issues encountered in psychiatric settings and the institution of mental healthcare. Additionally, it is crucial to cover the comprehensive skill set required for becoming a diagnostician, which professional counselors must use to practice in private settings.

Example Assignment: Culturally Informed Diagnostic Report

Assignment Directions: Choose a client case (real or hypothetical) and write a comprehensive diagnostic report that incorporates cultural considerations. The report should include the following elements:

- Client Description: Provide a detailed description of the client's cultural background, presenting problem, and relevant personal history.
- Assessment Tools and Techniques: Discuss the assessment tools and techniques used, ensuring they are culturally appropriate and sensitive.
- Diagnostic Formulation: Present a diagnostic formulation that considers cultural factors and how they influence the client's symptoms and mental health.
- Treatment Recommendations: Propose culturally responsive treatment recommendations based on the diagnostic findings.
- Ethical Considerations: Identify and discuss any ethical considerations related to the client's cultural background and diagnosis.
- Reflection: Reflect on the process of conducting a culturally informed assessment and diagnosis, including any challenges and insights gained.

Length: 10 to 12 pages, double-spaced, APA format

Culturally Responsive Rubric

Criteria	Excellent (4)	Good (3)	Fair (2)	Needs Improvement (1)
Client Description	Comprehensive and insightful description of the client	Clear and detailed description of the client	Basic description of the client	Minimal or unclear description of the client
Assessment Tools and Techniques	Thorough discussion of culturally appropriate tools and techniques	Clear discussion of culturally appropriate tools and techniques	Basic discussion of tools and techniques with some cultural sensitivity	Minimal discussion of tools and techniques with little or no cultural sensitivity
Diagnostic Formulation	In-depth and culturally informed diagnostic formulation	Clear and culturally informed diagnostic formulation	Basic diagnostic formulation with some cultural considerations	Minimal or unclear diagnostic formulation with few cultural considerations
Treatment Recommendations	Detailed and specific culturally responsive recommendations	Clear and culturally responsive recommendations	Basic culturally responsive recommendations	Minimal or unclear culturally responsive recommendations
Ethical Considerations	Comprehensive identification and analysis of ethical considerations	Clear identification and analysis of ethical considerations	Basic identification and analysis of ethical considerations	Minimal identification and analysis of ethical considerations

(continued)

Culturally Responsive Rubric (continued)

Criteria	Excellent (4)	Good (3)	Fair (2)	Needs Improvement (1)
Reflection	In-depth reflection on process and insights gained	Clear reflection on process and insights gained	Basic reflection on process and insights gained	Minimal reflection on process and insights gained
Writing Quality	Clear, well-organized, and free of errors	Clear and organized, with few errors	Somewhat clear and organized, with several errors	Unclear or disorganized, with many errors
APA Format	Correct and consistent use of APA format	Mostly correct use of APA format	Some errors in APA format	Many errors in APA format

Research Methods in Counseling (Culturally Responsive Version)

This course equips students with the skills and knowledge necessary to conduct and critically evaluate research in counseling, with a special emphasis on cultural competence. Students will explore various research methodologies, including qualitative, quantitative, and mixed methods, and learn how to design and implement research studies that respect and reflect the cultural contexts of diverse populations. The course covers ethical considerations in conducting research with marginalized and underserved communities, ensuring that research practices are inclusive and culturally sensitive. Students will examine how cultural factors influence research questions, data collection, analysis, and interpretation. Through hands-on projects, case studies, and interactive discussions, students will develop the ability to conduct culturally informed research that contributes to the advancement of equitable and effective counseling practices.

Course Learning Objectives

- Design Inclusive Research Studies: Students will demonstrate the ability to design research studies that respect and reflect the cultural contexts of diverse populations, using qualitative, quantitative, and mixed methods.
- Ethical Conduct in Research: Students will understand and apply ethical principles in conducting research with marginalized and underserved communities, ensuring that research practices are inclusive and culturally sensitive.
- Analyze Cultural Influences in Research: Students will critically analyze how cultural factors influence research questions, data collection, analysis, and interpretation and help develop culturally informed research practices.
- Contribute to Equitable Counseling Practices: Students will conduct and evaluate research that contributes to the advancement of equitable and effective counseling practices, promoting social justice and cultural competence in the field.

CACREP (2024) Standards That Align With This Course

The primary set of *Standards* for this course is Section 3, subheading "H. RESEARCH AND PROGRAM" (p. 16). Review other *Standard* areas for corresponding course content that is covered in this course.

Example Assignment: Culturally Inclusive Research Proposal

Assignment Directions: Develop a research proposal that focuses on a counseling-related topic relevant to a specific cultural group or community. Your proposal should include the following elements:

- Research Topic: Clearly define the research topic and its significance to the chosen cultural group or community.
- Literature Review: Conduct a literature review that highlights previous research on the topic and identifies gaps that your study aims to address.
- Research Questions and Hypotheses: Formulate research questions and hypotheses that are culturally sensitive and relevant.
- Research Design and Methods: Describe the research design and methods you will use, ensuring that they are culturally appropriate and inclusive.
- Ethical Considerations: Discuss the ethical considerations involved in conducting research with the chosen cultural group or community, and how you will address them.
- Expected Outcomes and Implications: Outline the expected outcomes of your research and the potential implications for counseling practice and policy.

Length: 12 to 15 pages, double-spaced, APA format

Culturally Responsive Rubric

Criteria	Excellent (4)	Good (3)	Fair (2)	Needs Improvement (1)
Research Topic	Clearly defined and highly significant research topic	Clear and significant research topic	Basic definition and significance of the research topic	Minimal or unclear definition and significance of the research topic
Literature Review	Comprehensive and insightful literature review	Clear and detailed literature review	Basic literature review with some insights	Minimal or unclear literature review
Research Questions and Hypotheses	In-depth and culturally sensitive research questions and hypotheses	Clear and culturally sensitive research questions and hypotheses	Basic research questions and hypotheses with some cultural sensitivity	Minimal research questions and hypotheses with little or no cultural sensitivity

(continued)

Culturally Responsive Rubric (continued)

Criteria	Excellent (4)	Good (3)	Fair (2)	Needs Improvement (1)
Research Design and Methods	Thorough and culturally appropriate research design and methods	Clear and culturally appropriate research design and methods	Basic research design and methods with some cultural appropriateness	Minimal research design and methods with little or no cultural appropriateness
Ethical Considerations	Comprehensive identification and analysis of ethical considerations	Clear identification and analysis of ethical considerations	Basic identification and analysis of ethical considerations	Minimal identification and analysis of ethical considerations
Expected Outcomes and Implications	Detailed and specific expected outcomes and implications	Clear expected outcomes and implications	Basic expected outcomes and implications	Minimal or unclear expected outcomes and implications
Writing Quality	Clear, well-organized, and free of errors	Clear and organized, with few errors	Somewhat clear and organized, with several errors	Unclear or disorganized, with many errors
APA Format	Correct and consistent use of APA format	Mostly correct use of APA format	Some errors in APA format	Many errors in APA format

Multicultural Counseling Practices (Culturally Responsive Version)

This course explores the principles and techniques of multicultural counseling, emphasizing the importance of cultural competence and sensitivity in effective practice. Students will examine various cultural identities and experiences, including race, ethnicity, gender, sexual orientation, socioeconomic status, religion, and ability. The course highlights the impact of systemic oppression, privilege, and social justice issues on mental health and well-being. Students will learn strategies for building rapport and fostering therapeutic relationships with clients from diverse cultural backgrounds. Topics such as culturally adapted interventions, culturally specific models of counseling, and advocacy for marginalized communities are discussed. Through experiential learning, case studies, and self-reflection, students will develop the skills and knowledge necessary to provide respectful, inclusive, and effective counseling to clients from diverse cultural contexts.

Course Learning Objectives

- Understand Cultural Identities and Experiences: Students will demonstrate an understanding of various cultural identities and experiences, including race, ethnicity, gender, sexual orientation, socioeconomic status, religion, and ability, and how these factors impact mental health and counseling practices.

- Develop Culturally Responsive Interventions: Students will learn to design and implement counseling interventions that are culturally relevant and effective, addressing the unique needs and strengths of clients from diverse cultural backgrounds.
- Address Systemic Oppression and Privilege: Students will examine the impact of systemic oppression, privilege, and social justice issues on mental health and develop strategies for advocating for marginalized communities within the counseling context.
- Enhance Cultural Self-Awareness: Students will engage in self-reflection to understand their own cultural identities, biases, and assumptions, and learn how to integrate this awareness into their counseling practice to provide respectful and inclusive care.

CACREP (2024) Standards That Align With This Course

The primary *Standards* for this course are identified in Section 3, subheading "B. SOCIAL AND CULTURAL IDENTITIES AND EXPERIENCES" (p. 13). *Multicultural* course content is now integrated into all courses of the counselor education curricula. Consequently, specific *Standards* from each course are recommended for coverage in this course and consistently throughout the curricula. This exemplifies the paradigm shift that is evident in the evolving teaching practices among CES faculty. However, there is also resistance to such a paradigm shift, whereby some CES faculty, counselors-in-training, and senior professional counselors contest the notion that multiculturalism and social justice should be incorporated into professional practices.

Example Assignment: Multicultural Counseling Intervention Plan

Assignment Directions: Select a specific cultural group and develop a comprehensive counseling intervention plan tailored to their unique needs and experiences. Your intervention plan should include the following elements:

- Cultural Group Description: Provide a detailed description of the cultural group, including relevant historical, social, and cultural factors that impact their mental health.
- Needs Assessment: Conduct a needs assessment to identify the mental health challenges and strengths within the cultural group.
- Intervention Strategies: Develop culturally responsive counseling strategies and interventions that address the identified needs and leverage the group's strengths.
- Ethical Considerations: Discuss the ethical considerations involved in counseling this cultural group and how you will address them.
- Evaluation Plan: Create a plan to evaluate the effectiveness of the intervention, including culturally appropriate assessment tools and methods.

- Reflection: Reflect on the process of developing the intervention plan and any insights gained about multicultural counseling practices.

Length: 10 to 12 pages, double-spaced, APA format

Culturally Responsive Rubric

Criteria	Excellent (4)	Good (3)	Fair (2)	Needs Improvement (1)
Cultural Group Description	Comprehensive and insightful description of the cultural group	Clear and detailed description of the cultural group	Basic description of the cultural group	Minimal or unclear description of the cultural group
Needs Assessment	Thorough and culturally sensitive needs assessment	Clear and culturally sensitive needs assessment	Basic needs assessment with some cultural sensitivity	Minimal needs assessment with little or no cultural sensitivity
Intervention Strategies	Detailed and specific culturally responsive strategies	Clear culturally responsive strategies	Basic culturally responsive strategies	Minimal or unclear culturally responsive strategies
Ethical Considerations	Comprehensive identification and analysis of ethical considerations	Clear identification and analysis of ethical considerations	Basic identification and analysis of ethical considerations	Minimal identification and analysis of ethical considerations
Evaluation Plan	Thorough and culturally appropriate evaluation plan	Clear and culturally appropriate evaluation plan	Basic evaluation plan with some cultural appropriateness	Minimal evaluation plan with little or no cultural appropriateness
Reflection	In-depth reflection on process and insights gained	Clear reflection on process and insights gained	Basic reflection on process and insights gained	Minimal reflection on process and insights gained
Writing Quality	Clear, well-organized, and free of errors	Clear and organized, with few errors	Somewhat clear and organized, with several errors	Unclear or disorganized, with many errors
APA Format	Correct and consistent use of APA format	Mostly correct use of APA format	Some errors in APA format	Many errors in APA format

Group Counseling (Culturally Responsive Version)

This course examines the principles and practices of group counseling, with a strong emphasis on cultural competence and inclusivity. Students will explore the dynamics of group processes and the therapeutic benefits of group counseling, particularly for diverse populations. The course covers various theoretical approaches to group counseling, highlighting strategies for creating a culturally sensitive and supportive group environment. Students will learn techniques for facilitating groups that honor and respect the cultural backgrounds, values, and experiences of all members. Topics such as managing group diversity, addressing cultural biases, and promoting social justice within group settings are discussed. Through experiential learning, role-playing, and case studies, students will develop skills in leading and participating in culturally responsive group counseling sessions.

Course Learning Objectives

- Facilitate Multicultural Group Dynamics: Students will develop the ability to effectively facilitate group counseling sessions, understanding and managing the unique dynamics and therapeutic benefits of diverse groups.
- Create Inclusive Group Environments: Students will learn techniques for creating culturally sensitive and inclusive group environments where all members feel valued and respected.
- Address Cultural Biases in Group Settings: Students will develop strategies to identify and address cultural biases within group counseling, promoting equity and social justice.
- Apply Culturally Adapted Group Interventions: Students will practice and refine culturally adapted group counseling interventions that are relevant and effective for diverse populations.

CACREP (2024) Standards That Align With This Course

The primary *Standard* for this course is in Section 3, subheading "F. GROUP COUNSELING AND GROUP WORK" (p. 15). Other aligned *Standards* are in the sections for ethics, social and cultural, and assessment and diagnostic.

Example Assignment: Group Counseling Facilitation Plan

Assignment Directions: Design a facilitation plan for a group counseling session that is inclusive and culturally responsive. Your plan should include the following elements:

- Group Description: Provide a detailed description of the group, including the cultural backgrounds of the members and the primary focus of the group.
- Group Goals: Identify the goals for the group counseling sessions, considering the cultural needs and strengths of the group members.
- Facilitation Strategies: Develop strategies for facilitating group discussions and activities that are culturally sensitive and promote inclusivity and respect among group members.
- Addressing Cultural Biases: Identify potential cultural biases that may arise in group settings and propose strategies to address and mitigate these biases.
- Evaluation Plan: Create a plan to evaluate the effectiveness of the group counseling sessions, including culturally appropriate assessment tools and methods.

- Reflection: Reflect on the process of developing the facilitation plan and any insights gained about group counseling practices in multicultural settings.

Length: Eight to 10 pages, double-spaced, APA format

Culturally Responsive Rubric

Criteria	Excellent (4)	Good (3)	Fair (2)	Needs Improvement (1)
Group Description	Comprehensive and insightful description of the group	Clear and detailed description of the group	Basic description of the group	Minimal or unclear description of the group
Group Goals	Thorough and culturally sensitive identification of goals	Clear identification of goals with cultural sensitivity	Basic identification of goals with some cultural sensitivity	Minimal identification of goals with little or no cultural sensitivity
Facilitation Strategies	Detailed and specific culturally sensitive facilitation strategies	Clear culturally sensitive facilitation strategies	Basic culturally sensitive facilitation strategies	Minimal or unclear culturally sensitive facilitation strategies
Addressing Cultural Biases	Comprehensive identification and strategies to address cultural biases	Clear identification and strategies to address cultural biases	Basic identification and strategies to address cultural biases	Minimal identification and strategies to address cultural biases
Evaluation Plan	Thorough and culturally appropriate evaluation plan	Clear and culturally appropriate evaluation plan	Basic evaluation plan with some cultural appropriateness	Minimal evaluation plan with little or no cultural appropriateness
Reflection	In-depth reflection on process and insights gained	Clear reflection on process and insights gained	Basic reflection on process and insights gained	Minimal reflection on process and insights gained
Writing Quality	Clear, well-organized, and free of errors	Clear and organized, with few errors	Somewhat clear and organized, with several errors	Unclear or disorganized, with many errors
APA Format	Correct and consistent use of APA format	Mostly correct use of APA format	Some errors in APA format	Many errors in APA format

SPECIALIZATION COURSES

Psychopathology (Culturally Responsive Version)

This course provides a comprehensive examination of mental health disorders, with a strong emphasis on cultural competence and sensitivity. Students will explore the etiology, diagnosis, and treatment of various psychopathologies, considering how cultural factors influence the manifestation and understanding of mental health conditions. The course covers the *Diagnostic and Statistical Manual of Mental Disorders*, Fifth Edition, Text Revision (*DSM-5-TR*) criteria, while also addressing the limitations and cultural biases inherent in the *DSM-5-TR* framework.

Course Learning Objectives

- Analyze Cultural Variations in Psychopathology: Students will demonstrate an understanding of how cultural beliefs and practices impact the expression, interpretation, and treatment of mental health disorders.
- Conduct Culturally Informed Assessments: Students will develop skills in conducting assessments that respect and incorporate clients' cultural contexts, ensuring accurate and fair evaluations.
- Integrate Cultural Factors in Diagnosis and Treatment: Students will learn to consider cultural factors in the diagnostic formulation and develop culturally adapted treatment plans for diverse populations.
- Address Stigma and Promote Resilience: Students will explore the role of cultural stigma in mental health and learn strategies to reduce stigma and promote culturally specific resilience factors in diverse communities.

Example Assignment: Culturally Informed Psychopathology Case Analysis

Assignment Directions: Choose a client case (real or hypothetical) and write a comprehensive case analysis that incorporates cultural considerations in the understanding and diagnosis of psychopathology. The analysis should include the following elements:

- Client Description: Provide a detailed description of the client's cultural background, presenting problem, and relevant personal history.
- Cultural Conceptualization of Psychopathology: Discuss how the client's cultural background influences the conceptualization and manifestation of their mental health condition.
- Diagnostic Formulation: Present a diagnostic formulation that considers cultural factors and how they influence the client's symptoms and mental health.
- Treatment Plan: Develop a culturally responsive treatment plan based on the diagnostic findings, including specific interventions and strategies.
- Ethical Considerations: Identify and discuss any ethical considerations related to the client's cultural background and diagnosis.
- Reflection: Reflect on the process of conducting a culturally informed case analysis and any insights gained about the role of culture in psychopathology.

Length: 10 to 12 pages, double-spaced, APA format

Culturally Responsive Rubric

Criteria	Excellent (4)	Good (3)	Fair (2)	Needs Improvement (1)
Client Description	Comprehensive and insightful description of the client	Clear and detailed description of the client	Basic description of the client	Minimal or unclear description of the client
Cultural Conceptualization of Psychopathology	In-depth discussion of cultural influences on psychopathology	Clear discussion of cultural influences on psychopathology	Basic discussion of cultural influences on psychopathology	Minimal or unclear discussion of cultural influences on psychopathology
Diagnostic Formulation	In-depth and culturally informed diagnostic formulation	Clear and culturally informed diagnostic formulation	Basic diagnostic formulation with some cultural considerations	Minimal or unclear diagnostic formulation with few cultural considerations
Treatment Plan	Detailed and specific culturally responsive treatment plan	Clear culturally responsive treatment plan	Basic culturally responsive treatment plan	Minimal or unclear culturally responsive treatment plan
Ethical Considerations	Comprehensive identification and analysis of ethical considerations	Clear identification and analysis of ethical considerations	Basic identification and analysis of ethical considerations	Minimal identification and analysis of ethical considerations
Reflection	In-depth reflection on process and insights gained	Clear reflection on process and insights gained	Basic reflection on process and insights gained	Minimal reflection on process and insights gained
Writing Quality	Clear, well-organized, and free of errors	Clear and organized, with few errors	Somewhat clear and organized, with several errors	Unclear or disorganized, with many errors
APA Format	Correct and consistent use of APA format	Mostly correct use of APA format	Some errors in APA format	Many errors in APA format

Addictions Counseling (Culturally Responsive Version)

This course explores the principles and practices of addictions counseling, with a strong emphasis on cultural competence and sensitivity. Students will examine the etiology, assessment, diagnosis, and treatment of substance use disorders and other addictive behaviors, considering how cultural factors influence these processes. The course highlights the importance of understanding clients' cultural backgrounds, values, and experiences in developing effective treatment plans.

Course Learning Objectives

- Understand Cultural Variations in Addiction: Students will demonstrate an understanding of how cultural beliefs and practices impact the development, manifestation, and recovery from addiction.
- Conduct Culturally Informed Assessments: Students will develop skills in conducting assessments that respect and incorporate clients' cultural contexts, ensuring accurate and fair evaluations.
- Develop Culturally Responsive Interventions: Students will learn to create and implement treatment plans that are culturally relevant and tailored to the unique needs of clients from diverse cultural backgrounds.
- Address Stigma and Promote Recovery: Students will explore the role of cultural stigma in addiction and learn strategies to reduce stigma and support culturally specific resilience factors in the recovery process.

Example Assignment: Culturally Responsive Addiction Treatment Plan

Assignment Directions: Select a client case (real or hypothetical) and develop a comprehensive addiction treatment plan that incorporates cultural considerations. The plan should include the following elements:

- Client Description: Provide a detailed description of the client's cultural background, presenting problem, and relevant personal history.
- Cultural Conceptualization of Addiction: Discuss how the client's cultural background influences their experience and understanding of addiction.
- Assessment and Diagnosis: Conduct a culturally informed assessment and provide a diagnosis, considering the client's cultural context.
- Treatment Interventions: Develop culturally responsive treatment interventions tailored to the client's needs and cultural background.
- Addressing Stigma: Identify strategies to address cultural stigma related to addiction and support the client's recovery process.
- Ethical Considerations: Discuss any ethical considerations related to the client's cultural background and treatment.
- Reflection: Reflect on the process of developing the addiction treatment plan and any insights gained about culturally responsive counseling.

Length: 10 to 12 pages, double-spaced, APA format

Culturally Responsive Rubric

Criteria	Excellent (4)	Good (3)	Fair (2)	Needs Improvement (1)
Client Description	Comprehensive and insightful description of the client	Clear and detailed description of the client	Basic description of the client	Minimal or unclear description of the client
Cultural Conceptualization of Addiction	In-depth discussion of cultural influences on addiction	Clear discussion of cultural influences on addiction	Basic discussion of cultural influences on addiction	Minimal or unclear discussion of cultural influences on addiction
Assessment and Diagnosis	Thorough and culturally informed assessment and diagnosis	Clear and culturally informed assessment and diagnosis	Basic assessment and diagnosis with some cultural considerations	Minimal or unclear assessment and diagnosis with few cultural considerations
Treatment Interventions	Detailed and specific culturally responsive interventions	Clear culturally responsive interventions	Basic culturally responsive interventions	Minimal or unclear culturally responsive interventions
Addressing Stigma	Comprehensive strategies to address cultural stigma	Clear strategies to address cultural stigma	Basic strategies to address cultural stigma	Minimal or unclear strategies to address cultural stigma
Ethical Considerations	Comprehensive identification and analysis of ethical considerations	Clear identification and analysis of ethical considerations	Basic identification and analysis of ethical considerations	Minimal identification and analysis of ethical considerations
Reflection	In-depth reflection on process and insights gained	Clear reflection on process and insights gained	Basic reflection on process and insights gained	Minimal reflection on process and insights gained
Writing Quality	Clear, well-organized, and free of errors	Clear and organized, with few errors	Somewhat clear and organized, with several errors	Unclear or disorganized, with many errors
APA Format	Correct and consistent use of APA format	Mostly correct use of APA format	Some errors in APA format	Many errors in APA format

Marriage and Family Counseling (Culturally Responsive Version)

This course examines the principles and practices of marriage and family counseling with a strong emphasis on cultural competence and sensitivity. Students will explore various theoretical approaches and techniques for working with couples and families from diverse cultural backgrounds. The course highlights the importance of understanding the cultural context of relationships, family dynamics, and community influences in counseling practice. Students will learn to recognize and address the unique challenges faced by couples and families from different cultural, ethnic, and socioeconomic backgrounds. Emphasis is placed on developing culturally responsive interventions that honor and respect clients' cultural values, traditions, and beliefs. The course also covers ethical and legal considerations in marriage and family counseling, with a focus on advocating for equity and access to mental health services for all clients. Through case studies, role-playing, and experiential learning, students will develop the skills and knowledge necessary to provide effective, culturally informed counseling to couples and families, promoting healthy relationships and fostering resilience within diverse communities.

Course Learning Objectives

- Understand Cultural Contexts in Relationships: Students will demonstrate an understanding of the cultural contexts that influence marriage and family dynamics, including cultural values, traditions, and beliefs.
- Develop Culturally Responsive Interventions: Students will learn to design and implement counseling interventions that are culturally relevant and effective for couples and families from diverse cultural backgrounds.
- Address Multicultural Family Dynamics: Students will explore the unique challenges and strengths of multicultural families and develop strategies to support their mental health and well-being.
- Promote Equity and Access: Students will learn to advocate for equitable access to mental health services for all couples and families, addressing systemic barriers and promoting social justice within the counseling context.

Example Assignment: Culturally Responsive Family Therapy Plan

Assignment Directions: Select a family (real or hypothetical) from a diverse cultural background and develop a comprehensive family therapy plan that incorporates cultural considerations. The plan should include the following elements:

- Family Description: Provide a detailed description of the family's cultural background, presenting issues, and relevant family history.
- Cultural Influences on Family Dynamics: Discuss how the family's cultural background influences their dynamics, communication patterns, and relationships.
- Assessment and Diagnosis: Conduct a culturally informed assessment of the family's presenting issues and provide a diagnosis, considering the cultural context.
- Therapeutic Interventions: Develop culturally responsive therapeutic interventions tailored to the family's needs and cultural background.
- Addressing Cultural Conflicts: Identify and propose strategies to address any cultural conflicts or challenges within the family.
- Ethical Considerations: Discuss any ethical considerations related to the family's cultural background and therapy.

- Reflection: Reflect on the process of developing the family therapy plan and any insights gained about culturally responsive counseling in family settings.

Length: 10 to 12 pages, double-spaced, APA format

Culturally Responsive Rubric

Criteria	Excellent (4)	Good (3)	Fair (2)	Needs Improvement (1)
Family Description	Comprehensive and insightful description of the family	Clear and detailed description of the family	Basic description of the family	Minimal or unclear description of the family
Cultural Influences on Family Dynamics	In-depth discussion of cultural influences on family dynamics	Clear discussion of cultural influences on family dynamics	Basic discussion of cultural influences on family dynamics	Minimal or unclear discussion of cultural influences on family dynamics
Assessment and Diagnosis	Thorough and culturally informed assessment and diagnosis	Clear and culturally informed assessment and diagnosis	Basic assessment and diagnosis with some cultural considerations	Minimal or unclear assessment and diagnosis with few cultural considerations
Therapeutic Interventions	Detailed and specific culturally responsive interventions	Clear culturally responsive interventions	Basic culturally responsive interventions	Minimal or unclear culturally responsive interventions
Addressing Cultural Conflicts	Comprehensive strategies to address cultural conflicts	Clear strategies to address cultural conflicts	Basic strategies to address cultural conflicts	Minimal or unclear strategies to address cultural conflicts
Ethical Considerations	Comprehensive identification and analysis of ethical considerations	Clear identification and analysis of ethical considerations	Basic identification and analysis of ethical considerations	Minimal identification and analysis of ethical considerations
Reflection	In-depth reflection on process and insights gained	Clear reflection on process and insights gained	Basic reflection on process and insights gained	Minimal reflection on process and insights gained
Writing Quality	Clear, well-organized, and free of errors	Clear and organized, with few errors	Somewhat clear and organized, with several errors	Unclear or disorganized, with many errors
APA Format	Correct and consistent use of APA format	Mostly correct use of APA format	Some errors in APA format	Many errors in APA format

Human Sexuality in Counseling (Culturally Responsive Version)

This course explores the complexities of human sexuality and its implications for counseling practice, with a strong emphasis on cultural competence and sensitivity. Students will examine various aspects of human sexuality, including sexual development, orientation, identity, behavior, and relationships, considering how cultural, social, and historical contexts shape these experiences. The course highlights the importance of understanding and respecting clients' diverse sexual identities and expressions in counseling.

Course Learning Objectives

- Understand Cultural Perspectives on Sexuality: Students will demonstrate an understanding of how different cultures view and experience sexuality, and the impact of these perspectives on clients' sexual health and well-being.
- Explore Sexual Identity and Orientation: Students will examine the spectrum of sexual identities and orientations, and the unique challenges faced by LGBTQ+ individuals, integrating this knowledge into their counseling practice.
- Address Sexual Health and Education: Students will develop culturally responsive approaches to addressing issues related to sexual health, education, and access to resources.
- Support Sexual Trauma and Healing: Students will learn to provide culturally sensitive interventions for clients who have experienced sexual trauma, promoting healing and recovery.

Example Assignment: Culturally Informed Sexual Health Education Program

Assignment Directions: Design a sexual health education program that is culturally informed and responsive to the needs of a specific cultural group. Your program should include the following elements:

- Cultural Group Description: Provide a detailed description of the cultural group, including relevant historical, social, and cultural factors that impact their views on sexuality.
- Needs Assessment: Conduct a needs assessment to identify the sexual health education needs and strengths within the cultural group.
- Program Content: Develop culturally relevant content for the sexual health education program, including topics such as sexual identity, orientation, consent, and sexual health practices.
- Educational Strategies: Propose culturally sensitive educational strategies and activities to engage the cultural group in the program.
- Evaluation Plan: Create a plan to evaluate the effectiveness of the program, including culturally appropriate assessment tools and methods.

- Ethical Considerations: Discuss any ethical considerations related to providing sexual health education to the cultural group.
- Reflection: Reflect on the process of developing the sexual health education program and any insights gained about culturally responsive sexual health education.

Length: 10 to 12 pages, double-spaced, APA format

Culturally Responsive Rubric

Criteria	Excellent (4)	Good (3)	Fair (2)	Needs Improvement (1)
Cultural Group Description	Comprehensive and insightful description of the cultural group	Clear and detailed description of the cultural group	Basic description of the cultural group	Minimal or unclear description of the cultural group
Needs Assessment	Thorough and culturally sensitive needs assessment	Clear and culturally sensitive needs assessment	Basic needs assessment with some cultural sensitivity	Minimal needs assessment with little or no cultural sensitivity
Program Content	Detailed and specific culturally relevant content	Clear culturally relevant content	Basic culturally relevant content	Minimal or unclear culturally relevant content
Educational Strategies	Comprehensive and culturally sensitive educational strategies	Clear and culturally sensitive educational strategies	Basic culturally sensitive educational strategies	Minimal or unclear culturally sensitive educational strategies
Evaluation Plan	Thorough and culturally appropriate evaluation plan	Clear and culturally appropriate evaluation plan	Basic evaluation plan with some cultural appropriateness	Minimal evaluation plan with little or no cultural appropriateness
Ethical Considerations	Comprehensive identification and analysis of ethical considerations	Clear identification and analysis of ethical considerations	Basic identification and analysis of ethical considerations	Minimal identification and analysis of ethical considerations
Reflection	In-depth reflection on process and insights gained	Clear reflection on process and insights gained	Basic reflection on process and insights gained	Minimal reflection on process and insights gained
Writing Quality	Clear, well-organized, and free of errors	Clear and organized, with few errors	Somewhat clear and organized, with several errors	Unclear or disorganized, with many errors
APA Format	Correct and consistent use of APA format	Mostly correct use of APA format	Some errors in APA format	Many errors in APA format

Counseling in Community Settings (Culturally Responsive Version)

This course focuses on the principles and practices of providing counseling services in diverse community settings, with a strong emphasis on cultural competence and social justice. Students will explore various models of community-based counseling, considering the unique needs and strengths of different cultural and socioeconomic groups. The course highlights the importance of understanding and addressing the cultural, social, and environmental factors that impact mental health and well-being in community contexts. Students will learn strategies for developing culturally responsive programs and interventions that promote mental health equity and access to care. Topics such as community assessment, program planning, and evaluation are covered, with a focus on culturally sensitive approaches. The course also addresses the role of counselors as advocates and change agents, working to dismantle systemic barriers and promote social justice in their communities. Through case studies, experiential learning, and community engagement projects, students will develop the skills and knowledge necessary to provide effective, culturally informed counseling services in a variety of community settings, ensuring that all individuals and families receive the support they need.

Course Learning Objectives

- Understand Community Contexts: Students will demonstrate an understanding of the cultural, social, and environmental factors that impact mental health and well-being within community settings.
- Develop Culturally Responsive Programs: Students will learn strategies for designing and implementing mental health programs and interventions that are culturally relevant and inclusive, addressing the unique needs of diverse populations.
- Advocate for Social Justice: Students will explore the role of counselors as advocates and change agents, working to dismantle systemic barriers and promote social justice in their communities.
- Engage in Community Assessment: Students will develop skills in conducting community assessments, identifying strengths and needs, and planning culturally sensitive interventions to support mental health and well-being.

Example Assignment: Community-Based Mental Health Program Proposal

Assignment Directions: Develop a proposal for a community-based mental health program that addresses the unique needs of a specific cultural group within a community. Your proposal should include the following elements:

- Community Description: Provide a detailed description of the community and the cultural group, including relevant historical, social, and cultural factors that impact their mental health.

- Needs Assessment: Conduct a needs assessment to identify the mental health challenges and strengths within the cultural group and community.
- Program Design: Develop a culturally responsive program design, including goals, objectives, and specific interventions or activities.
- Implementation Plan: Create a plan for implementing the program, including logistics, resources, and community partnerships.
- Evaluation Plan: Develop a plan to evaluate the effectiveness of the program, including culturally appropriate assessment tools and methods.
- Ethical Considerations: Discuss any ethical considerations related to providing mental health services to the cultural group and community.
- Reflection: Reflect on the process of developing the program proposal and any insights gained about community-based mental health counseling.

Length: 12 to 15 pages, double-spaced, APA format

Culturally Responsive Rubric

Criteria	Excellent (4)	Good (3)	Fair (2)	Needs Improvement (1)
Community Description	Comprehensive and insightful description of the community and cultural group	Clear and detailed description of the community and cultural group	Basic description of the community and cultural group	Minimal or unclear description of the community and cultural group
Needs Assessment	Thorough and culturally sensitive needs assessment	Clear and culturally sensitive needs assessment	Basic needs assessment with some cultural sensitivity	Minimal needs assessment with little or no cultural sensitivity
Program Design	Detailed and specific culturally responsive program design	Clear culturally responsive program design	Basic culturally responsive program design	Minimal or unclear culturally responsive program design
Implementation Plan	Comprehensive and practical implementation plan	Clear and practical implementation plan	Basic implementation plan with some practical elements	Minimal or unclear implementation plan
Evaluation Plan	Thorough and culturally appropriate evaluation plan	Clear and culturally appropriate evaluation plan	Basic evaluation plan with some cultural appropriateness	Minimal evaluation plan with little or no cultural appropriateness
Ethical Considerations	Comprehensive identification and analysis of ethical considerations	Clear identification and analysis of ethical considerations	Basic identification and analysis of ethical considerations	Minimal identification and analysis of ethical considerations

(continued)

Culturally Responsive Rubric (continued)

Criteria	Excellent (4)	Good (3)	Fair (2)	Needs Improvement (1)
Reflection	In-depth reflection on process and insights gained	Clear reflection on process and insights gained	Basic reflection on process and insights gained	Minimal reflection on process and insights gained
Writing Quality	Clear, well-organized, and free of errors	Clear and organized, with few errors	Somewhat clear and organized, with several errors	Unclear or disorganized, with many errors
APA Format	Correct and consistent use of APA format	Mostly correct use of APA format	Some errors in APA format	Many errors in APA format

CLINICAL EXPERIENCE COURSES

Counseling Practicum (Culturally Responsive Version)

This course provides students with hands-on, supervised experience in a counseling setting, emphasizing the importance of cultural competence and sensitivity in practice. Students will apply the theories, skills, and techniques learned in their coursework to real-world counseling situations, working with clients from diverse cultural backgrounds. The practicum experience is designed to enhance students' clinical skills while fostering an understanding of the cultural, social, and systemic factors that influence mental health.

Key components of the course include:

- Supervised Practice: Students will engage in supervised counseling sessions, receiving feedback and guidance from experienced professionals to refine their skills.
- Cultural Competence Development: Emphasis will be placed on understanding and respecting the cultural contexts of clients, including their values, beliefs, and life experiences.
- Ethical Practice: Students will navigate ethical and legal considerations in counseling, with a focus on cultural sensitivity and advocacy for marginalized populations.
- Reflective Learning: Students will engage in reflective practices, such as journaling and supervision meetings, to critically examine their own cultural identities and biases, and to develop culturally responsive approaches to counseling.
- Case Management: Practical experience in case management, including developing treatment plans, documenting sessions, and coordinating care with other professionals.

Through this practicum, students will gain the confidence and competence needed to provide culturally responsive counseling services, ensuring that all clients receive equitable and effective care.

Course Learning Objectives

- Apply Theoretical Knowledge in Practice: Students will demonstrate the ability to apply counseling theories and techniques in real-world settings, working with clients from diverse cultural backgrounds.
- Develop Cultural Competence in Practice: Students will enhance their cultural competence by integrating culturally responsive approaches into their counseling practice, respecting and valuing clients' cultural contexts.
- Navigate Ethical and Legal Considerations: Students will practice navigating ethical and legal issues in counseling, with a focus on cultural sensitivity and advocacy for marginalized populations.
- Engage in Reflective Practice: Students will engage in reflective practices, such as journaling and supervision meetings, to critically examine their own cultural identities and biases, and develop culturally informed approaches to counseling.

CACREP (2024) Standards That Align With This Course

The 2024 CACREP *Standards* require that counseling students complete a supervised practicum experience totaling a minimum of 100 clock hours over a full academic term of at least 10 weeks. Of these hours, at least 40 must be direct service with actual clients to foster the development of counseling skills. Students must receive weekly supervision averaging 1 hour of individual or triadic supervision and participate in 1½ hours of group supervision per week. Supervision must be conducted by qualified faculty or site supervisors in accordance with CACREP guidelines (p. 35).

Example Assignment: Culturally Responsive Counseling Case Presentation

Assignment Directions: Select a client (real or hypothetical) from your practicum experience and develop a comprehensive case presentation that incorporates cultural considerations. Your presentation should include the following elements:

- Client Description: Provide a detailed description of the client's cultural background, presenting problem, and relevant personal history.
- Theoretical Approach: Explain the counseling theory or theories you applied in your work with the client, and how these theories were adapted to be culturally responsive.
- Assessment and Diagnosis: Conduct a culturally informed assessment and provide a diagnosis, considering the client's cultural context.
- Interventions and Techniques: Describe the counseling interventions and techniques you used, highlighting how they were tailored to the client's cultural background.
- Ethical Considerations: Identify any ethical considerations related to the client's cultural background and discuss how you addressed them in your counseling practice.
- Outcomes and Reflections: Reflect on the outcomes of your work with the client, any challenges you faced, and insights gained about culturally responsive counseling.

- Presentation: Prepare a 15-minute presentation summarizing your case, using visual aids to enhance your presentation.

Length: Eight to 10 pages, double-spaced, APA format (for the written portion)

Culturally Responsive Rubric

Criteria	Excellent (4)	Good (3)	Fair (2)	Needs Improvement (1)
Client Description	Comprehensive and insightful description of the client	Clear and detailed description of the client	Basic description of the client	Minimal or unclear description of the client
Theoretical Approach	Thorough explanation and cultural adaptation of theories	Clear explanation and cultural adaptation of theories	Basic explanation and some cultural adaptation of theories	Minimal or unclear explanation and cultural adaptation of theories
Assessment and Diagnosis	Thorough and culturally informed assessment and diagnosis	Clear and culturally informed assessment and diagnosis	Basic assessment and diagnosis with some cultural considerations	Minimal or unclear assessment and diagnosis with few cultural considerations
Interventions and Techniques	Detailed and specific culturally responsive interventions and techniques	Clear culturally responsive interventions and techniques	Basic culturally responsive interventions and techniques	Minimal or unclear culturally responsive interventions and techniques
Ethical Considerations	Comprehensive identification and analysis of ethical considerations	Clear identification and analysis of ethical considerations	Basic identification and analysis of ethical considerations	Minimal identification and analysis of ethical considerations
Outcomes and Reflections	In-depth reflection on outcomes, challenges, and insights	Clear reflection on outcomes, challenges, and insights	Basic reflection on outcomes, challenges, and insights	Minimal reflection on outcomes, challenges, and insights
Presentation	Clear, engaging, and well-organized presentation	Clear and organized presentation	Somewhat clear and organized presentation	Unclear or disorganized presentation
Writing Quality	Clear, well-organized, and free of errors	Clear and organized, with few errors	Somewhat clear and organized, with several errors	Unclear or disorganized, with many errors
APA Format	Correct and consistent use of APA format	Mostly correct use of APA format	Some errors in APA format	Many errors in APA format

Counseling Internship (Culturally Responsive Version)

The counseling internship provides advanced, supervised clinical experience in a professional counseling setting, with a strong emphasis on cultural competence and sensitivity. During this intensive internship, students will apply their theoretical knowledge and practical skills to work with clients from diverse cultural backgrounds, addressing a wide range of mental health issues. The internship is designed to deepen students' understanding of the cultural, social, and systemic factors that influence mental health and well-being.

Key components of the course include:

- Supervised Clinical Practice: Students will engage in extensive, supervised counseling sessions, receiving regular feedback and guidance from experienced supervisors to enhance their clinical skills.
- Cultural Competence Development: Emphasis will be placed on integrating culturally responsive approaches into all aspects of counseling, including assessment, intervention, and treatment planning.
- Ethical Practice: Students will navigate ethical and legal considerations in counseling, focusing on cultural sensitivity and advocacy for marginalized and underserved populations.
- Reflective Practice: Students will engage in continuous self-reflection and supervision meetings to critically examine their own cultural identities and biases, and to develop culturally informed counseling strategies.
- Case Management and Documentation: Students will develop practical experience in case management, including developing comprehensive treatment plans, documenting sessions, and coordinating care with other professionals and community resources.
- Professional Development: Students will participate in professional development activities, such as attending workshops, conferences, and trainings focused on cultural competence and social justice in counseling.

Through this internship, students will gain the advanced skills and experience necessary to provide effective, culturally responsive counseling services, preparing them for professional practice in diverse community settings.

Course Learning Objectives

- Integrate Theoretical Knowledge and Practice: Students will demonstrate the ability to apply counseling theories and techniques in a professional setting, working with clients from diverse cultural backgrounds.
- Develop Advanced Cultural Competence: Students will enhance their cultural competence by incorporating culturally responsive approaches into all aspects of their counseling practice, including assessment, intervention, and treatment planning.
- Navigate Ethical and Legal Issues: Students will practice addressing ethical and legal issues in counseling, with a focus on cultural sensitivity and advocacy for marginalized and underserved populations.

- Engage in Reflective Practice and Supervision: Students will participate in continuous self-reflection and supervision meetings to critically examine their own cultural identities and biases, thereby developing culturally informed counseling strategies.
- Conduct Case Management and Documentation: Students will gain practical experience in case management, including developing comprehensive treatment plans, documenting sessions, and coordinating care with other professionals and community resources.

CACREP (2024) Standards That Align With This Course

Following successful completion of the practicum, counseling students must engage in a supervised internship totaling at least 600 clock hours in settings aligned with their specialized practice area. Of these hours, a minimum of 240 must be direct service with actual clients, allowing students to refine their counseling competencies in real-world contexts. The internship also includes opportunities to lead or co-lead counseling or psychoeducational groups, and students are expected to become familiar with a range of professional activities and resources. Supervision and evaluation are integral throughout the experience, ensuring that students demonstrate the ability to integrate and apply their knowledge effectively (p. 36).

Example Assignment: Comprehensive Counseling Internship Portfolio

Assignment Directions: Throughout your counseling internship, compile a comprehensive portfolio that demonstrates your ability to integrate cultural competence into your counseling practice. Your portfolio should include the following elements:

- Case Studies: Document at least three detailed case studies of clients from diverse cultural backgrounds, including cultural considerations, assessment, diagnosis, interventions, and outcomes.
- Reflective Journals: Maintain weekly reflective journals that capture your experiences, challenges, and insights related to culturally responsive counseling during your internship.
- Supervision Notes: Include notes and feedback from your supervision sessions that highlight your development and application of cultural competence in your practice.
- Professional Development: Document any professional development activities related to cultural competence, such as workshops, training sessions, or conferences attended.
- Ethical Dilemmas: Analyze any ethical dilemmas encountered during your internship that involved cultural considerations, including how you resolved them and the impact on your practice.
- Final Reflection: Write a final reflection that synthesizes your learning experiences and growth in culturally responsive counseling throughout your internship.

Length: Varies by component; final reflection should be five to seven pages, double-spaced, APA format

Culturally Responsive Rubric

Criteria	Excellent (4)	Good (3)	Fair (2)	Needs Improvement (1)
Case Studies	Comprehensive and insightful case studies with cultural considerations	Clear and detailed case studies with cultural considerations	Basic case studies with some cultural considerations	Minimal or unclear case studies with few cultural considerations
Reflective Journals	Thorough and reflective weekly entries capturing cultural insights	Clear and reflective weekly entries capturing cultural insights	Basic weekly entries with some cultural insights	Minimal or unclear weekly entries with few cultural insights
Supervision Notes	Comprehensive and insightful supervision notes with cultural feedback	Clear and detailed supervision notes with cultural feedback	Basic supervision notes with some cultural feedback	Minimal or unclear supervision notes with little cultural feedback
Professional Development	Thorough documentation of professional development activities	Clear documentation of professional development activities	Basic documentation of professional development activities	Minimal or unclear documentation of professional development activities
Ethical Dilemmas	In-depth analysis of ethical dilemmas with cultural considerations	Clear analysis of ethical dilemmas with cultural considerations	Basic analysis of ethical dilemmas with some cultural considerations	Minimal or unclear analysis of ethical dilemmas with few cultural considerations
Final Reflection	In-depth and comprehensive final reflection synthesizing learning experiences	Clear and detailed final reflection synthesizing learning experiences	Basic final reflection with some synthesis of learning experiences	Minimal or unclear final reflection with little synthesis of learning experiences
Writing Quality	Clear, well-organized, and free of errors	Clear and organized, with few errors	Somewhat clear and organized, with several errors	Unclear or disorganized, with many errors
APA Format	Correct and consistent use of APA format	Mostly correct use of APA format	Some errors in APA format	Many errors in APA format

TEXTBOOKS AND ASSIGNED READING FOR THE COURSES

Table 5.2 offers a textbook and article listing for the courses covered in this chapter.

TABLE 5.2 Contemporary Textbooks and Reading Assignments That Align With the Courses Covered in This Chapter.

Course	Textbooks	Assigned Readings (Examples)
Foundations in Counseling	Gerig, M. S. (2020). *Foundations for clinical mental health counseling: An introduction to the profession* (3rd ed.). Pearson. Sue, D. W., Sue, D., Neville, H. A., & Smith, L. (2019). *Counseling the culturally diverse: Theory and practice* (8th ed.). Wiley.	Peters, H. C., Luke, M., Bernard, J., & Trepal, H. (2019). *Culturally responsive strengths-based therapy: The journey to becoming a culturally responsive therapist.* Springer Publishing Company.
Counseling Theories and Techniques	Corey, G. (2016). *Theory and practice of counseling and psychotherapy* (10th ed.). Cengage Learning. Flynn, S. V., & Castleberry, J. J. (2023). *Counseling theories and case conceptualization: A practice-based approach.* Springer.	Cain, D. J., & Haley, J. (2021). *Integrative approaches to psychotherapy: A comprehensive guide to theory and practice.* Springer Publishing Company.
Ethics and Professional Issues in Counseling	Remley, T. P., & Herlihy, B. (2020). *Ethical, legal, and professional issues in counseling* (6th ed.). Pearson.	Barnett, J. E. (2019). The ethical practice of psychotherapy: Clearly within our reach. *Psychotherapy, 56*(4), 431–440. https://doi.org/10.1037/pst0000272
Counseling Across the Life Span	Santrock, J. W. (2021). *Life-span development* (16th ed.). McGraw-Hill Education.	Kuther, T. L., & Burnell, K. (2019). A life span developmental perspective on psychosocial development in midlife. *Adultspan Journal, 18*(1), Article 3. https://mds.marshall.edu/adsp/vol18/iss1/3
Career Development in Counseling	Niles, S. G., & Harris-Bowlsbey, J. (2021). *Career development interventions* (6th ed.). Pearson.	Zunker, V. G. (2020). *Career counseling: A holistic approach* (10th ed.). Cengage Learning.
Assessment and Diagnosing in Counseling	Hays, D. G. (2023). *Assessment in counseling: Procedures and practices* (7th ed.). American Counseling Association. Sattler, J. M., & Ryan, J. J. (2021). *Assessment of children: Cognitive foundations and applications* (6th ed.). Sattler Publisher.	Martin-Key, N. A., Spadaro, B., Funnell, E., Barker, E. J., Schei, T. S., Tomasik, J., & Bahn, S. (2022). The current state and validity of digital assessment tools for psychiatry: SYSTEMATIC review. *JMIR Mental Health, 9*(3), e32824. https://doi.org/10.2196/32824
Research Methods in Counseling	Balkin, R. S., & Kleist, D. M. (2022). *Counseling research: A practitioner-scholar approach* (2nd ed.). American Counseling Association.	Wittenborn, A. K., Blow, A. J., Holtrop, K., & Parra-Cardona, J. R. (2019). Strengthening clinical research in marriage and family therapy: Challenges and multilevel solutions. *Journal of Marital and Family Therapy, 45*(1), 20–32. https://doi.org/10.1111/jmft.12338
Multicultural Counseling Practices	Ivey, A. E., Ivey, M., & Zalaquett, C. P. (2024). *Essentials of intentional counseling and psychotherapy in a multicultural world* (4th ed.). Cengage.	Tanaka-Matsumi, J. (2022). Counseling across cultures: A half-century assessment. *Journal of Cross-Cultural Psychology, 53*(7–8), 957–975. https://doi.org/10.1177/00220221221111810

(continued)

TABLE 5.2 Contemporary Textbooks and Reading Assignments That Align With the Courses Covered in This Chapter *(continued)*

Course	Textbooks	Assigned Readings (Examples)
Group Counseling	Bernard, J. M., Greene, B., & Wampold, J. A. (2022). *Group counseling: Strategies and skills* (8th ed.). Cengage. Curtis, R. K., & Jacobs, M. D. (2023). *The essentials of group therapy* (2nd ed.). Wiley.	Wang, L. F., Kivlighan, D. M., Wei, M., Kivlighan, D. M., Hung, Y. L., & Koay, E. Y. Y. (2023). Changes in group counseling engagement and conflict and growth in emotional cultivation for children and adolescents. *Journal of Counseling Psychology, 70*(2), 159–171. https://doi.org/10.1037/cou0000648
Psychopathology	Barlow, D. H. (2021). *Clinical handbook of psychological disorders: A step-by-step treatment manual* (6th ed.). The Guilford Press.	Bradley, L., Noble, N., & Hendricks, B. (2023). *DSM-5-TR:* Salient changes. *The Family Journal, 31*(1), 5–10. https://doi.org/10.1177/10664807221123558
Addictions Counseling	Brady, K. T., Levin, F. R., Galanter, M., & Kleber, H. D. (2021). *The American Psychiatric Association publishing textbook of substance use disorder treatment* (6th ed.). American Psychiatric Association Publishing. Capuzzi, D., & Stauffer, M. D. (2020). *Foundations of addictions counseling* (4th ed.). Pearson.	Stubbe, D. E. (2024). Addressing stigmas that hinder addiction treatment and recovery. *Focus, 22*(4), 501–504. https://psychiatryonline.org/doi/pdf/10.1176/appi.focus.20240023
Marriage and Family Counseling	Nichols, M. P., & Davis, S. (2020). *Family therapy: Concepts and methods* (12th ed.). Pearson.	D'Aniello, C., & Fife, S. T. (2020). A 20-year review of common factors research in marriage and family therapy: A mixed methods content analysis. *Journal of Marital and Family Therapy, 46*(1), 5–25. https://doi.org/10.1111/jmft.12427
Human Sexuality in Counseling	Carroll, J. L. (2021). *Sexuality now: Embracing diversity* (4th ed.). Cengage Learning. Yarber, W. L., & Lasswell, B. R. (2022). *Human sexuality: Diversity in contemporary America* (10th ed.). McGraw-Hill Education.	Döring, N., Le, T. D., Vowels, L. M., Vowels, M. J., & Marcantonio, T. L. (2024). The impact of artificial intelligence on human sexuality: A five-year literature review 2020–2024. *Current Sexual Health Reports. 17,* Article 4. https://doi.org/10.1007/s11930-024-00397-y
Counseling in Community Settings	Gladding, S. T., & Newsome, D. W. (2020). *Clinical mental health counseling in community and agency settings* (5th ed.). Pearson. Munson, M. R. (2021). *Community mental health: Challenges for the 21st century* (2nd ed.). Cengage Learning.	Heetderks-Fong, E., & Bobb, A. (2024). Community mental health workers: Their workplaces, roles, and impact. *Community Mental Health Journal. 60,* 1547–1556. https://doi.org/10.1007/s10597-024-01306-2

(continued)

TABLE 5.2 Contemporary Textbooks and Reading Assignments That Align With the Courses Covered in This Chapter *(continued)*

Course	Textbooks	Assigned Readings (Examples)
Counseling Practicum and Internship	Jungers, C. M., Scott, J., & Gregoire, J. (2024). *Practicum and internship: Textbook and resource guide for counseling and psychotherapy* (7th ed.). American Counseling Association.	Ikonomopoulos, J., Cavazos Vela, J., Smith, W. D., & Dell'Aquila, J. (2023). Examining the practicum experience to increase counseling students' self-efficacy. *The Professional Counselor*. 6(2), 161–173. doi:10.15241/ji.6.2.161

CHAPTER RESOURCES

Culturally Responsive Counselor Educator Skills

CRCE Skills to Further Develop From This Chapter	
1. Develop cultural self-awareness and examine personal biases.	11. Develop skills for culturally sensitive assessment and diagnosis.
2. Understand diverse cultural worldviews and experiences.	12. Learn to advocate for equity and social justice.
3. Design inclusive course descriptions and learning objectives.	13. Practice culturally informed research methods.
4. Select culturally diverse and representative course materials/readings.	14. Build skills for addressing cultural conflicts and microaggressions.
5. Create culturally relevant assignments and activities.	15. Enhance abilities to create inclusive group counseling environments.
6. Construct fair and unbiased assessment rubrics.	16. Develop culturally adapted interventions and treatment planning.
7. Incorporate discussions of power, privilege, and systemic oppression.	17. Improve cross-cultural communication and relationship building.
8. Use culturally responsive teaching methods and facilitation skills.	18. Learn to integrate cultural factors in case conceptualization.
9. Adapt counseling theories/techniques for diverse populations.	19. Enhance cultural humility and lifelong multicultural learning.
10. Address ethical considerations in multicultural counseling.	20. Develop abilities to provide culturally responsive supervision.

Note: The objective of these skills is infusing cultural responsiveness throughout all aspects of counselor education, from course design to implementation to evaluation. This cultural responsiveness helps prepare counselors-in-training to work effectively with diverse client populations, better understand themselves in the process of learning, and encourage critical thinking skills that encompass the sociopolitical-cultural climate and landscape in a shared society.

CRCE, culturally responsive counselor educator.

CONTENT SUMMARY	
This chapter presents scholarly insights into the process of reframing core and specialization courses that constitute the primary components of counselor education curricula. The outline to the right delineates the elements addressed in the chapter. It is recommended to use the previously noted CRCE Skills Textbox as a reference when developing content for your courses.	• Developing course description • Creating learning objectives that are based on the most current revision of the CACREP *Standards* (2024) • Building course assignments • Designing parallel rubrics to the assignments • Determining current textbooks for the courses • Developing sample reading assignments that are not in the textbooks

Advanced Reflection Questions

1. How do the course objectives reflect and respect the diverse cultural backgrounds of students?
2. In what ways do the assignments promote cultural awareness and inclusivity?
3. How are the rubrics designed to be fair and unbiased across different cultural contexts?
4. What strategies are used in the assigned readings to highlight diverse perspectives and experiences?
5. How do the course materials encourage students to critically reflect on their own cultural biases and assumptions?
6. What measures are taken to ensure that the course content is accessible and relevant to students from various cultural backgrounds?
7. How do the assignments and rubrics support the development of culturally responsive counseling practices?
8. In what ways do the course objectives and readings foster an inclusive and equitable learning environment?
9. How can the course materials be improved to better address the needs of culturally diverse students?

Further Reading

Tripp, L. O., & Collier, R. M. (2019). *Culturally responsive teaching and learning in higher education*. Information Science Reference. https://doi.org/10.4018/978-1-5225-9989-0

Crosby-Cooper, T. (2020). *Implementing culturally responsive practices in education.* IGI Global. https://doi.org/10.4018/978-1-7998-3331-4

REFERENCES

Council for Accreditation of Counseling and Related Educational Programs. (2024). *2024 CACREP standards*. Council for Accreditation of Counseling and Related Educational Programs.

Haskins, N. H., Harris, J. A., Parker, J., Nambiar, A., & Chin, P. (2023). Teaching anti-racist counseling theories: Black liberation narrative therapy. *Counselor Education and Supervision, 62*(4), 355–367. https://doi.org/10.1002/ceas.12286

CHAPTER 6

CULTURALLY RESPONSIVE TEACHING IN THE ERA OF ARTIFICIAL INTELLIGENCE

Therefore, while AI can be a supportive tool, it should not replace the professional judgment of professional counselors. It is recommended that AI be used as an adjunct to, rather than a replacement for, the expertise provided by professional counselors.

—American Counseling Association

LEARNING OBJECTIVES After studying this chapter, you will be able to:

- Acquire a comprehensive understanding of emerging and contemporary AI programs and tools used in counselor education and learn how these tools can be appropriately implemented by faculty.
- Develop the ability to analyze the ethical responsibilities associated with the use of AI in counseling, identify potential challenges in implementing AI, and propose viable solutions to these challenges, aligning with the strategies proposed by the American Counseling Association (ACA).
- Develop the competencies to effectively implement AI tools in assessment and evaluation processes and formulate strategies to maintain relevance and efficacy in an AI-driven educational environment.

SNAPSHOT: A counselor educator's career experience

During a counseling session with an adolescent client who was discussing experiences of stress and academic assignments, the client recounted an instance where she was required to "write an essay by hand." In her explanation for the manual writing requirement, as opposed to typing, she indicated that this directive was her teacher's method of ensuring students were not using artificial intelligence (AI) to complete the assignment. After this session and with the parent of the client, this dialogue prompted a reflection on students in my own course, where I had recently completed grading an assignment and observed that the majority of submitted papers exhibited significant similarities in format and content. This observation led to speculation regarding the potential use of AI in completing the assignment. At the commencement of the previous fall semester, I received updated content for course syllabi that focused on AI and its ethical use. Initially, I did not anticipate that this would be a concern for counselor education and supervision (CES) faculty; however, it has become apparent that it is indeed a relevant issue for the profession.

INTRODUCTION

As artificial intelligence (AI) continues to evolve, its influence on counselor education and the profession of counseling is becoming increasingly significant. From curriculum design to clinical training, AI offers transformative possibilities that can enrich teaching, supervision, assessment, and professional practice. This chapter explores five key dimensions of AI integration within counselor education. First, it examines how AI-enhanced training and supervision can create immersive, interactive learning environments that support skill development and reflective practice. Second, it considers AI-driven assessment and evaluation, highlighting how adaptive feedback and data-informed insights can improve student learning outcomes. Third, it addresses the ethical complexities of AI use, including concerns around privacy, algorithmic bias, and the preservation of human-centered counseling values. Fourth, it explores AI's emerging role in counseling practice, demonstrating how intelligent tools can assist counselors while maintaining relational integrity. Finally, the chapter looks ahead to future innovations, considering how AI may reshape counselor education and professional identity in the years to come. Together, these subtopics offer a comprehensive and culturally responsive framework for understanding AI's impact on counselor preparation and the counseling profession.

INTEGRATIVE ARTIFICIAL INTELLIGENCE IN COUNSELING TRAINING AND SUPERVISION

The integration of AI in counselor training and supervision represents a significant paradigm shift in educational methodology, offering innovative approaches to enhance the learning experience. AI-driven simulations and virtual reality technologies can create immersive role-playing scenarios that enable students to practice and refine their counseling skills in a controlled, low-risk environment. These tools can provide immediate, detailed feedback, assisting students in identifying areas for improvement and monitoring their progress over time. Furthermore, AI can support supervisors by automating routine administrative tasks, such as scheduling and record-keeping, thereby allowing them to allocate more time to providing personalized guidance and support. This subtopic examines the various applications of AI in improving the efficacy and efficiency of counselor training and supervision, ultimately contributing to the preparation of graduates who are better equipped to meet the demands of the profession.

Helpful resources for faculty looking to integrate AI into counselor education training and supervision include:

- American Counseling Association (ACA) AI Work Group Recommendations: The ACA has developed guidelines and recommendations for the ethical and inclusive use of AI in counseling education (ACA, n.d.-a, n.d.-b). These resources provide best practices and emphasize the importance of maintaining ethical standards and promoting diversity, equity, and inclusion (DEI).

- University-Specific Guidelines: Faculty should consult their institution's guidelines on the acceptable use of AI technologies. These policies are continuously updated to address ethical, legal, and academic integrity concerns.
- Interdisciplinary Collaboration: Engaging in interdisciplinary collaboration with experts in AI, computer science, and counseling can foster a holistic approach to integrating AI into counselor education (Broadwater & Moore, 2022). This collaboration can help ensure that AI tools are ethically sound, culturally sensitive, and meet the clinical needs of students and clients.

ARTIFICIAL INTELLIGENCE–DRIVEN ASSESSMENT AND EVALUATION

AI-driven assessment and evaluation offer significant advancements in counselor education by providing personalized and data-informed feedback. These AI-based tools can analyze student performance in real-time, identifying strengths and areas requiring improvement with a level of precision and efficiency that traditional methods often lack. Machine learning algorithms can track patterns and trends in student interactions, assignments, and practice sessions, enabling faculty to tailor their pedagogical strategies to better address individual student needs. Furthermore, AI can support formative assessments by offering timely feedback and adaptive learning paths, facilitating student engagement and progress. This subtopic examines the potential benefits of AI-driven assessment and evaluation in enhancing the efficacy of counselor education programs and improving student outcomes.

Helpful resources for faculty looking to integrate AI into assessment and evaluation include:

- Chatbots and Virtual Assistants: Tools like ChatGPT and Google Bard can assist in providing initial counseling support, answering frequently asked questions, and offering resources to students.
- AI-Powered Assessment Tools: Platforms like Kira Talent and HireVue can be used for conducting interviews and assessments and providing automated feedback to students.
- Learning Management Systems (LMS) With AI Integration: Systems like Canvas and Blackboard often have AI features that can track student progress, provide personalized learning paths, and offer predictive analytics to identify students who may need additional support.
- Data Analytics Tools: Tools like Tableau and Power BI can help faculty analyze student data, identify trends, and make data-driven decisions to improve educational outcomes.
- AI-Enhanced Research Tools: Tools like Semantic Scholar and Google Scholar can assist faculty and students in finding relevant research articles, papers, and resources more efficiently.

OTHER COMMON ARTIFICIAL INTELLIGENCE RESOURCES GROWING IN USE

- AI for Accessibility and Inclusion: Tools like Otter.ai for real-time captioning and translation, and ReadSpeaker for text-to-speech and speech-to-text capabilities, can enhance accessibility for students with disabilities.
- AI-Enhanced Research Support: Platforms like Mendeley for literature review and Plotly for advanced data visualization can aid in academic research by streamlining processes and uncovering valuable insights.
- AI in Research Administration: Tools like ResearchGate for identifying funding opportunities and Grants.gov for automated grant management can optimize research administration processes.
- Predictive Analytics: Tools like Course Signals and Early Alert Systems can help identify at-risk students and provide timely interventions to support their success.
- Adaptive Learning Platforms: Platforms like DreamBox Learning and Smart Sparrow offer personalized learning experiences tailored to individual student needs.

ETHICAL CONSIDERATIONS AND CHALLENGES

The integration of AI in counselor education presents significant ethical considerations and challenges that necessitate careful navigation. Primary concerns include data privacy, wherein the collection, storage, and utilization of student information must adhere to legal and ethical standards to safeguard individuals' privacy and confidentiality. Furthermore, biases inherent in AI algorithms have the potential to perpetuate or exacerbate existing inequities if left unaddressed, underscoring the importance of developing and implementing AI tools with a commitment to fairness and inclusivity. The human element of counseling, which relies on empathy, intuition, and interpersonal connections, cannot be fully replicated by AI, posing a challenge to maintaining the core values of the profession (Chan, 2023). This subtopic examines these ethical considerations and challenges, offering guidance on how to address them responsibly while harnessing AI's potential benefits.

Solutions to Ethical Issues and Challenges That May Surface With the Use of Artificial Intelligence

The implementation of strategies to address the ethical considerations and challenges associated with the integration of AI in counselor education programs encompasses several key approaches. The following are a few solutions:

- Developing Comprehensive Policies: Institutions should create and regularly update comprehensive policies that address data privacy, confidentiality, and ethical use of AI tools. These policies should be aligned with legal standards and ethical guidelines, such as those provided by the ACA.
- Ensuring Transparency and Informed Consent: Faculty and students should be transparent about the use of AI, explaining its what its purpose is, what its limitations are,

and how it works. Obtaining informed consent from students and clients is crucial, allowing them to opt out if they choose.

- Providing Training and Education: Offering training sessions and workshops on the ethical use of AI can help faculty and students understand the technology's capabilities and limitations. This includes understanding how to evaluate AI content for accuracy and bias.
- Implementing Human Oversight: AI tools should be used as aids, not replacements for human judgment. Counselors must maintain responsibility for clinical decisions and ensure that AI-generated recommendations are reviewed and applied appropriately.
- Promoting DEI: AI tools should be evaluated for biases and designed to promote DEI. This involves incorporating diverse perspectives in the development and implementation of AI systems and ensuring that they do not perpetuate existing inequities.
- Regularly Reviewing and Updating AI Practices: Institutions should continuously monitor and review their AI practices to ensure they remain ethical and effective. Such review includes staying informed about the latest developments in AI and adjusting practices as needed.

With the implementation of these strategies, counselor education programs can responsibly integrate AI while upholding ethical standards and promoting the well-being of students and clients (Parsons et al., 2024).

ARTIFICIAL INTELLIGENCE IN COUNSELING PRACTICE AND CLIENT INTERACTION

AI possesses the potential to transform counseling practice and client interaction, offering innovative tools that can enhance the quality and accessibility of counseling services (Sheikh et al., 2023). AI-powered chatbots and virtual assistants can provide immediate, continuous support to clients, facilitating the bridging of gaps in care and offering timely interventions. These tools can assist with initial assessments, provide psychoeducation, and offer resources and self-help strategies, thereby enabling counselors to focus on more complex and personalized care. Furthermore, AI can analyze large data sets to identify trends and patterns in client behavior, offering valuable insights that can inform treatment planning and improve outcomes. This subtopic examines the various ways AI can support and enhance counseling practice, ensuring that both counselors and clients benefit from its integration.

Helpful resources for integrating AI in counseling practice and client interaction include:

- Chatbots and Virtual Assistants: Tools like Woebot and Replika offer AI-powered chatbot services that provide initial support, psychoeducation, and self-help strategies to clients.
- AI-Powered Assessment Tools: Platforms like TheraNest and Quenza can assist counselors in conducting assessments, tracking client progress, and providing personalized feedback.

- Data Analytics Tools: Tools like Tableau and Power BI can help counselors analyze client data, identify trends, and make data-driven decisions to improve treatment outcomes.
- Virtual Counseling Platforms: Platforms like BetterHelp and Talkspace offer AI-enhanced virtual counseling services, allowing clients to access support from licensed counselors online.
- AI-Enhanced Research Tools: Tools like Semantic Scholar and Google Scholar can assist counselors in finding relevant research articles, papers, and resources more efficiently.
- AI-Powered Role-Playing Simulations: Tools like Mursion offer AI-driven simulations where students can practice counseling skills in a virtual environment with AI-generated clients. This helps students develop their skills in a controlled, risk-free setting.
- Virtual Reality (VR) Counseling Simulations: Platforms like Oculus Rift and HTC Vive can be used to create immersive VR environments for students to practice counseling sessions, enhancing their ability to handle various scenarios.

FUTURE DIRECTIONS AND INNOVATIONS

As AI technology continues to advance, its potential applications in counselor education are poised to expand significantly, potentially leading to substantial innovations in the field. One promising direction is the development of more sophisticated AI-driven simulations that provide realistic, immersive experiences for students to practice their counseling skills. Furthermore, advancements in natural language processing (NLP) and machine learning could result in more accurate and personalized AI tools for assessment, feedback, and intervention planning. The integration of AI with wearable technology and biofeedback may offer novel approaches to monitor and support clients' mental health in real-time. Moreover, as ethical AI development becomes a priority, it is anticipated that more tools will be designed with a focus on inclusivity, fairness, and cultural sensitivity. This subtopic explores these future directions and innovations, highlighting the potential developments that may arise for AI in counselor education and practice.

REMAINING RELEVANT IN THE ERA OF ARTIFICIAL INTELLIGENCE

The work of Joseph E. Aoun (2017), *Robot-Proof: Higher Education in the Age of Artificial Intelligence*, holds significant relevance for both novice and experienced faculty members in counselor education. The publication emphasizes the critical nature of human literacy, data literacy, and technological literacy in preparing students for a future in which AI plays a prominent role. Aoun posits that a "robot-proof" education should prioritize the development of students' creative and critical thinking skills, enabling them to innovate, generate, and discover solutions beyond the capabilities of even sophisticated AI systems.

BOX 6.1 Highlights from *Robot-Proof: Higher Education in the Age of Artificial Intelligence* (Aoun, 2017)

- Humanics: Aoun introduces the concept of "humanics," a new discipline that combines technological literacy, data literacy, and human literacy. This framework aims to prepare students to work alongside smart machines while leveraging their unique human capabilities.
- Lifelong Learning: The book emphasizes the importance of lifelong learning as a means to adapt to the rapidly changing job market. Aoun advocates for a social compact between universities, government, employers, and learners to support continuous education.
- Creativity and Critical Thinking: Aoun argues that a "robot-proof" education should focus on developing students' creative and critical thinking skills, enabling them to invent, create, and discover solutions that even sophisticated AI cannot.
- Experiential Learning: The book highlights the value of experiential learning, where students apply their knowledge in real-world settings, gaining practical experience and skills that are essential for their professional lives.
- **Ethical Considerations:** Aoun addresses the ethical implications of AI in education, stressing the need for transparency, informed consent, and the responsible use of AI tools to ensure fairness and inclusivity.
- **Future of Work:** The book explores how the nature of work is changing because of advancements in AI and automation and how higher education must evolve to prepare students for future job markets that require new skills and literacies

This approach promotes lifelong learning and adaptability, which are essential qualities for faculty to cultivate in their students. By incorporating these literacies into the curriculum, faculty can assist students in maintaining relevance and competitiveness in a rapidly evolving job market. Aoun presents a series of key highlights, which are summarized in Box 6.1.

CONCLUSION

This chapter examines AI integration into culturally responsive teaching (CRT) in counselor education, focusing on five subtopics. It begins with AI in training and supervision, highlighting AI-driven simulations and automated feedback systems for skill enhancement. It then discusses AI-driven assessment and evaluation, emphasizing real-time analysis and personalized feedback to improve student outcomes. Ethical considerations are addressed, focusing on data privacy, algorithmic biases, and maintaining the human element in counseling. The role of AI in practice and client interaction is explored, with a highlight of AI-powered chatbots, virtual assistants, and data analytics for informed treatment planning. Finally, the chapter investigates future directions, including advancements in AI technology, natural language processing, and ethical AI development, emphasizing the importance of ethical, inclusive, and culturally responsive AI integration in counselor education.

CHAPTER RESOURCES

Culturally Responsive Counselor Educator Skills

CRCE Skills to Further Develop From This Chapter	
Digital Literacy	This involves understanding how AI technologies work and being comfortable with various digital tools and platforms that integrate AI.
Data Analysis	This involves the ability to interpret and use data generated by AI tools to inform teaching practices, assess student performance, and personalize learning experiences
AI Tool Proficiency	This involves mastering specific AI tools and software used for educational purposes, such as LMS that incorporate AI, AI-powered grading platforms, and virtual teaching assistants.
Curriculum Design With AI	This involves developing and designing curriculum content that integrates AI capabilities, such as personalized learning pathways, adaptive learning modules, and AI-driven assessment methods.
Student Data Security	This involves implementing and maintaining robust data security measures to protect student information and ensure compliance with privacy regulations when using AI tools in educational settings.

CRCE, culturally responsive counselor educator; LMS, learning management systems.

CONTENT SUMMARY

- This chapter provides an overview of the potential applications of artificial intelligence (AI) in counselor education. The integration of AI in counselor training and supervision is described through AI-driven simulations and virtual reality for immersive learning experiences. Additionally, AI programs for automated feedback systems and their benefits are presented.
- AI-driven assessment and evaluation is discussed in relation to specific tools for real-time analysis and personalized feedback, as well as machine learning algorithms for tracking student progress. Ethical considerations and challenges are addressed, including solutions for data privacy and ethical standards, and the issue of biases in AI algorithms.
- In relation to remaining "robot proof," the preservation of the human element in counseling and careers in counselor education and supervision (CES) and counseling is discussed according to Aoun (2017).

Advanced Reflection Questions

1. What methods can doctoral-level counselor educators use to critically assess the efficacy and ethical considerations of various AI tools used in counselor training, and what standards should be implemented to ensure these technologies promote inclusive and fair learning outcomes?
2. In what ways can AI-based approaches be integrated with conventional teaching methods in counselor education programs, and how can doctoral-level educators strike a balance between using AI to improve experiential learning while maintaining the crucial human aspects of counselor training?
3. Given the swift progress in AI technology, how can doctoral-level counselor educators foresee and ready themselves for AI's long-term effects on the counseling field, and what strategic measures can be taken to continually update and enhance training programs to keep pace with emerging AI innovations and ethical guidelines?

Further Reading

American Counseling Association. (n.d.). *Best practices for ethical AI use for counseling students*. https://www.counseling.org/resources/research-reports/artificial-intelligence-counseling/for-students

Chan, T. (2023). *AI and ethics in counseling: Navigating the future*. https://professionaleducation.web.baylor.edu/news/story/2025/ai-ethics-navigating-future

National Board for Certified Counselors. (2024). *Ethical principles for artificial intelligence in counseling*. https://www.nbcc.org/assets/ethics/EthicalPrinciples_for_AI.pdf

Russell, S. J., & Norvig, P. (2020). *Artificial intelligence: A modern approach* (4th ed.). Pearson.

Tegmark, M. (2017). *Life 3.0: Being human in the age of artificial intelligence*. Alfred A. Knopf.

REFERENCES

American Counseling Association. (n.d.-a). *Integrating AI and LLMs into counseling education: Ethical and inclusive approaches*. Retrieved from https://www.counseling.org/resources/research-reports/artificial-intelligence-counseling/for-faculty

American Counseling Association. (n.d.-b). *Recommendations for practicing counselors and their use of AI*. Retrieved from https://www.counseling.org/resources/research-reports/artificial-intelligence-counseling/recommendations-for-practicing-counselors

Aoun, J. E. (2017). *Robot-proof: Higher education in the age of artificial intelligence*. MIT Press.

Broadwater, A. R., Brown, C. L., & Moore, M. (2022). An integrative pedagogical approach to teaching counseling supervision. *Journal of Counselor Preparation and Supervision, 15*(2). https://digitalcommons.sacredheart.edu/jcps/vol15/iss2/3

Chan, T. (2023). *Best practices for ethical AI use for counseling students.* American Counseling Association. Retrieved from https://www.counseling.org/resources/research-reports/artificial-intelligence-counseling/for-students

Parsons, J., Romero, D., White, M., & Callery, P. (2024). *AI in counselor education: Ethical challenges and solutions.* Association for Counselor Education and Supervision (ACES). Retrieved from Multibriefs.

Sheikh, A., D'Alfonso, S. A., & Woodcock, K. (2023). *Recommendations for practicing counselors and their use of AI.* American Counseling Association. https://www.counseling.org/resources/research-reports/artificial-intelligence-counseling/recommendations-for-practicing-counselors

INDEX